THE ORIGINS OF SOME ANGLO-NORMAN FAMILIES

BY

THE LATE LEWIS C. LOYD

AND EDITED BY

CHARLES TRAVIS CLAY

AND

DAVID C. DOUGLAS

Originally Published
as Volume CIII of
The Publications of the Harleian Society
Leeds, England
1951

Reprinted
Genealogical Publishing Co., Inc.
Baltimore, 1975, 1980, 1985, 1992

Library of Congress Cataloging in Publication Data
Loyd, Lewis Christopher, 1875-1947.
The origins of some Anglo-Norman families.
Reprint of the 1951 ed. published by Leeds, which was issued as v. 103 of the Publications of the Harleian Society.
Bibliography: p.
1. Great Britain—Genealogy. 2. Normandy—Genealogy. I. Title. II. Series: Harleian Society, London. Publications, v. 103.
CS432.N7L69 1975 929'.2'0942 74-18109
ISBN 0-8063-0649-1

Made in the United States of America

INTRODUCTION

Lewis Christopher Loyd, from whose manuscript collections the present volume has been compiled, was born at Abington Rectory, Northampton, on 27 September 1875. He was the eldest of the three sons of the Rev. Lewis Haig Loyd, and was educated at Eton from 1889 to 1894, and at Trinity College, Cambridge, taking his degree in 1897. He was called to the Bar by the Inner Temple in 1901, and practised on the Midland Circuit. In 1917 he entered the Department of the Treasury Solicitor, and retired at the end of March, 1936. On the outbreak of war in September, 1939, he rejoined his department, and finally retired in the early part of 1946, about eighteen months before his death on 17 August 1947.

His early years were spent in Northamptonshire, where his father held several benefices, being rector of Orlingbury for the last few years of the century ; and when he started his researches into feudal history it was to Northamptonshire and to the honour of Ferrers that his interests were primarily directed. Then came his intensive exploration of the medieval history of Normandy, not only as a result of many visits and walking tours through the less frequented parts, but by means of the fine library of Norman books which he accumulated in his rooms in Chelsea. Thomas Stapleton's edition in 1840 and 1844 of the Norman Exchequer Rolls, and Round's *Calendar of Documents in France,* published in 1899, had laid foundations for his work ; but he owed even more to the Norman historians, especially Léopold Delisle, of whose unrivalled authority he would speak with admiration.

There were three fields of research to which Mr. Loyd gave special attention. These were the new edition of *The Complete Peerage* ; the manuscript known as the Hatton Book of Seals ; and the collection of material which forms the basis of the present volume.

As to the first, his wide knowledge of Anglo-Norman sources and genealogy was placed unreservedly—except with a deep-seated desire for anonymity—at the disposal of the editor. The introductions to volume vii, published in 1929, and to succeeding volumes, record grateful acknowledgements for his assistance. Although his desire for anonymity was often obeyed, his name occurs frequently in contributions for which he was primarily responsible. To him was due such important material as the charter evidence for the early part of the article on the earldom of Leicester, and the early parts of the articles on Lovel of Titchmarsh, Mortimer of Wigmore, the earldom of Richmond, and the families of St. John. 'A note on the relationship between the families of Mortimer and Warenne,' which he contributed as the first appendix to volume ix, is an admirable example of the value of his critical handling of documentary material ; and his account of Roger de Montgomery, first earl of Shrewsbury, together with an appendix on the date of the creation of the earldom, was among the last pieces of work which he was able to undertake.

His work on the Hatton Book of Seals has been happily made available in the edition of *Sir Christopher Hatton's Book of Seals*, which was issued as a tribute to Sir Frank Stenton on the occasion of his seventieth birthday in 1950. In her preface to the volume Lady Stenton, with whose name Lewis Loyd's is associated on the title-page, records the course of his work from 1936 to his last illness, describing the complexity of the task, the wide range of the charters in date and district, and his unique knowledge of feudal genealogy both in England and Normandy. That his prolonged and careful work on this manuscript has been enshrined in a printed volume of such intrinsic interest is due to her.

On rare occasions Mr. Loyd was persuaded to contribute to the proceedings of a local society. Two important papers, one on 'The origin of the family of Warenne,' and the other on 'The origin of the family of Aubigny of Cainhoe,' were printed by the Yorkshire Archæological Society[1] and the Bedfordshire Historical Record Society[2] respectively. Apart from these the only signed contributions which have been traced are a note forming a postscript to a paper on the castles of Conisborough and Mortemer,[3] and one on the Pierrepont family to which reference is made in the section relating to that family in the present volume.

But with characteristic generosity he placed at the unrestricted disposal of others the fruits of his own work[4]; and in the prefatory pages of several volumes his name is recorded with gratitude, sometimes, perhaps, with a restraint and lack of detail which accorded with his own wishes. It was his own opinion, shared by those who owed so much to him, that an attack on problems ranging from the time of Domesday to the end of the twelfth century, especially those which required a correlation of English and Norman sources, could not be made with any measure of success except in close co-operation.

During the latter part of his life, Mr. Loyd became engaged upon an important new line of research. Its object was to supply express documentary evidence as to the place of origin beyond the seas of those feudal families which between the Norman Conquest and the loss of Normandy became possessed of land in England. The labour directed to these investigations extended over many years. As early as 1938 the work was well advanced, and from 1941 onwards he was sending at regular intervals to one of the editors of the present volume sheets embodying his conclusions on particular families. As these accumulated, Mr. Loyd entered them in a manuscript volume arranged in alphabetical sections to which he was wont to refer collo-

[1] *Yorks. Arch. Journal*, xxxi (1933), pp. 97–113.

[2] *Publications*, xix (1937), pp. 101–109.

[3] By Harold Sands and Hugh Braun in *Yorks. Arch. Journal*, xxxii, pp. 146–159.

[4] As an example of this his unpublished memorandum on the dignitaries in the six Norman secular cathedrals in the eleventh and twelfth centuries was placed at the disposal of Miss Kathleen Edwards for her *English Secular Cathedrals in the Middle Ages* (1949). The editors of the present volume could cite a number of similar examples.

quially as his 'Address Book.' It is this 'Address Book,' which at the time of his death had come to include entries relating to three hundred and fifteen families, that is the basis of the volume here printed.

The scope of the 'Address Book,' and the critical methods employed in its compilation, appear clearly in a letter which Mr. Loyd wrote to Sir Frank Stenton on 18 March 1945. He had lately been taking stock, he said, of what he had been able to do up to date; and he enclosed a summary of his results. " The people I treat of," he wrote, " are those who were settled in England at any time between 1066 and 1205. As regards the identification of the places, I have treated mere identity of name as insufficient evidence and have only included cases where some corroborative evidence is available. The amount and quality of such corroboration is largely conditioned by the name in question; where it is apparently unique or extremely rare I have taken a small amount of corroboration as sufficient, but I have regarded some as necessary, however obvious the identification may seem on the name alone; if one departs from some such rule one soon slides into guessing, of which I feel that there has been more than enough already. Even on the identifications I send you work remains to be done in the shape of verification. Many of my books are refugees at Lockinge, including my Pipe Rolls and Norman cartularies, and when I get them back I must check my facts; in some cases I hope to be able to strengthen the evidence, in others I shall no doubt find that my identification is wrong. What I send you is therefore provisional, but I confess that I shall be surprised if the errors come to as much as 10%. I may say, by the way, that in the case of what is perhaps the most interesting identification, that of Mandeville earl of Essex, the proof is in my opinion complete and amounts practically to demonstration.

" To make a few comments: I think that my list shows the danger of assuming that all Normans in England bearing the same territorial name came from the same place in Normandy; Mandeville, Balliol, Sancto Audoeno, Noyers and Chanfleur (Campo Florido) are sufficient instances. How often does one read 'Another branch of the family is found in ———shire,' but no evidence is forthcoming that it is the same family. 'Campus Floridus' should be a warning.

"An interesting class of men seems to me to emerge, those who were not of any particular importance in Normandy but who became so in England; whose fortunes were made by the Conquest. At the head of these seems to stand Roger Bigot . . . . . .[1]

"A similar case is Hugh de Port of Basing; all I can trace to him is land held by the service of three knights of the bishop of Bayeux. Both Bigot and Port were very important under-tenants of Odo [bishop of Bayeux] in 1086, and it looks as if it was he who made their fortune, *i.e.* put them on the road. Lacey held land for the service of two knights of the bishop of Bayeux; I have not traced any other lands held in Normandy, though there may well have been such: it looks as if Odo may well have put Lacey, both

[1] Here follow some notes the substance of which is incorporated in the section on BIGOT in the present volume.

of Hereford and Pontefract, on the road to fortune, though I don't think that they held of him in England. In *Domesday Monachorum* Douglas has said something about Odo's influence on the Norman settlement in England —it may well have been even more far-reaching.

" I have added an (incomplete) list of Norman overlords and their under-tenants in England,[1] which may assist as a partial key to the whole. Among these under-tenants I would remark on Schorchebofe ; men of this name were under-tenants both of Lacey of Pontefract and Lacey of Hereford, and take their name from a hamlet in the parish of Lassy. This seems sufficient to connect the two lines of Lacey. Lastly there is a summary of the numbers from each department.[2] After making all allowance for the incompleteness of my work, I think that the proportions are probably not far out, though the Eure may perhaps be under-represented. The early forfeiture of William FitzOsbern's lands and the absence of a return from the earl of Leicester in 1166 deprive us of a good deal of evidence . . . . . . "

It is clear that after the return of his books from his brother's house at Lockinge, where they had been sent for safety during the war, Mr. Loyd made a revision of the evidence for the purpose of the verification to which he alluded in his letter. He then cancelled in pencil about twenty families with such observations as ' evidence inadequate ' or ' not proved ' ; and with one or two exceptions, such as Aldrie and Meisi, these are not included in the present volume. His standards of proof, or of a reasonable degree of proof, were so high that he cancelled the entry for Brus as derived from Brix, dept. Manche, arr. and cant. Valognes, which, though it has been usually accepted,[3] he discarded as the evidence ' hardly seems sufficient.'

At about the same time he had come to the conclusion that the results of his research might be of sufficient interest to justify their committal to print ; and it is within the bounds of possibility that he might have consented to allow his name to appear on the title-page. It was presumably with the intention of putting the material into a more appropriate form with a view to publication that he started a new series of sheets giving a fair copy, as it may be called, of some of the material collected in the 'Address Book.' Of these new sheets about seventy were compiled. They have been used in the present volume for those particular families, with slight amendments mainly for the sake of uniformity. For the remaining families, about two hundred and forty-five in number, the material in the 'Address Book ' has been placed in the same kind of form of which the sheets had provided a model. A few references have been added to publications issued since his death, to which, as is reasonably certain, he would have himself referred.

Of the three hundred and fifteen families which are now included, the places of origin of two hundred and ninety-nine are spread over the five

[1] This forms the basis of the second index to the present volume.

[2] The revised numbers of these, which include considerable additions since the date of his letter, are given below.

[3] This derivation is given without reserve in *Complete Peerage*, new ed., ii, 358.

departments of Normandy as follows[1] :

Calvados	95
Seine-Inférieure	93
Manche	50
Eure	47
Orne	15

The places of origin of the remaining sixteen, which include four in Britanny, three in the Somme, and three in the Pas-de-Calais, lie outside the bounds of Normandy.

A bibliography, showing the wide range of sources used by Mr. Loyd, is given at the end of these introductory notes. In addition to the index of families, names and places, a second index gives the list of Norman overlords and their under-tenants in England, to which allusion has been made above ; and this is followed by a list of places in Normandy which formed the *caput* of a barony or honour. The map, for which we are indebted to Miss Norah Davenport, shows the various places which are the subject of identification in the text. Our thanks are also due to Sir Frank Stenton for his welcome interest in the work both before and after Mr. Loyd's death, and for his advice on several points. The book as it now appears is, however, essentially, and in all major respects, the work of Mr. Loyd himself, and the editors would wish its publication to be regarded as their tribute to the memory of a great scholar.

CHARLES CLAY

DAVID DOUGLAS

March, 1951

[1] The one extra is due to the fact that two places, one in Calvados and one in the Manche, are given for Paynel.

SELECT SHORT-TITLE BIBLIOGRAPHY OF WORKS CITED

Antiquus cartularius ecclesiae Baiocensis (*Livre Noir*), ed. V. Bourrienne, 2 vols. (Soc. Hist. Norm., 1902, 1903)

Archives de l'Eure. Inventaire Sommaire, Série H. (Evreux, 1893)

Beaucousin, A., *Registre des fiefs et arrière-fiefs du bailliage de Caux en* 1503 (Soc. Hist. Norm., 1891)

Beaurepaire, Ch. de, *Notes historiques et archéologiques* (Rouen, 1883)

Beaurepaire, Ch. de, *Recueil de Chartes de l'abbaye de Saint-Victor-en-Caux* (Soc. Hist. Norm. *Mélanges*, 5e. Série, 1898, *rectius* 1901)

Bertrand de Broussillon, *La Maison de Craon. Etude historique accompagnée du cartulaire de Craon,* 2 vols. (Paris, 1893)

Bertrand de Broussillon, *La Maison de Laval. Etude historique accompagnée du cartulaire de Laval et de Vitré,* 5 vols. (Paris, 1895-1903)

Béziers, M., *Mémoires pour servir à l'état historique et géographique du diocèse de Bayeux,* ed. G. Le Hardy, 3 vols. (Soc. Hist. Norm., 1894, 1895, 1896)

Blosseville, le marquis de, *Dictionnaire topographique du département de l'Eure* (Paris, 1878)

Bonnin, Th., *Cartulaire de Louviers,* 5 vols. in 6 (Evreux, 1870-1883)

Book of Fees, commonly called Testa de Nevill, reformed from the earliest MSS. by the Deputy Keeper of the Records, 3 vols. (London, 1920-1931)

Bréard, Ch., *L'abbaye de Notre-Dame de Grestain* (Rouen, 1904)

Brooks, E. St. J., *Nowers of Wymington* (Beds. Hist. Rec. Soc. xiv, 1931)

Brunel, C., *Recueil des Actes des Comtes de Pontieu* (Coll. de Docs. Inédits, Paris, 1930)

Calendar of Ancient Deeds in the Public Record Office, 6 vols. (London, 1890-1915)

Calendar of Charter Rolls preserved in the Public Record Office, 6 vols. (London, 1903-1927)

Calendar of Documents preserved in France illustrative of the history of Great Britain and Ireland, ed. J. Horace Round, vol. i (all published) (London, 1899)

Calendar of Miscellaneous Inquisitions, 3 vols. (London, 1916-1937)

Cartulaire de Fontenay-le-Marmion, ed. G. Saige (Monaco, 1895)

Cartulaire des Iles Normandes (Soc. Jersiaise. 6 fascicules, 1919-1924)

Cartulaire de Montmorel, ed. M. Dubosc (Saint-Lô, 1878)

Cartulaire de .... Saint Martin de Pontoise, ed. J. Depoin, 2 vols. (Soc. Hist. du Vexin, 1895, 1901)

Cartulaire ... de Saint-Michel-du-Tréport, ed. Laffleur de Kermaingant (Paris, 1880)

Cartulaire de la Sainte-Trinité-de-Rouen, ed. A. Deville. (This is pp. 403-487 in *Cartulaire de Saint Bertin,* ed. M. Guérard, Coll. de Docs. Inédits, Paris, 1841)

Cartulaire de la Sainte-Trinité-de-Beaumont-le-Roger, ed. E. Deville (Paris, 1912)

Cartulaire.... de la Trinité de Vendôme, ed. Ch. Métais, 5 vols. (Paris, 1893-1904)

Cartularium monasterii Sancti Iohannis Baptistae de Colecestria, ed. S. A. Moore, 2 vols. (Roxburghe Club, 1897)

Cartulary of the Abbey of Old Wardon, ed. G. H. Fowler (Beds. Hist. Rec. Soc., xiii, 1930)

Caumont, A. de, *Statistique monumentale du Calvados*, 5 vols. (vol. i 're-impression,' 1898; vols. ii-v, 1850-1867, Paris)

Charpillon et Caresme, *Dictionnaire historique de toutes les communes du département de l'Eure*, 2 vols. (Les Andelys, 1868, 1879)

Charters and documents illustrating the history of the cathedral city and diocese of Salisbury. Selected by W. R. Jones, and edited by W. D. Macray (Rolls Series, 1891)

Chartulary of the Priory of St. Pancras of Lewes, ed. L. F. Salzman, 2 vols. (Sussex Rec. Soc. xxxviii, xl, 1932, 1934)

Chronicle of Melrose, facsimile edition by A. O. and M. O. Anderson (London, 1936)

Clay, C. T., *The Family of Amundeville* (Lincs. Architectural and Archaeological Soc. *Reports*, iii, pt. ii, 1945)

Clay, C. T., *Notes on the Family of Amundeville* (*Archaeologia Aeliana*, 4th ser. xxiv, 1946)

Cochet, J. B. D., *Répertoire archéologique du département de la Seine-Inférieure* (Paris, 1871)

Coleman, J., *The Descent of the Manor of Allerton* (Somerset. Arch. Soc. *Proc.* xlv, pt. 2, 1899)

Complete Peerage of England, Scotland, Ireland, Great Britain and the United Kingdom (new edition, London, 1910—in progress)

Coquelin, F. B., *Histoire de l'abbaye de Saint-Michel-du-Tréport*, ed. C. Lormier, 2 vols. (Soc. Hist. Norm., 1879, 1888)

Cottineau, L. H., *Répertoire topo-bibliographique des abbayes et prieurés*, 2 vols. (Macon, 1936, 1937)

Coucher Book of Furness Abbey, vol. ii, ed. J. Brownbill (Chetham Soc., N.S., lxxiv, lxxvi, lxxviii, 1915, 1916, 1919)

Couppey, L., *L'abbaye de Notre-Dame-du-Voeu près Cherbourg: chronique des Abbés* (Evreux, 1913)

Curia Regis Rolls, ed. C. T. Flower, 8 vols. (London, 1922—in progress)

Darsy, F. I., *Picquigny et ses seigneurs* (Abbeville, 1860)

Davis, H. W. C., *Regesta Regum Anglo-Normannorum*, vol. i (Oxford, 1913)

Delisle, Léopold, *Documents relating to the abbey of Furness* (*Journal* of Brit. Arch. Assoc., vii, 1851)

Delisle, Léopold, *Cartulaire normand de Philippe-Auguste, Louis viii, Saint Louis et Philippe-le-Hardi*. (This is included in vol. xvi of the *Mémoires* of the Soc. des Antiq. de Normandie, Caen, 1852)

Delisle, Léopold, *Catalogue des Actes de Philippe-Auguste avec une introduction sur les sources, les caractères et l'importance de ces documents* (Paris, 1856)

Delisle, Léopold, *Chronique de Robert de Torigni.... suivie de divers opuscules historiques*, 2 vols. (Soc. Hist. Norm., 1872, 1873)

Delisle, Léopold, *Histoire du Château et des Sires de Saint-Sauveur-le-Vicomte* (Valognes, 1867)

Delisle, Léopold, et Berger, Emile, *Recueil des actes de Henri II, roi d'Angleterre et duc de Normandie, concernant les provinces françaises et les affaires de France,* 4 vols. and atlas of plates (Paris, 1909-1927)

Deville, A., *Essai historique et descriptif sur l'église et l'abbaye de Saint-Georges-de-Bocherville, près Rouen* (Rouen, 1827)

Deville, E., *Analyse d'un ancien cartulaire... de Saint-Etienne de Caen* (*Notice sur quelques manuscrits normands conservés à la bibliothèque Sainte-Geneviève* No. iv; Evreux, 1905)

Diceto, Ralph de, *Opera Historica,* ed. W. Stubbs, 2 vols. (Rolls Series, 1876)

Domesday Book, seu Liber Censualis Willelmi Primi regis Angliae, ed. Abraham Farley, 2 vols. (London, 1783). The supplementary volumes (vols. "iii" and "iv") were edited by H. Ellis in 1816.

Douglas, David C., *Companions of the Conqueror* (*History,* xxviii, 1943)

Douglas, David C., *Domesday Monachorum of Christ Church, Canterbury* (London, 1944)

Douglas, David C., *Feudal Documents from the abbey of Bury St. Edmunds* (Brit. Acad., 1932)

Douglas, David C., *The Rise of Normandy* (Brit. Acad., 1947)

Douglas, David C., *Social Structure of Medieval East Anglia* (Oxford, 1927)

Du Buisson-Aubenay, *Itinéraire de Normandie,* ed. A. A. Porée (Soc. Hist. Norm., 1911)

Duchesne, André, *Histoire généalogique de la Maison de Montmorency et de Laval* (Paris, 1624)

Ekwall, E., *Concise Oxford Dictionary of English Place-Names* (Oxford, 1936)

English Place-Name Society, Publications (Oxford, 1924—in progress)

Estaintot, le vicomte de, *Récherches sur Auffay* (Dieppe, 1879)

Eyton, R. W., *Antiquities of Shropshire,* 12 vols. (London, 1854-1860)

Farrer, W., and Clay, C. T., *Early Yorkshire Charters,* 8 vols. and index vol. to vols. i-iii (Edinburgh, 1914-1916, and Yorks. Arch. Soc., 1938-1949)

Farrer, W., *Feudal Cambridgeshire* (Cambridge, 1920)

Farrer, W., *Lancashire Pipe Rolls and early charters* (Liverpool, 1902)

Farrer, W., *Honors and Knights' Fees,* 3 vols. (London, 1923, 1924; Manchester, 1925)

Fowler, G. H., *Bedfordshire in* 1086: *an analysis and synthesis of Domesday Book* (Beds. Hist. Rec. Soc., 4to Ser., i, 1922)

Fowler, G. H., *Early records of Turvey and its neighbourhood* (Beds. Hist. Rec. Soc. xi, 1927)

Fowler, G. H., and Hughes, M. W., *A Calendar of the Pipe Rolls of the reign of Richard I for Buckinghamshire and Bedfordshire* (Beds. .Hist. Rec. Soc. vii, 1923)

Freeman, E. A., *History of the Norman Conquest,* 5 vols. and index vol. (London, 1867 etc.)

Galbraith, V. H., *Documents illustrating monastic foundation charters of the eleventh and twelfth centuries* (*Camb. Historical Journal,* iv, 1934)

Galbraith, V. H., *An episcopal land-grant of* 1085 (*Eng. Hist. Rev.,* xliv, 1929)

Gallia Christiana—vol. xi—(Paris, 1874)

Gerville, Ch. D. de, *Récherches sur les anciens châteaux du département de la Manche* (*Mém.* Soc. Antiq. Norm., ii (1825) and v (1830))

Gesta Stephani regis Anglorum, ed. R. Howlett (*Chronicles .... of Stephen, Henry II and Richard I*, vol. iii, Rolls Series, 1886)

Glanville, L. de, *Histoire du prieuré de Saint-Lô de Rouen*, 2 vols. (Rouen, 1890, 1891)

Gurney, Daniel, *The record of the House of Gournay*, 2 vols. (Printed for private circulation, London, 1848)

Harcourt, L. W. V., *His Grace the Steward and Trial of Peers* (London, 1907)

Haskins, C. H., *Norman Institutions* (Harvard U.P., 1925)

Sir Christopher Hatton's Book of Seals, ed. L. C. Loyd and D. M. Stenton (Oxford, 1950)

Hippeau, C., *Dictionnaire topographique du département du Calvados* (Paris, 1866)

Histoire de Guillaume le Maréchal, ed. Paul Meyer, 3 vols. (Paris, 1891-1901)

Historia Coenobii Mortui-maris (*Recueil des Historiens des Gaules et de la France*, xxiii)

Historia et cartularium monasterii sancti Petri Gloucestriae, ed. W. H. Hart, 3 vols. (Rolls Series, 1863-1867)

Historical Manuscripts Commission: Duke of Rutland, vol. iv (1905); Earl of Essex (Various Collections, vol. vii, 1914); Lord De L'Isle and Dudley, vol. i (1925); R. R. Hastings, vol. i (1928)

Houth, E., *Recueil des chartes de Saint-Nicaise-de Meulan* (Soc. Hist. de Pontoise et du Vexin, 1924)

Howden, Roger of, *Chronica Rogeri de Hoveden*, ed. W. Stubbs, 4 vols. (Rolls Series, 1868-1871)

Hutchins, John, *The history and antiquities of the county of Dorset*, ed. W. Shipp and J. W. Hodson, 4 vols. (London, 1861-1873)

Inquisitions and assessments relating to Feudal Aids .... preserved in the Public Record Office, 6 vols. (London, 1899-1920)

Jeayes, I. H., *Descriptive catalogue of Derbyshire charters* (London, 1906)

Jeayes, I. H., *Descriptive catalogue of the charters .... of the Gresley family* (London, 1895)

Jumièges, William of, *Gesta Normannorum Ducum*, ed. J. Marx (Soc. Hist. Norm., 1914)

Lancaster, W. T., *Ripley and the Ingilby family* (Privately printed, 1918)

Lawrie, Archibald, *Early Scottish charters prior to A.D.* 1153 (Glasgow, 1905)

Le Cacheux, P., *Chartes du prieuré de Longueville* (Soc. Hist. Norm., 1934)

Lecanu, C. A. F., *Histoire du diocèse de Coutances et Avranches* (2nd ed., Coutances, 1877)

Lees, B. A., *Records of the Templars in England* (Brit. Acad., 1935)

Lemarignier, J. F., *Etude sur les privilèges d'exemption ..... des abbayes normandes* (Paris, 1937)

Le Prévost, A., *Mémoires et notes pour servir à l'histoire du département de l'Eure*, ed. L. Delisle et L. Passy, 3 vols. (Evreux, 1862-1869)

Liber S. Mariae de Dryburgh, ed. C. Innes (Bannatyne Club, lxxxvii, 1847)

Liber Niger Scaccarii, ed. T. Hearne, 2 vols. (Oxford, 1728; 2nd ed. London, 1774)

Lincolnshire Domesday and the Lindsey Survey, ed. C. W. Foster and T. Longley (Lincoln Rec. Soc., 1924)

Longnon, A., *Pouillés de la province de Rouen* (Paris, 1903)

Lot, F., *Etudes critiques sur l'abbaye de Saint-Wandrille* (Paris, 1913)

Loyd, L. C., *The origin of the family of Aubigny of Cainhoe* (Beds. Hist. Rec. Soc. xix, 1937)

Loyd, L. C., *The origin of the family of Warenne* (*Yorks. Arch. Journal*, xxxi, 1933)

Loyd, L. C., *The provenance of the Pierrepoint family* (*Sussex Notes and Queries*, vii, 1939)

Mabillon, Jean, *De Re Diplomatica* (Paris, 1681; supplement, Paris, 1704)

Madox, T., *Formulare Anglicanum: a collection of ancient charters and instruments of various kinds* .... (London, 1702)

Magni Rotuli Scaccarii Normanniae sub regibus Angliae, ed. T. Stapleton, 2 vols. (London, Society of Antiquaries, 1840)

Magni Rotuli Scaccarii Normanniae sub regibus Angliae [ed. Léchaudé D'Anisy] (Paris, 1846). (This is part of vol. xv of the *Mémoires* of the Soc. Antiq. Norm.)

Magni Rotuli Scaccarii Normanniae sub regibus Angliae; pars secunda, ed. Léchaudé D'Anisy and A. Charma (Caen, 1852). (This is part of vol. xvi of the *Mémoires* of the Soc. Antiq. Norm.)

Malicorne, J., *Documents et courte notice sur l'abbaye de Bival* (Rouen, 1897)

Maxwell-Lyte, H., *Dunster and its lords* (Exeter, 1882)

Monasticon Anglicanum . . . originally published in Latin by Sir William Dugdale . . . A new edition by John Caley, Henry Ellis and the Rev. Bulkeley Bandinel, 6 vols. in 8 (London, 1817-1830)

Morice, Pierre-Hyacinthe, *Mémoires pour servir de preuves à l'histoire ecclésiastique et civile de Bretagne*, 3 vols. (Paris, 1742, 1744, 1746)

Nichols, John, *The History and Antiquities of the county of Leicester*, 4 vols. in 8 (London, 1795-1815)

Northumberland: *A History of Northumberland*, 15 vols. (Newcastle-upon-Tyne, 1893-1940)

Orderici Vitalis angligenae . . . historiae ecclesiasticae libri tredecim, ed. A. Le Prévost, 5 vols. (Paris, 1838-1855)

Patte, V., *Histoire de Gisors* (Gisors, 1896)

Percy Chartulary, ed. Miss M. T. Martin (Surtees Soc. cxvii, 1911)

Pipe Roll Society, Publications (London, 1884—in progress)

Porée, A. A., *Histoire de l'abbaye du Bec*, 2 vols. (Evreux, 1901)

Pouillé de l'ancien diocèse de Séez redigé en 1763 *par Jacques Savary*, 2 vols. (Soc. hist. et arch. de l'Orne, 1903, 1908)

Powicke, F. M., *Loss of Normandy* (Manchester, 1913)

Poynton, E. M., *Charters relating to the Priory of Sempringham* (*Genealogist*, xv-xvii, 1899-1901)

Querimoniæ Normannorum (*Recueil des Historiens des Gaules et de la France*, xxiv)

Raine, J., *History of Blyth* (Westminister, 1860)

Recueil des Historiens des Gaules et de la France, 24 vols. (Paris, 1738-1904)

Red Book of the Exchequer, ed. H. Hall, 3 vols. (Rolls Series, 1896)

Registrum antiquissimum of the Cathedral Church of Lincoln, ed. C. W. Foster and K. Major (Lincoln Record Soc., 1931—in progress)

Rotuli de dominabus et pueris et puellis de xii comitatibus [1185], ed. J. H. Round (Pipe Roll Soc. xxxv, 1913)

Rotuli de oblatis et finibus in turri Londiniensi asservati, ed. T. D. Hardy, 2 vols. (London, 1835, 1836)

Rotuli Normanniae in Turri Londiniensi asservati..., ed. T. D. Hardy (London, 1835)

Round, J. H., *A Bachepuz charter* (*Ancestor*, xii, 1905)

Round, J. H., *The Commune of London and other studies* (Westminster, 1899)

Round, J. H., *The families of St. John and of Port* (*Genealogist*, xvi, 1900)

Round, J. H., *Family of De Clare* (*Dict. Nat. Biog.* x, 1887)

Round, J. H., *Family Origins and other studies* (London, 1930)

Round, J. H., *Feudal England* (London, 1895)

Round, J. H., *Geoffrey de Mandeville* (London, 1892)

Round, J. H., *A great marriage settlement* (*Ancestor*, xi, 1904)

Round, J. H., *Helion of Helion's Bumpstead* (Essex Arch. Soc. *Trans.* viii, 1903)

Round, J. H., *King's serjeants and officers of state* (London, 1911)

Round, J. H., *Peerage and Pedigree*, 2 vols. (London, 1910)

Round, J. H., *The Ports of Basing and their priory* (*Genealogist*, xviii, 1902)

Round, J. H., *Studies in Peerage and Family history* (Westminster, 1901)

Round, J. H., *The value of Ancient Deeds* (*Ancestor*, vi, 1903)

Russell, J., *The Haigs of Bemersyde* (Edinburgh, 1881)

Salter, H. E., *Facsimiles of early charters in Oxford muniment-rooms* (Oxford, 1929)

Salter, H. E., *Newington Longueville charters* (Oxfordshire Rec. Soc., 1921)

Sauvage, E., *Les chartes de fondation du prieuré de Bacqueville-en-Caux* (Rouen, 1882)

Sauvage, R. N., *L'abbaye de Saint-Martin-de Troarn* (Caen, 1911)

Scripta de feodis ad regem spectantibus et de militibus ad exercitum vocandis e Philippi Augusti regestis excerpta (*Recueil des Historiens des Gaules et de la France*, xxiii)

Société des Antiquaires de Normandie: Mémoires (First Series, 10 vols. with atlas of plates, Caen, 1825-1837; vol. xv, Paris, 1846; vol. xvi, Caen, 1852)

Société de l'Histoire de Normandie: Mélanges, 14 vols. (Rouen—Paris, 1891-1938)

Stapleton, T., *Observations upon the succession to the barony of William of Arques* (*Archaeologia*, xxxi, 1846)

Stenton, F. M., *Documents illustrative of the social and economic history of the Danelaw* (Brit. Acad., 1920)

Stenton, F. M., *Facsimiles of early charters from Northamptonshire collections* (Northants. Rec. Soc. iv, 1930)

Stenton, F. M., *The first century of English feudalism* (Oxford, 1932)

Textus Roffensis, ed. T. Hearne (Oxford, 1720)

Toussaints Du Plessis, *Description géographique et historique de la Haute Normandie*, 2 vols. (Paris, 1740)

Vernier, J. J., *Chartes de Jumièges*, 2 vols. (Soc. Hist. Norm., 1915)

Victoria History of the Counties of England (London, 1900—in progress)

Wace, *Roman de Rou*, ed. H. Andresen, 2 vols. (Heilbron, 1877, 1879)

Warner, G. F., and Ellis, H., *Facsimiles of royal and other charters in the British Museum*, vol. i (all published) (London, 1903)

Willelmi Malmesbiriensis de gestis pontificum Anglorum, libri quinque, ed. N. E. S. A. Hamilton (Rolls Series, 1870)

THE ORIGINS OF SOME ANGLO-NORMAN FAMILIES

ABERNON.

Abenon: Calvados, arr. Lisieux, cant. Orbec.

In 1086 Roger de Abernon or Arbernum held in Moulsey Prior (*Molesham*) in East Moulsey, Surrey, and in Freston (*Frestuna*), Suffolk, of Richard Fitz Gilbert.[1] In 1166 Ingeram de Abernon held four knights' fees of the honour of Clare,[2] and gave the church of Freston to the priory of Stoke-by-Clare.[3] Abenon, of which the old form is Abernon, is 5 kil. S of Orbec, the *caput* of Richard Fitz Gilbert's Norman honour. In the thirteenth century Abenon was held of Richard Marshal, then in possession of the Norman lands of the house of Clare.[4]

ABETOT, ABITOT.

Abbetot: Seine-Inf., arr. Le Havre, cant. Saint-Romain.

Urse de Abetot, Domesday tenant-in-chief and sheriff of Worcestershire, is a well-known person; his first recorded occurrence in England is in 1067.[5] The overlords of Abbetot were the chamberlains of Tancarville. In a charter of William duke of the Normans, which cannot be later than the summer of 1066, certain gifts to the church of St-Georges-de-Boscherville are stated to have been confirmed by the chamberlain Ralf son of Gerold (of Tancarville), the name of Urso 'de Abetot' as a witness to the confirmation being added in another hand above the line in the cartulary.[6] By a charter of the time of Henry I William the chamberlain of Tancarville gave to Boscherville, 'in Abetot ecclesiam et decimam et terram pertinentem ecclesiae et quatuor acras quae sunt inter ecclesiam et domum Roberti filii Ursi.'[7] Taking into account the fact that Urse is not a common name and that there is no other Abbetot in Normandy, these charters seem sound evidence of Urse's origin. Robert son of Urse may be the Robert de Abetot whose wife Lesza gave land to the priory of Ste-Barbe-en-Auge, a house of which the Tancarvilles were patrons.[8] Urse was succeeded in England by his son Roger, who forfeited his lands *c.* 1114.

[1] *D.B.*, i, 35; ii, 395b; *V.C.H. Surrey*, i, 318; *V.C.H. Suffolk*, i, 533.

[2] *Red Bk. Exch.*, p. 405.

[3] *Mon. Ang.*, vi, 1660.

[4] *Querimoniæ Normannorum* in *Rec. Hist. France*, xxiv, 44.

[5] Davis, *Regesta*, no. 10.

[6] A. Deville, *Essai sur . . . Saint-Georges de Bocherville*, p. 67; for the interlineations see note on p. 69. The charter in its present form presents difficulties, but comparison with other charters of confirmation for the abbey suggests the truth of its substance

[7] *Mon. Ang.*, vi, 1066. The grantor died in or before 1129.

[8] *Cal. Docs. France*, no. 568; cf. *Cal. Chart. Rolls*, 1300-26, p. 309.

The gift of the church and tithe of Abbetot by William de Tancarville mentioned above seems really to have been a confirmation, since a charter of Henry II confirmed the gift by Ralf the chamberlain of William the Conqueror of the church and tithe together with seven acres of land and the tithe of all assarts between Abbetot and Colbosc.[1] No other evidence as to Urse in Normandy has come to light, and it seems probable that Abbetot was held by the Tancarvilles in demesne and that Urse was in origin a man of no importance who made his way as a soldier of fortune, a view quite consistent with the reputation he earned in Worcestershire.

ACQUIGNY, AKENY, DE ACHIGNEIO.

Acquigny: Eure, arr. and cant. Louviers.

The family held of Tosny in Whittlesford, co. Cambridge, and Garsington, co. Oxford.[2] Richard de Achigneio witnessed a Norfolk charter of Ralf de Tosny *c.* 1115, and one of Roger de Tosny *c.* 1125.[3] Acquigny is 16 kil. W of Tosny. Roger de Tosny gave to the abbey of Conches *c.* 1035 'ecclesiam de Achineio cum offerendis et decimis de annona.'[4] The castle of Acquigny was in the hands of the lords of Tosny and the known facts as to its history in the twelfth century suggest that the place was held by them in demesne[5]; while it is clear that this family came from Acquigny, there is no evidence that they held it as under-tenants.

AINCOURT, DEINCOURT, EINCURIA, ETC.

Ancourt: Seine-Inf., arr. Dieppe, cant. Offranville.

Walter de Aincourt was a substantial Domesday tenant-in-chief, notably in Lincolnshire and Northamptonshire. In the early thirteenth century the representative of the family was his descendant Oliver.[6] In the feodary of 1212-1220 in the Registers of Philip Augustus under the rubric ' Ballivia domini Gaufridi de Capella,' *i.e.* the bailiwick of Caux in which Ancourt lay, is the entry ' Terra Oliveri de Eincuria unum feodum apud Eincuriam.'[7] Oliver had remained in England and adhered to John; Ancourt would therefore be in the French king's hand. The epitaph of William son of Walter de Aincourt, the Domesday tenant-in-chief, preserved in Lincoln Cathedral, describes Walter as kinsman of Remigius bishop of Lincoln[8]: it is to be noted that Remigius had been a monk and almoner of Fécamp and that the abbot of Fécamp was patron of the church of Ancourt.[9] In 1870 the remains of the castle were to be seen near the church.[10]

[1] Delisle et Berger, *Rec. des Actes de Henri II*, ii, 190. The original gift of the four acres beside the church was probably that of William de Tancarville.

[2] Farrer, *Feudal Cambridgeshire*, p. 260.

[3] D. C. Douglas, *The Social Structure of Mediaeval East Anglia*, pp. 254-5.

[4] *Gall. Christ.*, xi, Instr. 128.

[5] A. Le Prévost, *Mém. et Notes . . . . de l'Eure*, i, 89.

[6] *Complete Peerage*, new ed., iv, 118 *n.*

[7] *Rec. Hist. France*, xxiii, 640d.

[8] F. M. Stenton, *English Feudalism*, p. 32 *n.*

[9] A. Longnon, *Pouillés de la province de Rouen*, p. 40.

[10] Cochet, *Rép. arch. . . . de la Seine-Inf.*, col. 55.

ALDRIE.

[?] Audrieu: Calvados, arr. Caen, cant. Tilly-sur-Seules.

In 1086 William de Aldrie was an under-tenant of William of Eu in Wiltshire.[1] A William de Audreio gave the church of Loucelles to St. Stephen's, Caen, the gift being mentioned in Henry II's general confirmation charter of 1156-57.[2] Loucelles is the next parish to Audrieu. The identification is not established beyond all doubt, but in the absence of any other known place of the name it is in the highest degree probable.[3] There was a castle at Audrieu.[4]

AMBLIE.

Amblie: Calvados, arr. Caen, cant. Creully.

The history of this family has been carefully worked out by Farrer.[5] Between 1100 and 1120 Ralf de Ambli, with the consent of his lord Eudo dapifer, gave two thirds of the tithes of his demesne in Elmsett, Suffolk, to the abbey of St. John at Colchester[6]: this gift was confirmed by a charter of Richard I in 1189.[7] In 1166 Geoffrey de Amblia held two knights' fees of Henry son of Gerold the chamberlain as of the honour of Eudo dapifer.[8] This Geoffrey gave the abbey four acres of land in exchange for the tithes given by Ralf de Amblia, whom he calls his grandfather.[9] The family became extinct in the male line about the middle of the thirteenth century.

Amblie is 10 kil. E by S of Ryes, Eudo's place of origin.

AMUNDEVILLE.

Mondeville: Calvados, arr. and cant. Caen.

An account of the family, whose principal interests lay in Lincolnshire,[10] has been given by C. T. Clay in *Lincs. Architectural and Archæological Soc. Reps.*, vol. iii, part ii (1945–47), pp. 109–36.[11] Evidence is there given for the descent from Goslin the dapifer, also described as 'Goslanus, de Amundavilla dapifer,' whose office as the bishop of Lincoln's steward, which he was holding in 1115–18 and 1130, was inherited successively by his two eldest sons Walter and William. Goslin's predecessor in many of the family's Lincolnshire holdings, and probably his father,

1 *D.B.*, i, 71b.

2 *Cal. Docs. France*, no. 453. William's charter, in which he is styled 'Guillelmus filius Alberti de Aldreio,' the gift being probably made during the abbacy of Eudo (1108-40), is pd. in E. Deville, *Analyse d'un ancien cartulaire . . . . de Saint-Etienne de Caen*, p. 48.

3 Mr. Loyd has the entry deleted in pencil—' cancelled, evidence inadequate '—presumably for the identification of the D. B. under-tenant; and it is included here with that reservation.

4 A. de Caumont, *Statistique monumentale du Calvados*, i, 313.

5 *Honors and Knights' Fees*, iii, 174-7.

6 *Cartularium Monasterii . . . de Colecestria* (Roxburghe Club), p. 283.

7 *Cal. Chart. Rolls*, 1226-57, p. 424.

8 *Red Bk. Exch.*, p. 354.

9 *Cartularium . . .*, p. 283.

10 Another family, in all probability a younger line, whose name is preserved in Coatham Mundeville, co. Durham, is the subject of a paper by the same writer in *Arch. Aeliana*, 4th ser., xxiv, pp. 60–70.

11 The evidence for the identification, here given in summary, was collected with Mr. Loyd's co-operation.

was Goislan, a Domesday under-tenant in Lincolnshire both of the bishop of Lincoln and the bishop of Durham; and there are strong grounds for identifying the latter with Juclinus de Amundivilla who was a witness on behalf of the abbey of Fécamp in the determination of a suit in 1085. Remigius bishop of Lincoln in 1086, formerly a monk and almoner of Fécamp, had been in charge of ten knights supplied by the abbot for the invasion of England. In 989–90 duke Richard I gave Amundivilla to the abbey of Fécamp; and *c.* 1350 the church of Amondevilla in the diocese of Bayeux was of the exemption of Fécamp. There is no other church of a similar name in that diocese.[1]

ANGENS.

Angiens: Seine-Inf., arr. Yvetot, cant. Fontaine-le-Dun.

Hugh de Angens witnessed a charter of Henry Biset for Breamore priory 1187–*c.* 1208.[2] An inspeximus by Richard the dean and the chapter of Salisbury of an agreement between Andrew prior of Maiden Bradley and Margaret sister of Henry Biset shows that agreement to have been made in the presence of Hugh de Angens, William his son, Randulf de Angens and others 'liberi homines tenementi de Bradele.'[3] By a charter issued in his court at Cany, the *caput* of his Norman honour, Henry Biset confirmed to Longueville priory the gifts of his predecessors including the church of Angiens.[4]

ANISY.

Anisy: Calvados, arr. Caen, cant. Creully.

In 1130 William de Anesia occurs on the Wiltshire pipe roll as pardoned 16*s.* 6*d.* for danegeld[5]; later evidence shows him to have been a royal dispenser holding Dilton in Westbury and Bratton, Wilts, by serjeanty.[6] By a charter of about the end of Henry I's reign this William with the consent of his eldest son William surrendered Sherfield English, Hants, to his lord Henry de Port of Basing who enfeoffed William's younger son Richard to hold it by the service of one knight[7]; since William speaks of Sherfield as his acquisition (*acatum*), he must have been the first feoffee. In 1166 Richard de Anesia is returned as holding one knight's fee of John de Port of Basing,[8] and the fee descended in this younger line. In 1212 John de Anesye held half a knight's fee in Stratton, Wilts, of the honour of Kington.[9] Anisy is 28 kil. ESE of Port-en-Bessin; and the Registers of Philip Augustus show an Alan de Anisy holding

[1] Mr. Loyd notes that much nearer to Fécamp lies Emondeville, Seine-Inf., arr. Yvetot, cant. Ourville; but a pre-conquest charter of duke William shows that it belonged to Jumièges (Vernier, *Chartes de Jumièges*, i, 87), and there was no connexion with the abbey of Fécamp.

[2] *Sir Christopher Hatton's Book of Seals*, ed. L. C. Loyd and Lady Stenton, no. 216.

[3] *Sarum Charters* (Rolls Ser.), pp. 74–5.

[4] P. Le Cacheux, *Chartes du Prieuré de Longueville* (Soc. Hist. Norm.), no. 34.

[5] *Pipe Roll* 31 *Hen. I*, p. 23.

[6] *Bk. of Fees*, p. 1225.

[7] *Sir Christopher Hatton's Book of Seals*, no. 301.

[8] *Red Bk. Exch.*, p. 208.

[9] *Ibid.*, p. 600. The honour of Kington had been held by Port of Mapledurwell (*q.v.*).

land there in 1212–20, formerly of the earl of Chester[1]; but in view of the facts that no other place of the name is to be found in Normandy, and that other Port under-tenants in England took their names from places at a substantial distance from Port-en-Bessin,[2] the identification seems reasonably certain.

APPEVILLE.

Appeville-le-Petit: Seine-Inf., arr. Dieppe, cant. Offranville, comm. Hautot-sur-Mer.

In 1086 Walter de Appevile held land in Folkestone, Kent, of William of Arques, who held the manor of Odo bishop of Bayeux.[3] Appeville is 6 kil. NW of Arques. A charter of Robert I duke of Normandy, dated 1030, confirmed to the abbey of the Holy Trinity of Rouen among the gifts of Goscelin the *vicomte*, its founder, 'capellam de Appavilla.'[4] The *pouillé* of 1337 shows the abbot of St. Catherine's (*i.e.* the Holy Trinity) as patron of the church.[5] William of Arques was the son of Goscelin's daughter and his eventual heir.[6]

ARGUGES.

Argouges-sur-Mosles: Calvados, arr. Bayeux, cant. Trevières, comm. Russy.[7]

In 1166 Odo de Arguges held half a knight's fee of the new feoffment of Adam de Port of Mapledurwell.[8] Argouges-sur-Mosles is 5 kil. S by W of Port-en-Bessin. There is also an Argouges-sur-Aure (Calvados, arr. Bayeux, cant. Ryes, comm. Vaux-sur-Aure) lying 6 kil. SE of Port-en-Bessin, and it is impossible to decide between them with certainty. At the same time the weight of evidence seems to be somewhat strongly in favour of Argouges-sur-Mosles, since the patronage of the church pertained to the abbey of Cerisy,[9] of which the family of Port were benefactors, and no less than four under-tenants of Port of Mapledurwell in 1166 took their name from Le Fresne also in the commune of Russy.[10] An interesting note by Round will be found in *The Ancestor*,[11] in which he suggests that the notorious Adam de Stratton was of this family; he derives it, however, from either Argouges (Manche, arr. Avranches, cant. St-James) or alternatively Argueil (Seine-Inf., arr. Neufchâtel), without giving his reasons.

ARQUES, DE ARCHIS.

Arques-la-Bataille: Seine-Inf., arr. Dieppe, cant. Offranville.

William of Arques has been the subject of an exhaustive study by

1 *Rec. Hist. France*, xxiii, 620k, 634b.

2 See remarks *sub* PORT of Basing.

3 *D.B.*, i, 9b.

4 *Cartulaire de la Sainte-Trinité de Rouen*, ed. A. Deville, no. 1.

5 A. Longnon, *Pouillés de la province de Rouen*, p. 35.

6 D. C. Douglas, *Domesday Monachorum*, p. 43.

7 A. Longnon, *Pouillés de la province de Rouen*, index, *s.v.* A. de Caumont places it in the adjacent commune of Mosles (*Statistique monumentale du Calvados*, iii, 649).

8 *Red Bk. Exch.*, p. 280.

9 Longnon, *op. cit.*, p. 119.

10 See FRESNE.

11 Vol. vi, pp. 177–8.

Professor D. C. Douglas in the introduction to his edition of *The Domesday Monachorum of Christ Church Canterbury*,[1] where full references are given to the authorities; and it is unnecessary to go over the ground again. Briefly he held Folkestone, Kent, and was the son of Godfrey *vicomte* of Arques.[2] The identity of the tenant of Folkestone is established by the fact that it passed to Nigel de Monville who had married his daughter and coheiress[3] Emma. He must not be confused with William of Arques, a monk of Molême who was a counsellor of Robert Curthose,[4] and still less with William count of Arques, the uncle of William the Conqueror. The ruined castle at Arques-la-Bataille is well known.

AUBERVILLE.

Auberville-sur-Yère: Seine-Inf., arr. Dieppe, cant. Eu, comm. St-Martin-le-Gaillard.

In 1166 William de Auberville held four and a half knights' fees of the old feoffment in Kent of William of Avranches,[5] who had inherited the English lands of his great-grandfather William of Arques, the Domesday tenant of Odo bishop of Bayeux.[6] In 1130 Hugh de Albertivilla occurs on the Kentish pipe roll.[7] Since there is no place of the name in the department of La Manche, whence came the Avranches family, it is to the Seine-Inférieure and the neighbourhood of Arques that one must look for the original home of this family. At first sight Auberville-sur-Eaulne (Seine-Inférieure, arr. Dieppe, cant. and comm. Envermeu) suggests itself, since it lies only 11 kil. E of Arques, but there is no other evidence to suggest a connexion between it and William of Arques. On the other hand Auberville-sur-Yère is barely one kilometre E of Canéhan, which was part of the original endowment of the abbey of the Holy Trinity of Rouen given by its founder Goscelin the *vicomte*,[8] the maternal grandfather of William of Arques; and William was his eventual heir.[9] Other evidence tends to strengthen this identification. A charter of 1058 by William (of Arques) and Gilbert, sons of Godfrey *vicomte* of Arques, for Holy Trinity is attested by Osbern de Alberti Villa, the only other witnesses being the cook and seneschal of the abbey.[10] This Osbern witnessed a number of other gifts to the abbey which are in no way connected with the Arques family. One, however, is a grant by Hugh Talbot of the tithe of 'Sanreith' which appears to be Sangroy in

[1] Pp. 42–44.

[2] *Cartulaire de la Sainte-Trinité de Rouen*, ed. A. Deville, no. 25; William de Jumièges, *Gesta Normannorum Ducum*, lib. viii, c. 37 (by Robert of Torigny), ed. Marx, p. 325.

[3] In writing 'sole daughter and heiress' Professor Douglas overlooked the fact that William of Arques had another daughter, Maud, married to William the chamberlain of Tancarville, who inherited his Norman lands (William of Jumièges, *u.s.*); this point was not, however, relevant to his argument.

[4] *Ord. Vit.*, ed. Le Prévost, iii, 322, 354.

[5] *Red Bk. Exch.*, p. 192.

[6] See AVRANCHES.

[7] *Pipe Roll* 31 *Hen. I*, pp. 64, 67.

[8] *Cartulaire de la Sainte-Trinité de Rouen*, ed. A. Deville, no. 1.

[9] See APPEVILLE.

[10] A. Deville, *op. cit.*, no. 25.

Touffreville-sur-Eu, formerly sur-Criel, a commune adjoining Canéhan.[1] The witnesses are mostly local men and include Osbern de Alberti Villa and Heddo de Canaan [Canéhan].[2] In the result, while the possibility of this family having come from Auberville-sur-Eaulne cannot be entirely excluded, the evidence points strongly to Auberville-sur-Yère.

AUBIGNY, ALBINI, ETC., earls of Arundel.

Saint-Martin d'Aubigny: Manche, arr. Coutances, cant. Periers.

The early history of the family will be found in *The Complete Peerage*, s.n. MOWBRAY, new ed., vol. ix, pp. 366–7. The details of their benefactions to the abbey of Lessay as confirmed by a charter of Henry II, 1185–1188,[3] identify St-Martin d'Aubigny with the Aubigny which was the *caput* of their Norman honour; thus the 'ecclesiam de Folgeriis' is Feugères, 2½ kil. SE of Aubigny, the 'feria Sancti Christofori' mentioned in conjunction with the 'forum Albinneii' is St-Christophe-d'Aubigny, a parish now united to that of St-Martin,[4] and 'Marchesis' is Marchésieux, 5 kil. NE of Aubigny. There is no trace of a feudal castle at Aubigny itself, but Gerville found nearby at Le Mesnil-Vigot the remains of a considerable castle with a well-defined motte, then known as 'le château de St-Clair.'[5]

AUBIGNY, ALBINI, ETC., of Cainhoe, co. Bedford.

Saint-Martin d'Aubigny: Manche, arr. Coutances, cant. Periers.

Nigel d'Aubigny was a Domesday tenant-in-chief at Cainhoe and elsewhere in Bedfordshire. His origin has been discussed by the present writer,[6] and the conclusion reached that he was a member of the same family as Aubigny of Arundel and derived his name from St-Martin d'Aubigny. His exact position in the pedigree has not been established with certainty, but the probabilities point somewhat strongly to his having been a younger brother of Roger d'Aubigny the father of William d'Aubigny, founder of the line of Arundel; if so, he was probably brother of Richard d'Aubigny, abbot of St. Albans.

AUBIGNY (BRITO), of Belvoir.

Saint-Aubin d'Aubigné: Ille-et-Vilaine.

For this identification see J. H. Round in Hist. MSS. Comm., *Duke of Rutland*, vol. iv, p. 107.

[1] It is not identified by Deville. A charter of Henry II in the Archives of Seine-Inférieure, printed by J. Malicorne *L'Abbaye de Bival* (pp. 60–64), confirms to that abbey a grant by a later Hugh Talbot of a rent charged on the mill of 'Sanrai.' The charter was transcribed for the author by Ch. de Beaurepaire and he, the highest possible authority on such a point, identifies 'Sanrai' with Sangroy (*op. cit.*, p. 63*n*). The charter in its present form is highly suspicious, but there seems little reason to doubt the fact of the grant.

[2] A. Deville, *op. cit.*, no. 56.

[3] Delisle et Berger, *Rec. des Actes de Henri II*, ii, 302; *cf.* a charter of William d'Aubigny, the second earl of Arundel, for the abbey of Lessay (*Mon. Ang.*, iv, 645).

[4] Lecanu, *Hist. du diocèse de Coutances* (2nd ed. 1877), ii, 353–4.

[5] 'Sur les anciens châteaux . . de la Manche' in *Mém. Soc. Ant. Norm.*, vol. ii (1825), p. 239.

[6] L. C. Loyd, 'The origin of the family of Aubigny of Cainhoe' in *Beds. Hist. Rec. Soc.*, vol. xix (1937), pp. 101–109.

An offshoot of the parent stock was represented by William de Albigneio, who was a benefactor of the abbey of Vieuville in Britanny *c.* 1200,[1] and the father of Philip d'Aubigny, bailiff of the Channel Islands *temp.* Henry III. This family frequently occurs in the dioceses of Dol and Rennes. An account is given in *The Complete Peerage,* s.n. DAUBENEY, new ed., vol. iv, pp. 93 *et seq.*

AUFFAY, ALFAIT, ALTIFAGIUM.

Auffay: Seine-Inf., arr. Dieppe, cant. Tôtes.

Gulbert of Auffay fought at the battle of Hastings, but refused the Conqueror's offer of lands in England.[2] Gulbert's grandson Jordan married Juliana daughter of Godescalch who had come to England with Adelaide the second queen of Henry I,[3] and the king gave Norton Ferris in Kilmington, Somerset, to Jordan in marriage with Juliana.[4] Thereafter Richard and John of Auffay occur on the Pipe Rolls as holding land in Somerset; these can be shown to be the son and grandson of Jordan, and this combined with the mention of Juliana in the entry in the *Book of Fees* establishes the identity of these Somerset landowners with the lords of Auffay. The deep ditches and thick walls of the castle existed in the nineteenth century, but by 1870 only the motte remained.[5]

AUKENVILLA.

Auquainville: Calvados, arr. Lisieux, cant. Livarot.

Hugh de Aukenvilla witnessed a charter of earl Robert de Ferrers for Maurice son of Geoffrey of Tilty, Essex, dated 26 Sept. 1139.[6] In the reign of Henry II two brothers Henry and Thomas de Auchenvilla, the earl's chaplains, witnessed charters of earl William de Ferrers.[7] Auquainville was a fief of the barony of Ferrières, and its fiefs in this neighbourhood were known as 'la branche d'Auquainville.'[8] Close to the church is a large motte[9]; this in the circumstances was probably in the hands of the lord of Ferrières.

There is no record of English lands held by the family, but since the English and Norman lands of Ferrers descended in different lines after the death of Henry de Ferrers in the late eleventh century, it must have been settled in England.

[1] Morice, *Hist. de Bretagne, Preuves,* vol. i, col. 776.

[2] *Ord. Vit.,* ed. Le Prévost, iii, 44.

[3] *Ibid.,* iii, 47. Orderic gives an elaborate account of the family, as to which he would be well-informed, since Gulbert founded a priory at Auffay in 1079 as a cell of St-Evroul. See also D'Estaintot, *Recherches sur Auffay* (1879), particularly the charter of Richard of Auffay on pp. 3 and 4; also *Gall. Christ.,* xi, 823.

[4] *Bk. of Fees,* p. 81.

[5] Cochet, *Rép. arch. . . . de la Seine-Inf.,* col. 85.

[6] Hist. MSS. Comm., *Earl of Essex* (*Various Collections,* vol. vii), p. 310.

[7] Jeayes, *Gresley Charters,* no. 7; *Mon. Ang.,* iv, 221; *Cal. Docs. France,* nos. 584–6; and *cf.* Jeayes, *Derbyshire Charters,* no. 1360.

[8] 'Aveu' for the barony of Ferrières in 1604; see A. Le Prévost, *Mém. et Notes . . . de l'Eure,* ii, 100.

[9] A. de Caumont, *Statistique monumentale du Calvados,* v, 703.

AUMALE, ALBEMARLA.

Aumale: Seine-Inf., arr. Neufchâtel, cant. Aumale.

An adequate account of the counts of Aumale will be found in *The Complete Peerage*, new ed., vol. i, pp. 350 *et seq.* The lands of the counts in France do not seem to have been of great extent. An examination of those mentioned in three charters[1] relating to the abbey of St. Martin of Aumale shows nearly all of them to be within a radius of 10 kil. of Aumale, mostly in Normandy but some on the eastern side of the river Bresle and therefore outside the limits of the duchy. This suggests that Aumale may not have been, strictly speaking, a Norman *comté*. This seems to support the suggestion made by the writer of the article in *The Complete Peerage* that the countship of Stephen the first count may have been due to the fact that he was the son of Odo the dispossessed count of Champagne and therefore of comital rank.

AVILERS.

Auvilliers: Seine-Inf., arr. and cant. Neufchâtel.

By a charter *temp.* William I Robert Malet confirmed to Eye priory among the gifts of his men those of Hugh de Avilers, namely, two thirds of the tithes of Brome, Suffolk, and of Shelfhanger, Norfolk.[2] There is reason to believe that Conteville (Seine-Inf., arr. Neufchâtel, cant. Aumale) was a fief of Robert Malet and that it was from this place that his Suffolk under-tenant took his name.[3] Auvilliers lies 11 kil. NW of Conteville, and since there is no other place of the name in the department of the Seine-Inférieure there is a strong probability that it was from this place that Hugh came.

The family continued in England, for in 1212 Bartholomew de Auviliers was holding Brome and Shelfhanger of the king by serjeanty.[4] It would appear therefore that the superiority over these lands was not granted out again with the rest of the honour of Eye after the forfeiture of Robert Malet.

AVRANCHES, DE ABRINCIS.

Avranches: Manche.

In 1166 William de Abrincis held twenty-one and a half knights' fees of the old feoffment and two and a half of the new, the majority being in Kent.[5] These, or the bulk of them, represented the lands of William of Arques, the Domesday tenant-in-chief, William's father Rualon of Avranches having married Maud daughter and heir of Nigel de Monville by Emma daughter and coheiress of William of Arques.[6] Since Rualon was sheriff of Kent in 1130 he was then in possession of these lands.[7]

[1] A charter of Stephen count of Aumale dated 1115 (*Early Yorks. Charters*, iii, no. 1304); one of William count of Aumale *c.* 1160–1162 (*ibid.*, no. 1307); one of Henry II, 1181–1182 (Delisle et Berger, *Rec. des Actes de Henri II*, ii, 210).

[2] *Mon. Ang.*, iii, 405. These gifts were confirmed by Henry II (*Cal. Chart. Rolls*, 1341–1417, p. 364).

[3] See CONTEVILLE.

[4] *Bk. of Fees*, pp. 131, 138.

[5] *Red Bk. Exch.*, p. 192. The text is corrupt but this seems to be the effect: see the editor's note.

[6] Round, *Geoffrey de Mandeville*, p. 397.

[7] *Pipe Roll* 31 *Hen. I*, pp. 63, 65.

In 1172 William de Abrincis held one fee of the honour of Mortain in the bailiwick of Cerences.[1] A charter of Henry II of 1185–88 confirmed to the abbey of Lessay the gift of William de Abrincis of a quarter of the church of St-Sauveur-Landelin, the chapelry of his house and twenty-six acres of land, etc.[2] St-Sauveur is 24 kil. N of Cerences; this locates William's Norman fee. The original return of his fees made by the abbot of Le Mont-St-Michel in 1172 shows that William de Abrincis did homage to the abbot Robert de Torigni on his accession in 1158 for the land of Noient (Manche, arr. Avranches, cant. Pontorson, comm. Macey), and was holding that land in 1172 for three quarters of a third of a fee.[3] Macey is 14 kil. S of Avranches. The identity of this Norman William with the Kentish tenant-in-chief of 1166 is clinched by the occurrence among his English under-tenants of a Richard de Milers holding two fees of the old feoffment and a Humphrey de Milliers holding one of the new.[4] There is a Millières 8 kil. NW of St-Sauveur-Landelin, but no such place in Seine-Inférieure whence William of Arques and Nigel de Monville came. These people must have been enfeoffed by the Avranches family.

Bachepuis, Bachepuz, Bagpuz.

Bacquepuits: Eure, arr. and cant. Evreux.

The family were well-known and extensive under-tenants of the Ferrers earls of Derby, and descended from Ralf [de Bachepuz] who in 1086 held of Henry de Ferrers in Berkshire and Derbyshire.[5] The distance of Bacquepuits from Ferrières-St-Hilaire, the *caput* of the Norman barony, is 35 kil., and moreover it was held of the counts of Evreux.[6] On the other hand the count of Evreux received but little land in England at the Conquest, and in 1086 he held lands of small extent in Berkshire and Oxfordshire, on none of which were there enfeoffed under-tenants. In such circumstances it would be natural that a man from Bacquepuits seeking fortune overseas should attach himself to a neighbouring baron who had obtained such vast estates in England as had Henry de Ferrers. When to this is added the fact that no other Bacquepuits is known to exist the provenance may be considered to be reasonably certain.

Bacon.

Le Molay (formerly Le Molay-Bacon): Calvados, arr. Bayeux, cant. Balleroy.

In 1166 Robert Bacun, William Bacun and Alexander de Kerdentone held four knights' fees of the old feoffment of William de Montfichet.[7] Le Molay is 9 kil. N of Montfiquet. In the abbacy of Gilbert (1079–1101)

1 *Red Bk. Exch.*, p. 643; *cf.* p. 636 *n.*

2 Delisle et Berger, *Rec. des Actes de Henri II*, ii, 301.

3 *Rec. Hist. France*, xxiii, 703 e, j.

4 *Red Bk. Exch.*, p. 193.

5 Mr. Loyd had probably in mind the paper by Round, 'A Bachepuz Charter,' in *Ancestor*, xii, 152–5.

6 For Bacquepuits see A. Le Prévost, *Mém. et Notes . . . de l'Eure*, i, 158; Charpillon et Caresme, *Dict. hist. de l'Eure*, i, 183.

7 *Red Bk. Exch.*, p. 349.

William Bacun gave to St. Stephen's abbey, Caen, his part in the churches of Sept-Vents (Calvados, arr. Bayeux, cant. Caumont), which lies 20 kil. S of Le Molay.[1] Roger Bacon surrendered the church and tithe of Planquery to Philip de Harcourt, bishop of Bayeux (1142–63),[2] who gave it to the priory of Le Plessis-Grimould.[3] Planquery is 12 kil. S of Le Molay. With the consent of Henry bishop of Bayeux (1165–1205) William Bacon gave to the abbey of Ardennes the advowsons of the churches of Le Breuil (2 kil. NE of Le Molay) and Blay (3 kil. NE of Le Molay),[4] and in 1260 Roger Bacon, lord of Le Molay, confirmed this gift of William his grandfather.[5] In 1172 Roger Bacon held a quarter of Campigny (5 kil. E of Le Molay).[6] The under-tenants of William de Montfichet must have been a younger branch of the family, since the lord of Le Molay in 1166 was clearly the Roger Bacon who surrendered the church of Planquery to the bishop of Bayeux between 1142 and 1163 and was holding Campigny in 1172.

William Bacon, 'a Norman,' held one quarter of Bradwell near the Sea, Essex, which he had received in marriage with a daughter of Thomas Bardolf,[7] and Dunsford, Devon,[8] both of which were forfeited on the loss of Normandy. He seems to have been the lord of Le Molay mentioned above.

Bailleul, de Bailiolio.

Bailleul-sur-Eaulne (now Bailleul-Neuville): Seine-Inf., arr. Neufchâtel, cant. Londinières.

In 1166 Gilbert de Bailiolio held three knights' fees of the old feoffment of the count of Eu.[9] A charter of king Stephen confirmed to Lewes priory the tithe of Geoffrey de Balliol in Bibleham (in Mayfield, Sussex).[10] A charter of Henry II, 1181–89, confirmed to St. Mary's church at Eu the church of Le Bosc-Geffroy, 6½ kil. NE of Bailleul, and tithes in Normandy and England given by Geoffrey de Baillol and Gilbert his heir.[11] There was a medieval castle near the church.[12]

The family of Balliol, kings of Scotland, came from Bailleul, dept. Somme, arr. Abbeville, cant. Hallencourt; see the elaborate history of that family in *Northumberland County History*, vol. vi.

Bailleul, Balgiole.

Bailleul-en-Gouffern: Orne, arr. Argentan, cant. Trun.

In Domesday Book Rainald de Balgiole occurs as a tenant-in-chief in Staffordshire and can safely be identified with the Rainald who occurs

[1] E. Deville, *Analyse d'un ancien cartulaire . . . de Saint-Etienne de Caen*, p. 28.

[2] *Cal. Docs. France*, no. 545. This must be the Roger whose gift to the abbey of Mortain Henry II confirmed *c.* 1174 (*ibid.*, no. 791).

[3] *Mém. Soc. Ant. Norm.*, viii, 153, no. 1363.

[4] *Ibid.*, vii, 3, no. 13. This William witnessed *Cal. Docs. France*, no. 485 in 1190 and no. 538 in 1201.

[5] *Mém. Soc. Ant. Norm.*, vii, 23, no. 238.

[6] *Red Bk. Exch.*, p. 645.

[7] *Bk. of Fees*, pp. 121, 615.

[8] *Ibid.*, p. 612.

[9] *Red Bk. Exch.*, p. 203.

[10] *Cal. Docs. France*, no. 1391, p. 511.

[11] Delisle et Berger, *Rec. des Actes de Henri II*, ii, 386; *Cal. Docs. France*, no. 1419.

[12] Cochet, *Rép. arch. . . . de la Seine-Inf.*, col. 222.

there as the under-tenant of Roger de Montgomery, earl of Shrewsbury, in Staffordshire and Shropshire, since a charter of earl Roger confirms to the abbey of St-Evroul tithe in Bailleul given by Rainald de Bailol and his wife Amiera, earl Roger's niece.[1] In 1247 a Gilo 'de Balloto,' knight, stated that the land which he held in Bailleul-en-Gouffern was held of the count of Alençon or his heirs[2]; they were the successors in title of earl Roger; *cf.* Tait in *V.C.H. Shropshire,* i, 104.

BALLON, DE BALADONE, ETC.

Ballon: Sarthe, arr. Le Mans, cant. Ballon.

An account of the family is given by Round in *Peerage and Family History,* pp. 181 *et seq.*, where there is cited a charter of Hamelin de Ballon to the abbey of St. Vincent, Le Mans, 1087–1100, in which he distinctly states that he was born at the castle of Ballon.[3]

BASSET.

Montreuil-au-Houlme: Orne, arr. Argentan, cant. Briouze.

In recounting the invasion of Normandy by Geoffrey count of Anjou in 1136 Orderic states that he took Carrouges and Ecouché, and then, after coming to an agreement with the garrison of Asnebec, attacked 'arcem de Mosterolo,' where he was repulsed.[4] A glance at Geoffrey's route on the map shows this to be Montreuil-au-Houlme. Orderic goes on to describe Montreuil as follows: 'Ricardus enim cognomento Bassetus, cujus in Anglia vivente Henrico potentia, utpote capitalis justiciarii, magna fuerat, in parvo feudo, quod parentum successivo jure in Normannia obtinuerat; . . . . Firmissimum ergo ex quadris lapidibus turrim apud Mosterolum construxit.'[5] This identifies Richard as the son of Ralf Basset also justiciar, and Montreuil as the original home of the family. Montreuil is 35 kil. NW by W of Domfront, and it is possible that Ralf Basset the father first came to the notice of the future king when he was lord of Domfront in the reign of William II.

BAUDEMONT, otherwise DE BOSCO.

Baudemont: Eure, arr. Les Andelys, cant. Ecos.

Henry I gave Mutford, Suffolk, to Baldric de Bosco in augmentation of his barony of 'Baldemund'[6]: this was before 1130, when Baldric occurs on the Pipe Roll under Suffolk as pardoned 56*s.* for danegeld.[7] Accounts of the family are to be found in Powicke, *The Loss of Normandy,* pp. 489–491; Stapleton, *Magn. Rot. Scacc. Norm.*, vol. ii, pp. cxi–cxiv; and Le Prévost, *Mém. et Notes . . . . de l'Eure,* i, 188–189. The style 'de Bosco' was derived from the adjacent fief of Bus, now Bus-St-Rémy. Baldric was succeeded by Goel de Baudemont, apparently his son, who in 1172 owed the service of one knight for his lands in

1 *Ord. Vit.*, ed. Le Prévost, ii, 414.
2 *Querimoniae Normannorum* in *Rec. Hist. France,* xxiv, 64.
3 *Cal. Docs. France,* no. 1045.
4 Ed. Le Prévost, v, 68.
5 *Ibid.*, pp. 68–9.
6 *Bk. of Fees,* p. 135.
7 *Pipe Roll* 31 *Hen. I*, p. 99.

Normandy.[1] He left a daughter and heir, Hildeburgh, who married 1st Osbert son of Roger de Cailly by whom she had two daughters, coheirs of their parents, and 2ndly Robert de Pinkeny. In the lists of 1204–8 in the Registers of Philip Augustus is the entry, ' Robert de Pinquigni Baskevillam et Baudemont de feodo Vernonis.'[2] A charter dated 1211 shows Hildeburgh and her second husband, Robert de Pinkeny, making a gift to St-Ouen of Rouen.[3]

BAVENT, BADVENT, ETC.

Bavent: Calvados, arr. Caen, cant. Troarn.

Among the fees of the old feoffment in the *carta* of Hubert de Ria of 1166 is the entry, ' Hugo Comes ij milites et dimidium, scilicet feodum Huberti de Bauvent.'[4] William the second abbot of St. Stephen's, Caen (1070–1079), bought the land of Ralf Pitot at Bavent ' concedente domino suo Huberto de Ria.'[5] Rannulf de Bavent and William his son gave two acres of land in Bavent to St. Stephen's, apparently during the abbacy of Eudo (1108–1140).[6] The overlordship of the Ryes family in Bavent establishes Hubert's provenance.

BEAUMONT, DE BELLOMONTE.

Beaumont-le-Roger: Eure, arr. Bernay, cant. Beaumont.

The well-known Roger de Beaumont held Sturminster Marshal, Dorset, in 1086[7]; it descended to the counts of Meulan through Roger's eldest son, Robert count of Meulan. That Roger took his name from Beaumont is a part of the general history of Normandy.[8] It follows that Roger's descendants, the counts of Meulan, the earls of Leicester, and the earls of Warwick all derive from Beaumont-le-Roger.[9]

BELMEIS, BEAUMEIS, ETC.

Beaumais-sur-Dive: Calvados, arr. Falaise, cant. Morteaux.

In the twelfth century this family furnished two bishops of London and a number of dignitaries and canons of St. Paul's cathedral. There are elaborate accounts of the family by Stubbs[10] and Eyton.[11] Richard de Belmeis, the founder of the family, was a follower of Roger de Montgomery and, according to Orderic,[12] sheriff of Shropshire. In 1108 he became bishop of London, having founded an important Shropshire family descending from his brother Walter. Beaumais-sur-Dive appears to have been a fief of Grandmesnil,[13] from which it was only 12 kil.

[1] *Red Bk. Exch.*, p. 636.
[2] *Rec. Hist. France*, xxiii, 714b.
[3] Le Prévost, *op. cit.*, p. 189.
[4] *Red Bk. Exch.*, p. 400.
[5] E. Deville, *Analyse d'un ancien cartulaire . . . de Saint-Etienne de Caen*, p. 13.
[6] *Ibid.*, *p.* 45.
[7] *D.B.*, i, 80.
[8] Express evidence is to be found in *Cal. Docs. France*, nos. 368–70.
[9] See *Complete Peerage*, new ed., vii, 522 *et seq.*
[10] *Ralph de Diceto* (Rolls Ser.), Introduction, p. xxi *et seq.*
[11] *Shropshire*, ii, 193 *et seq.*
[12] Ed. Le Prévost, iv, 275.
[13] *Cal. Docs. France*, no. 607; a charter of Robert earl of Leicester, son of the countess Parnel, the heiress of the Norman honour of Grandmesnil.

distant, but it is in the Hiesmois of which Roger was hereditary *vicomte*, 20 kil. W of Vimoutiers, an early and important Montgomery possession, and 12 kil. E of Noron held of Montgomery by William Pantulf, also an under-tenant in Shropshire. The only other Beaumais is in Seine-Inférieure (arr. Dieppe, cant. Offranville, comm. Aubermesnil) and far removed from the Montgomery sphere of influence. There seems to be no doubt about the identification, which is accepted by Stubbs.

BELNAI, BEUNAI.

Beaunay: Seine-Inf., arr. Dieppe, cant. Tôtes.

In 1166 Jordan de Belnai held two knights' fees of the old feoffment of the honour of Giffard.[1] In 1143 Helias de Belnai and Ingelran his brother and Lambert Porchet and William his brother restored to Longueville priory the church of Ste-Geneviève; the charter was afterwards read over at the gate of the castle of Longueville in the presence of earl Walter Giffard who confirmed it.[2] At some date after 1166 Gerard de Beaunai confirmed this church to the priory, and also the chapel of Belmesnil which Jordan de Beunai, his father, had given.[3] Beaunay and Ste-Geneviève are contiguous; Belmesnil is 4 kil. NW of Beaunay. Near the church of Beaunay is a large motte.[4]

BERNERS.

Bernières-sur-Mer: Calvados, arr. Caen, cant. Douvres.

In 1086 Ralf was an under-tenant of Eudo Dapifer in Dunmow, Essex.[5] An account of the family and its connexion with Dunmow is given by Farrer, *Honors and Knights' Fees*, iii, 213 *et seq.*, who shows that Ralf was Ralf de Berners. In 1166 a Ralf de Berners or Bernieres was returned among the knights of Eudo Dapifer as holding half a knight's fee of Henry son of Gerold.[6] Bernières is 15 kil. E of Ryes, Eudo's place of origin.

BIGOT.

Dept. Calvados.

A full account of Roger Bigot, a great Domesday tenant-in-chief in East Anglia and ancestor of the earls of Norfolk, will be found in the new edition of *The Complete Peerage*, vol. ix, pp. 575–579.

In the Bayeux Inquest of 1133 is the entry, 'Feodum Hugonis Bigoti in Logis et in Savenayo vavassoria, sed servit pro milite dimidio.'[7] Savenay is in the commune of Courvaudon (Calvados, arr. Vire, cant. Villers-Bocage); in it was a fief known as 'le fief Bigot.'[8] A Domesday under-tenant of Roger Bigot took his name from Savenay.[9] Les Loges (Calvados, arr. Vire, cant. Aunay-sur-Odon) is 17 kil. W of Courvaudon.

[1] *Red Bk. Exch.*, p. 312.
[2] P. Le Cacheux, *Chartes du Prieuré de Longueville*, no. 3.
[3] *Ibid.*, no. 51.
[4] Cochet, *Rép. arch. . . . de la Seine-Inf.*, col. 85.
[5] *D.B.*, ii, 50.
[6] *Red Bk. Exch.*, p. 355.
[7] *Rec. Hist. France*, xxiii, 701c.
[8] M. Béziers, *Mémoires . . . du diocèse de Bayeux* (Soc. Hist. Norm.), ii, 361.
[9] See SAVENIE.

In 1453 the fief of Les Loges was held of the bishop of Bayeux as of the barony of La Ferrière-Hareng by the service of a quarter of a knight's fee.[1] In addition to this vavassoria held of the bishop of Bayeux there is reason to believe that Roger Bigot held lands in the Val d'Auge, including Corbon, probably of the duke in chief.[2]

Attention should be drawn to a passage in Wace's Roman de Rou,[3] where in his enumeration of the combatants at the battle of Hastings he speaks of

L'ancestre Hue le Bigot
Qui aueit terre a Maletot
E as Loges et a Chanon.

Speaking generally this catalogue of Wace's seems to be historically worthless, but he was a canon of Bayeux cathedral and his statements as to persons and still more as to places cannot be entirely neglected. As regards Les Loges he is right. Maltot (Calvados, arr. Caen, cant. Evrecy) is 16 kil. NE of Savenay, Roger's fief, and 9 kil. SW of Caen, where Wace had been a 'clerc lisant,' but his statement is the only evidence to connect it with Bigot. Canon (Calvados, arr. Lisieux, cant. Mézidon) is 9 kil. SW of Corbon; although not actually in the Val d'Auge it may well have been part of the Bigot lands there mentioned above.[2] On the whole, therefore, Wace's statements appear in this case to be founded on fact. The circumstance that Wace appears to have been ignorant of the name of Hugh Bigot's Conquest ancestor, in reality his father Roger, suggests that the family was of minor importance in Normandy.

To sum up, Roger Bigot was a man of Calvados. His lands in Normandy were of but moderate extent and he made the fortunes of himself and his descendants in England, and through the Conquest. One cannot help suspecting that he was enabled to do this by his Norman overlord, Odo bishop of Bayeux, of whom in 1086 he was holding something like twenty manors in Suffolk.[4]

Biset.

Cany: Seine-Inf., arr. Yvetot, cant. Cany.

Manasser Biset was a steward of Henry II,[5] and was a member of his entourage before his accession to the throne, witnessing his charters at Château-du-Loir and Falaise in the period Sept. 1151–Jan. 1153.[6] He came to England with Henry and thereafter was one of the most frequent witnesses of his acts until his death in 1176–77.[7] He married

[1] M. Béziers, *op. cit.*, ii, 292. It will be noticed that in 1133 the total service of Savenay and Les Loges was half a knight.

[2] See Corbun.

[3] Ed. H. Andresen, vol. ii, p. 370, ll. 8571–3.

[4] *D.B.*, ii, 373–378b.

[5] Delisle, *Rec. des Actes de Henri II, Introduction*, p. 403.

[6] Delisle et Berger, *Rec. des Actes de Henri II*, i, 38, 40.

[7] As early as Mich. 1156 he held lands in Hants (*Pipe Roll 2 Hen. II*, p. 54) and other counties. He last figures on the roll of 22 Hen. II; on the succeeding roll his place is taken by his son, then a minor.

Alice de Cany, sister and heir of Gilbert de Falaise lord of Cany,[1] by whom he had a son and heir, Henry Biset, who on the loss of Normandy adhered to king John. It cannot be said that Cany was the place of origin of the Biset family, but it is worth while to record the part of Normandy with which Manasser was connected; moreover the fact that in 1166 he held one knight's fee of the old feoffment of the honour of Giffard in England[2] suggests a connexion with the Pays de Caux.

Bohun.

St-Georges de Bohon: Manche, arr. St-Lô, cant. Carentan. The Bohuns of Midhurst who actually held Bohon in the twelfth century descended in the male line from Savaric son of Cana and the *vicomtes* of Beaumont in Maine. The earls of Hereford who descended in the paternal line from Bohun were a younger branch. The motte existed in its entirety in 1830.[3]

Bois, de Bosco.

Bois-Arnault: Eure, arr. Evreux, cant. Rugles. Bois-Arnault was held of the honour of Breteuil by a family whose heads for more than two centuries were named Ernald. The earliest ascertained ancestor is Ernald 'Popeline filius,' who at some time before 1066 gave the church of Corneuil (Eure, arr. Evreux, cant. Damville) to the abbey of Lyre with the consent of his lord William Fitz Osbern, the lord of Breteuil, there being mention of Ernald's son, also named Ernald.[4] By another charter he gave the tithe of his demesne at Champ-Dominel (cant. Damville).[5] At a later date an Ernald de Bosco confirmed to the abbey the above gifts of his ancestors and also half the tithe of Bois-Arnault.[6] There is no trace of the family having settled in England in the time of William Fitz Osbern, but in 1130 Ernald de Bosco was holding Thorpe Arnold, co. Leicester, of the earl of Leicester[7]; he must have been enfeoffed at a date later than the earl's acquisition by marriage of the honour of Breteuil, that is after 1120.[8] Thereafter they are found witnessing charters of the earls both in England and Normandy. A record of the first years of the thirteenth century shows Bois-Arnault and its members as held of the honour of Breteuil by the service of $9\frac{5}{6}$ knights,[9] while in England they held $19\frac{1}{4}$ fees of the earldom of Leicester.[10] They also held a moiety of Little Houghton and Brafield, co. Northampton, and other lands

[1] Charters of Gilbert and Alice for Longueville priory (P. Le Cacheux, *Chartes du Prieuré de Longueville*, nos. 5, 33); of Alice for Jumièges (Vernier, *Chartes de Jumièges*, i, 179); Obituary of Longueville (*Rec. Hist. France*, xxiii, 435b).

[2] *Red Bk. Exch.*, p. 312.

[3] Gerville in *Mém. Soc. Ant. Norm.*, v, 308.

[4] A. Le Prévost, *Mém. et Notes . . . de l'Eure*, i, 347.

[5] *Ibid.*, i, 485.

[6] *Ibid.*, iii, 382.

[7] *Pipe Roll* 31 *Hen. I*, p. 88.

[8] *Complete Peerage*, new ed., vii, 529–30.

[9] *Rec. Hist. France*, xxiii, 705c.

[10] In 1166 the earl of Leicester made no return of his fees. This figure is taken from a return of the knights' fees belonging to Roger de Quincy, earl of Winchester, coheir of the earls of Leicester of the first line, who died in 1264 (Hist. MSS. Comm., *R. R. Hastings*, i, 331).

of the honour of Huntingdon, acquired by marriage with Emma daughter and coheir of Payn of Houghton.[1] On the separation of England and Normandy the Ernald of the day remained in England and his Norman lands were confiscated, and Philip Augustus granted certain of his lands to Roger des Essarts in 1203.[2] In 1219 the same king granted lands formerly held by Ernald de Bosco in Bois-Arnault and elsewhere to Robert de Los.[3]

BOLEBEC.

Bolbec: Seine-Inf., arr. Le Havre, cant. Bolbec.

Between 1067 and 1076 Roger Porchet, Hugh de Bolebec and others gave the church of St. Michael at Bolbec to the abbey of Bernay, Hugh's portion being a quarter; the gift was confirmed by Walter Giffard as overlord.[4] In 1086 Hugh de Bolebec was holding lands in Hartwell, and elsewhere in Buckinghamshire, of Walter Giffard.[5] The return of 1166 shows that Hugh de Bolebec (died 1164–65) had held twenty knights' fees of the old feoffment of the English honour of Giffard.[6] The complications of the Bolebec pedigree in the twelfth century have been admirably elucidated by Round in the introduction to the *Rotuli de Dominabus*.[7] At the beginning of the thirteenth century the lands passed by the marriage of the heiress to the earls of Oxford. Besides the extensive lands held of Giffard, Hugh de Bolebec held in chief a barony of which the *servitium debitum* was ten knights,[8] which passed on his death to his younger brother Walter, who in 1166 also held land in chief in Northumberland of which the *servitium debitum* was five knights.[9] On the other hand there are but few traces of the family in Normandy, but the Norman Exchequer Roll of 1180 shows that the farm of the Norman lands was then 40*li*. 16*s*. 1*d*.[10] It is perhaps significant that their attestations of the charters of their overlords are all to charters executed in England. The family appears to have been one originally of small account which owed its advancement to the Conquest.

[1] *V.C.H. Northants*, iv, 268; Farrer, *Honors and Knights' Fees*, ii, 303–5.

[2] Delisle, *Cartulaire Normand*, no. 71.

[3] *Ibid.*, no. 1220.

[4] A. Le Prévost, *Mém. et Notes . . . de l'Eure*, i, 286–7. The charter is calendared inadequately and in a misleading manner by Round (*Cal. Docs. France*, no. 412). It ends with a purported confirmation by William the Conqueror as king, dated at Lillebonne 1061. The witnesses are so mutually anachronistic as to show it to be spurious, quite apart from this impossible date. If, however, this clause be removed there remains a quite normal charter which seems open to no suspicion, and of which the limits of date are fixed by the mention of the *king's* forester and of Vitalis abbot of Bernay, who became abbot of Westminster in 1076.

[5] *D.B.*, i, 147, 147b. In the first entry the name is miswritten 'Molbec.' He is undoubtedly the Hugh who is entered as holding other lands of Giffard.

[6] *Red Bk. Exch.*, p. 312.

[7] *Pipe Roll Soc.*, vol. xxxv, pp. xxxix–xli.

[8] *Red Bk. Exch.*, p. 317; *cf.* Round, *Rot. de Dominabus*, p. xxxix.

[9] *Red Bk. Exch.*, p. 437.

[10] Stapleton, *Rot. Scacc. Norm.*, i, 67.

DE BORDINEIO.

Bordigny: Eure, arr. Evreux, cant. and comm. Breteuil. Reginald de Bordineo figures in the well-known treaty between Ranulf earl of Chester and Robert earl of Leicester as a man of the latter.[1] A charter of Henry II, 1156, confirmed to Leicester abbey the church of Church Langton, co. Leicester, 'ex dono Willelmi de Novo Mercato et Rogeri de Bordeni.'[2] The Leicestershire Survey shows Church Langton as land of the earl of Leicester.[3] In 1153 Reginald witnessed a charter of Henry duke of the Normans restoring his lands to Robert son of Robert earl of Leicester.[4] Bordigny lies on the edge of the forest of Breteuil, 2½ kil. N of Breteuil, the *caput* of the Norman honour of the earls of Leicester; and a charter of Henry II, 1155–58, confirmed to the abbey of Lyre, 'ex dono Rainaldi de Bordineio lx. solidos in fossa foreste et decimam molendinorum ipsius.'[5] The family could not have been enfeoffed in England until the earl of Leicester had obtained the honour of Breteuil by his marriage with Amice daughter of Ralf de Gael, which was later than November 1120.[6] The English lands were lost on the separation of England and Normandy. In 1272 'Dominus Guillelmus de Bordineio miles' was summoned to the host of Foix in respect of service due to the honour of Breteuil.[7] The family continued at Bordigny until the first quarter of the fourteenth century.[8]

BOSC-ROHARD, BOIS-ROHARD, BORARD, NEMUS-ROHARDI, ETC.

Bosc-le-Hard: Seine-Inf., arr. Dieppe, cant. Bellencombre. Dr. G. H. Fowler has given a good account of the family,[9] to which the reader is referred. In 1086 two brothers, William and Roger de Boscroard, held lands in Buckinghamshire of Robert de Todeni (Tosny) of Belvoir,[10] and the family continued until the end of the thirteenth century. In Normandy Ralf de Bosrohardi gave the church of Bosc-le-Hard to Longueville priory before 1155,[11] and before 1189 the same or another Ralf gave it the site of a grange there.[12] It is well established that Bosc-Rohard is the modern Bosc-le-Hard,[13] and it is 6 kil. NE of Clères, held by a family of that name who were under-tenants of the lord of Tosny.[14] Todeni of Belvoir was a younger branch of Tosny,[15] and

[1] F. M. Stenton, *English Feudalism*, p. 286.

[2] *Cal. Chart. Rolls*, 1300–26, p. 380.

[3] Round, *Feudal England*, p. 197.

[4] Delisle et Berger, *Recueil des Actes de Henri II*, i, 53.

[5] *Ibid.*, p. 168.

[6] *Complete Peerage*, new ed., vii, 529–30.

[7] *Rec. Hist. France*, xxiii, 747d.

[8] Charpillon et Caresme, *Dict. hist. de l'Eure*, i, 569.

[9] *Beds. Hist. Rec. Soc.*, xi, 72–4.

[10] *D.B.*, i, 149.

[11] P. Le Cacheux, *Chartes du Prieuré de Longueville*, no. 4.

[12] *Ibid.*, no. 35.

[13] So late as 1603 it is called Bos Rohard in the letters patent constituting it a barony (Toussaints Du Plessis, *Description de la Haute Normandie* (1740), ii, 352).

[14] *Red Bk. Exch.*, p. 642.

[15] See TOSNY.

the family is brought into still closer connexion with Clères by the fact that a family of that name held land of it in cos. York and Lincoln.[1] On a farm not far from the church of Bosc-le-Hard was the castle.[2]

Boscherville.

Boscherville: Eure, arr. Pont-Audemer, cant. Bourgtheroulde.

In 1135 Henry de Boskerville held three knights' fees of Ferrers; in 1166 they were held by his son John; and in 1135 William de Boskerville held three knights' fees of Ferrers, one of which was held in 1166 by his son Ralf.[3] An 'aveu' for the barony of Ferrières of 1604 shows that there was held of it 'un plain fief de haubert' in the parish of Boscherville called 'le fief de Boscherville'[4]; the identity with this Boscherville is established by the fact that it adjoins Bourgtheroulde, where the lords of Ferrières had an important interest in the middle ages.[5] It is to be noted that these facts, in addition to establishing the provenance of the under-tenants of 1135, carry back the connexion of the lords of Ferrières with Boscherville to the early twelfth century and probably to the days of Henry de Ferrers, the Domesday tenant-in-chief.

Bosville, Boesevilla, etc.

Beuzeville-la-Giffard: Seine-Inf., arr. Dieppe, cant. Bellencombre, comm. Beaumont-le-Hareng.

At some date before 1159 Elias de Boesevilla gave the church of Harthill, co. York, to Lewes priory[6]; and between 1159 and 1164 he gave all his land in Harthill to Reginald de Warenne to hold of him as he and his father Hugh had held it of earl de Warenne.[7] In the twelfth and thirteenth centuries Beuzeville appears as 'Boesevilla' and 'Bosavilla.' It is only 5½ kil. S of Bellencombre, the *caput* of the Warenne honour in Normandy, and it is contiguous to Grigneuzeville and Bracquetuit, both Warenne fiefs.[8] When it is added that there does not appear to be any other place of a similar name in the Warenne sphere of influence the identification seems a safe one.

Braiboue, Braibof.

Brébeuf: Calvados, arr. Caen, cant. Evrecy, comm. Vacogne.

In 1086 Hugh de Braiboue held Wateringbury (*Otrinberge*), Kent, of Odo bishop of Bayeux.[9] Brébeuf was a fief in the commune of Vacogne. It is not mentioned in the Bayeux Inquest of 1133, but a number of places nearby appear there as fiefs of the bishop of Bayeux; *e.g.* Bougy

[1] See Cleres. [2] Cochet, *Rép. arch. . . . de la Seine-Inf.*, col. 10.

[3] *Red Bk. Exch.*, p. 337.

[4] A. Le Prévost, *Mém. et Notes . . . de l'Eure*, ii, 96. The 'feudum loricae'—'fief del haubert'—is the French equivalent of the English knight's fee (see F. M. Stenton, *English Feudalism*, p. 14).

[5] Charpillon et Caresme, *Dict. hist. de l'Eure*, i, 519–21.

[6] *Early Yorks. Charters*, viii, no. 110. [7] *Ibid.*, no. 111.

[8] For Grigneuzeville see *infra*. For Bracquetuit, Ch. de Beaurepaire, *Rec. de chartes de l'Abbaye de Saint-Victor-en-Caux* (Soc. Hist. Norm., Mélanges 5e série), pp. 386, 388–9.

[9] *D.B.*, i, 8b; *cf.* Douglas, *Domesday Monachorum*, p. 102 and note.

4 kil. distant, Noyers 6 kil., St-Vaast 10 kil., Boulon 11 kil. The only other Brébeuf lay in Condé-sur-Vire between St-Lô and Torigny, in dept. La Manche, and therefore far from the lands of the bishopric of Bayeux. In 1166 a later Hugh held one fee of the old feoffment of John de Port of Basing,[1] being no doubt the successor of a Henry de Braiboue who witnessed a charter of Henry de Port for the abbey of Cerisy, 1120–30.[2] Brébeuf is some 35 kil. from Port-en-Bessin, but this tenure under Port supports the identification with Brébeuf in Vacogne as against Brébeuf in Condé-sur-Vire which is far removed from the lands of the bishopric; it must also be borne in mind that Port was an under-tenant of the bishop of Bayeux both in Normandy and England.

BRIOUZE, BRAIOSA, ETC.

Briouze: Orne, arr. Argentan, cant. Briouze.

From the time of Domesday the family of Briouze were lords of the rape of Bramber, Sussex. Their place of origin is established by a series of charters for the abbey of St. Florent at Saumur,[3] particularly by one *ante* 1080 in which William de Briouze gave to the church of St. Gervaise and St. Protaise at Briouze all his tithe except his demesne profit from the mills of Briouze, and also the church of St. Nicholas at his castle of Bramber.[4]

BROILG, BROY.

Brouay: Calvados, arr. Caen, cant. Tilly-sur-Seulles.

In his introduction to the Bedfordshire Domesday[5] Round points out that three, if not four, under-tenants of Beauchamp of Bedford derived their names from places within the single canton of Tilly-sur-Seulles; Wimund de Taissel from Tessel, William de Locels from Loucelles, and Serlo de Ros from Rots. The fourth is Osbert de 'Broilg,' who Round suggests may have derived from Brouay, pointing out however that the Domesday form is more suggestive of Breuil, a name borne by several places in Calvados, though not in the canton of Tilly. The usual name of the family, however, was Broy or a near variant thereof,[6] and Brouay occurs as Broe in 1177 and Broeium in 1251,[7] which points to the Domesday form being corrupt. The cumulative effect of the evidence seems sufficient to establish the identification with Brouay. As to the other three names there can be no doubt. These facts suggest further that the original home of the Beauchamps is to be sought in Calvados, but of the only two Beauchamps in that department one

[1] *Red Bk. Exch.*, p. 208.

[2] H. E. Salter, *Facsimiles of Oxford Charters*, no. 14.

[3] *Cal. Docs. France*, nos. 1110 *et seq.*

[4] *Ibid.*, no. 1112.

[5] *V.C.H. Beds.*, i, 201.

[6] See a note on the family by G. H. Fowler in his edition of the Wardon Abbey Cartulary (*Beds. Hist. Rec. Soc.*, vol. xiii, p. 352).

[7] C. Hippeau, *Dict. topogr. du Calvados*, p. 44.

is a fief in Moyaux, cant. Lisieux, 76 kil. E of Tilly-sur-Seulles, and the other in Vouilly, cant. Isigny, 32 kil. W of it, and it is impossible to draw any sound inference from such evidence.

DE BUCEIO, BOCEIO.

Boucé: Orne, arr. Argentan, cant. Ecouché.

The family held Kingston Bowsey or 'by Sea' (a modern corruption), Sussex, of Briouze from an early date. 'Randulfus Landrici de Boceio filius' witnessed a charter of William de Briouze for St. Florent de Saumur *ante* 1030[1]; and *temp.* William I Ralf de Boceio witnessed a letter of the same William de Briouze.[2] Boucé is 22 kil. E of Briouze, but only 9 kil. S of Ecouché (*Scocetum*), the church of which belonged to William de Briouze in the eleventh century.[3]

BUSLI, BUILLI, BULLI.

Bully: Seine-Inf., arr. and cant. Neufchâtel.

Before the Conquest Roger de Buslei sold the tithe of Buslei to the abbey of the Holy Trinity of Rouen; the witnesses included duke William, Robert count of Eu, Huelin de Drincourt, Richard de Drincourt and Thorald his brother.[4] Drincourt was the old name of Neufchâtel-en-Bray, from which Bully is less than 5 kil. distant. Roger founded the priory of Blyth, co. Nottingham, and in his charter of 1088 charged it with a yearly payment of 40*s.* to the Holy Trinity of Rouen.[5] The *Monasticon Anglicanum* omits the witnesses, but they are printed by Raine as follows: 'Gilbertus presbiter, Ricardus presbiter, Willielmus presbiter, Fulco de Lisoriis, Thoraldus frater ejus, Ernoldus de Buulli, Godefridus dapifer, Turoldus de Cheverchort, Claron, Radulfus Novi Fori, Paganus gladicus, Radulphus dispensator, W. de Drincort.'[6] Here again we have Roger's connexion with Holy Trinity and a witness coming from Drincourt (Neufchâtel); in addition Thorald de Chevercort took his name from Quiévrecourt, 4 kil. from Bully. In 1219 Alice countess of Eu executed a charter acknowledging the terms upon which Philip Augustus had restored the *comté* of Eu to her; it sets out that the king retained to himself the fief of Bully which Robert de Mellevilla held of him in the bailiwick of Neufchâtel.[7] Alice, the heiress of the family, was great-great-granddaughter of William count of Eu by Beatrix sister of Roger de Busli, a marriage by which Roger's honour of Tickhill came to the counts of Eu.

BYGORE.

La Biguerie: Eure, arr. Evreux, cant. Rugles, comm. Neaufles-sur-Risle.

In a return of knights' fees held of the earl of Leicester *c.* 1210–12

1 *Cal. Docs. France*, no. 1112.
2 *Ibid.*, no. 1110.
3 *Ibid.*, no. 1112.
4 *Cartulaire de la Sainte-Trinité de Rouen*, ed. A. Deville, no. xliii.
5 *Mon. Ang.*, iv, 623.
6 J. Raine, *History of Blyth*, pp. 29–30.
7 Delisle, *Cartulaire Normand*, p. 304.

Walerannus de Bygore is entered as holding a quarter of a fee.[1] La Biguerie lies near the western edge of the forest of Breteuil; and in the *Querimoniae Normannorum*[2] of 1247 it is stated that in the time of the earls of Leicester, lords of Breteuil, the men of La Biguerie (*Bigarria*) had the right of gathering wood in the forest; and in a list of fees of 1210–1220 in the Registers of Philip Augustus, Neaufles, in which it lay, is shown as held of the honour of Breteuil.[3] It is perhaps tempting to see in Waleran a man from Bigorre in Southern France, enfeoffed by Simon de Montfort, the Albigensian crusader, who obtained the honour and earldom of Leicester in about 1206, but this is impossible. Simon first went on crusade against the heretics in 1209 and he does not seem to have been in England at any subsequent date[4]; moreover in February 1207 his lands were taken into the king's hand.[5]

CAILLI, KAILLI, ETC.

Cailly: Seine-Inf., arr. Rouen, cant. Clères.

A family of Cailly were under-tenants of Warenne in Norfolk from the time of Domesday until the fourteenth century: the details are given by Farrer in *Honors and Knights' Fees*, vol. iii, pp. 382–384. Cailly is 15 kil. S of Bellencombre, the *caput* of the Norman honour of Warenne. It was not itself a fief of Warenne, but its situation combined with the fact that the christian name of Osbert occurs in the English line and in that of the lords of Cailly puts the identification beyond doubt. An account of the Norman line is given in Powicke, *The Loss of Normandy*, pp. 489–491. A careful examination shows that the two lines were distinct, though probably related.[6] There are remains of a castle at Cailly.[7]

CALCEIS, CAUCEIS.

Pays de Caux: Seine-Inf.

In 1166 Robert de (or le) Cauceis was a tenant of the new feoffment of William de Roumare, his land being then in the king's hand.[8] Henry II confirmed at Bur, 1166–73, an exchange made before him there between William de Roumare and Robert le Calceis, by which Robert gave to William all that he had of William's fee in England in Alkborough and Toynton St. Peter, co. Lincoln, and William gave to Robert all his demesne in Le Bourg-Dun, except the service of the knights holding of him there, and all he had in La Chapelle-sur-Dun, except the service of

[1] *Red Bk. Exch.*, p. 553. The list seems to contain elements of a somewhat earlier date. Matthew de Poteria who figures in it lost his English lands in 1204; see POTERIA, *infra*.

[2] *Rec. Hist. France*, xxiv, 34.

[3] *Ibid.*, xxiii, 617c.

[4] *Complete Peerage*, new ed., vii, 538–40.

[5] *Ibid.*, p. 538, note e.

[6] It is possible that the Osbert de Cailly, lord of Cailly, who witnessed a Jumièges charter in 1138 (Vernier, *Chartes de Jumièges*, i, 160) was identical with the Osbert who witnessed a Castleacre charter in the period 1121–35 (*Mon. Ang.*, v, 51); but this is improbable, and the charter evidence shows that from *c.* 1150 onwards the two lines must have been distinct.

[7] Cochet, *Rép. arch. . . . de la Seine-Inf.*, col. 280.

[8] *Red Bk. Exch.*, p. 378.

Walter de Cantelou and Richard de Dun, to hold by the service of one knight.[1] Robert de Calceis had granted marsh in Toynton St. Peter to the Templars, *temp.* Henry II.[2] A letter from Robert Calcensis to Henry II states that having taken the cross and going to Jerusalem he had entrusted his lands to his nephew William Calcensis to pay his debts and had made William heir of all his land to hold by the service testified by the king's charter concerning the agreement between himself and William de Roumare at Bur.[3]

This evidence seems to establish that this Robert was a man originating in and taking his name from the Pays de Caux, in which lie Le Bourg-Dun and La Chapelle. It is at least doubtful whether he is identical with Robert de Chauz who in 1166 was a considerable tenant-in-chief in Nottinghamshire.[4] That Robert was succeeded by his daughter and heir Maud; he was dead in 1185 and his latest occurrence on the Pipe Roll seems to be in 1168[5]; moreover the exchange between the former Robert and William de Roumare rather points to a man whose chief interests lay in Normandy.

CAMBREIS.

Broglie: Eure, arr. Bernay, cant. Broglie.

The original name of the place was Chambrais, which was changed to Broglie when it was acquired by the duc de Broglie of an Italian family. It is close to Ferrières-Saint-Hilaire and was held by the lords of Ferrières in demesne, finally superseding Ferrières as the *caput* of the barony. Henry de Cambreis held one knight's fee of Ferrers in 1135,[6] and witnessed earl Robert's foundation charter of Merevale abbey.[7]

CAMPEAUX, DE CAMPELLIS, CHAMPEUS.

Campeaux: Calvados, arr. Vire, cant. Beny-Bocage.

In 1086 Hervey held the manor of Skelbrook, co. York, under Ilbert de Lascy of Pontefract and four manors in Oxfordshire under Odo bishop of Bayeux.[8] Hervey de Campeaux and Robert his son made encroachments on the land of the abbey of Selby, for which Robert and his overlord Henry de Lascy made restitution by 1144–*c.* 1160.[9] Robert de Campeaux had been a party to the murder of William Maltravers in the interest of Ilbert de Lascy II, *c.* 1136.[10] Campeaux was held of the bishop of Bayeux by the Lascy family.[11]

1 Delisle et Berger, *Rec. des Actes de Henri II*, i, 559.

2 F. M. Stenton, *Danelaw Charters*, no. 522.

3 *Cal. Docs. France*, no. 277, dated by Round as ?1188; P. le Cacheux, *Chartes du Prieuré de Longueville*, no. 43.

4 *Red Bk. Exch.*, p. 343.

5 Lees, *Records of the Templars*, p. cci.

6 *Red Bk. Exch.*, p. 337.

7 *Mon. Ang.*, v, 482.

8 *Early Yorks. Charters*, iii, 229, where some notes on the family are given.

9 *Ibid.*, no. 1547.

10 *Ibid.*, p. 144 and no. 1455.

11 See LASCY.

CAMVILLE, CANVILLE.

Canville-les-Deux-Eglises: Seine-Inf., arr. Yvetot, cant. Doudeville. Richard de Camville (d. 1176) gave to the abbey of Jumièges the tithes of his land at Hautot-l'Auvray (the next parish to Canville) in a charter which mentions his two wives Adelicia and Milisent[1] and his brother Roger.[2] The Registers of Philip Augustus, 1204–8, record that Gerard de Canvilla held one fee 'apud Canvillam,'[3] and the entry of 1220 shows it to have been a member of the honour of Breteuil and in the king's hand.[4]

CANTELOU, DE KANTILUPO.

Canteleu: Seine-Inf., arr. Dieppe, cant. Bacqueville, comm. Luneray.

In 1166 Walter de Kantilupo held two knights' fees of the new feoffment of William de Roumare.[5] A charter of Henry II, issued between 1166 and 1172–3, confirmed an agreement for the exchange of lands between William de Roumare and Robert le Calceis, William giving to Robert all that he held in Le Bourg-Dun (Seine-Inf., arr. Dieppe, cant. Offranville) except the service rendered there by his knights, and in La Chapelle-sur-Dun (Seine-Inf., arr. Yvetot, cant. Fontaine-le-Dun) except the service of Walter de Cantelou and Richard de Dun.[6] Canteleu is 6 kil. S of Le Bourg-Dun and 7 kil. SE of La Chapelle. It seems certain that it was from this Canteleu that Walter took his name, as also Ralf de Kantilupo who in 1166 held one fee of the new feoffment of William de Roumare.[5]

An earlier member of the family appears to have been Gilbert de Cantelu who, described as seneschal of Robert son of Gerold (uncle and predecessor of William de Roumare I, earl of Lincoln), witnessed a charter of Robert to the abbey of Le Bec.[7]

CANTELU.

Canteloup: Calvados, arr. Caen, cant. Troarn.

By an agreement of 1142–53 Alexander de Cantelu delivered to the canons of Bruton, Somerset, in fee-farm all his rights in Bruton, namely the hundred and the market and the land of the court; and his gifts were confirmed by William the chamberlain of Tancarville.[8] In 1212 the prior of Bruton held the hundred and market of the king as of the fee of the chamberlain of Tancarville.[9] Canteloup is 8 kil. NW of Mézidon, the *caput* of the Tancarville barony in Western Normandy.[10]

[1] Milisent was the widow of Robert Marmion who died in 1143 or 1144; see *Complete Peerage*, new ed., viii, 506–7.

[2] Vernier, *Chartes de Jumièges*, ii, 1.

[3] *Rec. Hist. France*, xxiii, 714f.

[4] *Ibid.*, p. 643k.

[5] *Red Bk. Exch.*, p. 377.

[6] Delisle et Berger, *Rec. des Actes de Henri II*, i, 559.

[7] *Cal. Docs. France*, no. 376.

[8] *Cal. Docs. France*, no. 486.

[9] *Bk. of Fees*, p. 80.

[10] *Cf.* MEINNIL MALGERI.

CARLEVILLE.

Calleville: Eure, arr. Bernay, cant. Brionne.

A charter of Theobald archbishop of Canterbury recited a gift of tithe by Roger de Carlevilla to the priory of Stoke-by-Clare with the consent of his wife and his son Geoffrey.[1] Roger witnessed a charter of the second Richard FitzGilbert (1117–36)[2]; this with other attestations places him in the first quarter of the twelfth century. Calleville is 3 kil. E of Brionne.[3] The earliest recorded forms in Normandy are ' Carlevilla ' in 1216 and ' Karlevilla ' in 1221.[4]

CARON.

Cairon: Calvados, arr. Caen, cant. Creully.

In 1086 William de Caron, in addition to his holdings in Bedfordshire of Nigel d'Aubigny of Cainhoe and of the bishop of Lincoln, was an under-tenant of Eudo Dapifer in Clifton and elsewhere in that county.[5] Cairon is 15 kil. SE of Ryes, the home of Eudo's father Hubert de Rie. In 1166 Ranulf de Carun held three knights' fees of Hubert de Rie (who descended from a brother of Eudo), and with two others one fee of Robert d'Aubigny (Nigel's grandson).[6] Accounts of the family have been given by William Farrer[7] and G. H. Fowler.[8]

CARTERET, CARTRAI, CHARTRAI.

Carteret: Manche, arr. Valognes, cant. Barneville.

In 1166 Philip de Chartrai held thirteen or fourteen knights' fees of the old feoffment of William de Briouze as of the honour of Barnstaple, among Philip's knights being Richard de Chartrai.[9] Philip can be identified with Philip, seigneur of Carteret from *c.* 1130 to *c.* 1178. Carteret charters for the abbey of Le Mont-St-Michel and a pedigree of the family are given in *Cartulaire des Iles Normandes*, Soc. Jersiaise, pp. 50–62.

CASTELLON.

Castillon: Calvados, arr. Bayeux, cant. Balleroy.

In 1086 William de Castellon held two burgesses in Buckingham of the fee of the bishop of Bayeux.[10] Castillon is 11 kil. SW of Bayeux. The Bayeux Inquest of 1133 states that Odo bishop of Bayeux founded a prebend there, it being a part of the forfeited honour of Grimold de Plessis which had been granted to Odo by duke William.[11]

1 *Mon. Ang.*, vi, 1659–60.

2 *Ibid.*, p. 1660.

3 See NAZANDA.

4 Blosseville, *Dict. topogr. de l'Eure*, p. 43.

5 *D.B.*, i, 210, 210b, 212, 212b, 214b. Mr. Loyd suggests that the statement of the jurors (f. 210) that William's father had held T. R. E. is unlikely, and probably arose from a mistake; he gives a reference to Freeman, *Norman Conquest*, v, 755, where, however, the statement is accepted.

6 *Red Bk. Exch.*, pp. 324, 400.

7 *Honors and Knights' Fees*, iii, 258–60.

8 *Beds. Hist. Rec. Soc.*, xiii, 304 *et seq.*, where, however, the suggestion that the true form of the name is ' le Caron ' does not seem to be borne out by the evidence.

9 *Red Bk. Exch.*, p. 259.

10 *D.B.*, i, 143.

11 *Rec. Hist. France*, xxiii, 700c, 702d.

Chamflur, de Campo Flore.

Le Camp Fleuri: Seine-Inf., arr. Neufchâtel, cant. Aumale.

Sir Martin de Campo Flore was constable of Skipton in the period 1239–44, when the honour of Skipton was held by the count of Aumale.[1] Le Camp Fleuri is in the commune of Criquiers, 11½ kil. SSW of Aumale.

Champernowne, de Campo Arnulfi.

Cambernon: Manche, arr. and cant. Coutances.

In 1166 Henry de Camperburne held seven knights' fees of the old feoffment of Oliver de Tracy, and Jordan de Capernun held two knights' fees of William earl of Gloucester.[2] The latter holding is explained by the fact that Jordan's mother Mabira was a daughter of Robert earl of Gloucester and sister of earl William.[3] In 1172 Jordan de Campo Arnulfi owed the service of one knight in Normandy, having himself the service of two knights.[4] This entry is under the heading 'De vicecomitatu de Cerenciis,' and Cambernon (*Campus Arnulfi*) is 18 kil. N of Cerences; the context makes it probable that these fees were held of the *comté* of Mortain.[5] Between 1189 and 1199 Richard de Cambernof gave to the canons regular of Yvrandes the church of St-Cornier (dept. Orne, arr. Domfront, cant. Tinchebray), a gift confirmed by his brother Jordan de Champernon[6]; since the first witness to Richard's charter was John count of Mortain, and St-Cornier is 17 kil. ENE of Mortain, this seems to have been a tenure of that *comté*. Yvrandes was a cell of the priory of Plessis-Grimould. In the charter cited above,[7] *c.* 1170, Mabira confirmed to this priory the gift of her son Jordan de Campo Ernulfi of the church of Maisoncelles[-la-Jourdain, dept. Calvados, arr. and cant. Vire], which lies 12 kil. NW of St-Cornier.

Chandos, Candos.

Candos: Eure, arr. Pont-Audemer, cant. Montfort-sur-Risle, comm. Illeville-sur-Montfort.

In 1086 Roger de Candos was an under-tenant of Hugh de Montfort in Suffolk.[8] *Temp.* Henry I Robert de Candos founded Goldcliff priory, co. Hereford, as a cell to Le Bec[9]—which is near Montfort. He died in 1120, leaving sons Robert, Roger and Godard.[10] In 1123 Robert

1 *Early Yorks. Charters*, vii, 289.

2 *Red Bk. Exch.*, pp. 255, 291.

3 *Cal. Docs. France*, no. 547.

4 *Red Bk. Exch.*, p. 636.

5 It should be noted that Oliver de Tracy, Henry de Champernowne's overlord in England, also held land in the *vicomté* of Cerences, but since the Tracy family did not acquire the honour of Barnstaple till 1130–39 (see under Tracy) a tenant of the old feoffment is not likely to have been enfeoffed by them. The tenures in the *vicomté* of Cerences are more probably a coincidence, and cannot safely be put forward as confirmatory evidence of the origin of the family of Cambernon.

6 *Cal. Docs. France*, nos. 562–3.

7 *Ibid.*, no. 547.

8 *D.B.*, ii, 409b–410b.

9 *Cal. Chart. Rolls*, 1257–1300, pp. 361–3.

10 *Mon. Ang.*, ii, 60.

de Candos was castellan of Gisors.[1] A notification in the chartulary of Jumièges shows that Walter de Belmes granted tithe in Flancourt—close to Candos named above—which was confirmed by Hugh de Montfort[2]; a Hugh de Candos witnessed another grant in Flancourt[3]; and Robert de Belmes granted land at Candos.[3] Robert son of Roger de Candos confirmed gifts in Herefordshire to the abbey of Lyre.[4] Although there are other places named Candos in the Eure, and one near Duclair, dept. Seine-Inférieure, the combined evidence, especially that provided by the Flancourt references and the tenure under Montfort, makes the identification reasonably certain.

CHANFLEUR, DE CAMPO FLORIDO.

Le Champ-Fleuri: Calvados, arr. Vire, cant. Beny-Bocage.

In 1166 Thomas de Campo Florido held a knight's fee of the old feoffment and Lucas de Campo Florido one of the new feoffment of William de Mohun.[5] Le Champ-Fleuri, a hamlet of Ste-Marie-Laumont, is about 18 kil. SE of Moyon; and there does not seem to be another place of the name available in that district. The family gave its name to Huish Champflower, Somerset.

CHAWORTH, DE CADURCIS, DE CHAORCIIS, ETC.

Sourches: Sarthe, arr. Le Mans, cant. Conlie, comm. Saint-Symphorien.

For this identification and the castle of Sourches see J. H. Round in *Cal. Docs. France*, p. xlviii.

CHERBOURG, CESARIS BURGUM.

Cherbourg: Manche.

William d'Aubigny ' pincerna '[6] enfeoffed Peter de Cesaris Burgo of three knights' fees.[7] Although the name alone is sufficient for identification, it can be noted that William d'Aubigny held fiefs in the district, for a charter of his to the church of Rochester was witnessed by his knights, among whom were Ralf de Chiersburgh, Nigel del Wast and Richard Caneleu.[8] Le Vast and Canteloup are close to Cherbourg.[9] Ralf de Chieresburh was William d'Aubigny's butler.[10]

CHESNEY, DE CAISNETO, ETC.

Le Quesnay: Seine-Inf., arr. Neufchâtel, cant. and comm. Saint-Saëns.

In 1086 Ralf [de Chesney] was an under-tenant of William de Warenne in Sussex and Norfolk.[11] The elder line ended in an heiress Alice, who died before 1199, having married Geoffrey de Say, who died in 1214.[12]

[1] *Ord. Vit.*, ed. Le Prévost, iv, 451.

[2] Le Prévost, *Mém. et Notes . . . . de l'Eure*, ii, 108.

[3] *Ibid.*

[4] *Mon. Ang.*, vi, 1093.

[5] *Red Bk. Exch.*, pp. 226–7.

[6] See AUBIGNY, earls of Arundel.

[7] *Red Bk. Exch.*, p. 398.

[8] *Mon. Ang.*, i, 164.

[9] See *Beds. Hist. Rec. Soc.*, xix, 107.

[10] *Textus Roffensis*, ed. Hearne, p. 176.

[11] Farrer, *Honors and Knights' Fees*, iii, 313–4.

[12] *Ibid.*, p. 314.

In the Registers of Philip Augustus Geoffrey de Sai is recorded as having held half a fee in the 'terra de Quesneto[1]'; and the context shows the district. Geoffrey de Sai and Geoffrey his son by Alice de Kaisneio issued a charter dated 1 Jan. 1198[–9], giving to the hospital of St. Thomas the Martyr at Drincourt (Neufchâtel-en-Bray) the church of St. Nicholas of 'Monnouval,'[2] which can be identified as Menonval, 5½ kil. NE of Neufchâtel, of which the hospital at Neufchâtel was the patron in the thirteenth century.[3] Le Quesnay in St-Saëns is 14 and 17 kil. from these places respectively. Near St-Victor-en-Caux there are Grand and Petit Quesnay; but these lie much further south; moreover the former (in Saint-Saëns) is mentioned as a fief in 1503, the others not being then mentioned.[4]

CHESTER, earls of.

Hugh and Richard, first and second earls of Chester of the Norman line, were hereditary *vicomtes* of the Avranchin, dept. Manche, and their lands lay in that district, though it is not possible to point to a particular place as their original home.

Ranulf, third earl of Chester, and his descendants were hereditary *vicomtes* of the Bessin, dept. Calvados.

CHEVERCOURT, CAPRICURIA.

Quiévrecourt: Seine-Inf., arr. and cant. Neufchâtel.

In 1088 Thorold de Chevercort witnessed Roger de Busli's charter for Blyth priory; see under BUSLI. In 1208–13 Robert de Chevrecurt held two fees of the honour of Tickhill,[5] and in 1235–6 Bernard de Chevrecurt was holding of that honour in Wyfordby, co. Leicester.[6] Quiévrecourt is only 4 kil. from Bully. For this family see Nichols, *History of Leicestershire*, vol. ii, pt. i, pp. 395 *et seq.*

CHIRAY, DE CIERREIO.

Cierrey: Eure, arr. Evreux, cant. Pacy.

By a charter *c.* 1170–1175 Robert earl of Leicester gave to William de Chiray 10 librates of land in Burton Lazars, co. Leicester, to hold by the service of half a knight.[7] William witnessed a Lincolnshire charter of Ernald de Bosco in 1163,[8] and one of the earl of Leicester about the same time.[9] In Normandy he witnessed two charters of the earl for the abbey of Lyre,[10] and one for the priory of Les Deux Amants.[11] Cierrey is 8 kil. W of Pacy-sur-Eure, the *caput* of the honour of Pacy

1 *Rec. Hist. France*, xxiii, 640b.
2 *Cal. Docs. France*, no. 280.
3 *Rec. Hist. France*, xxiii, 271b.
4 Beaucousin, *Reg. des fiefs . . . . de Caux* (Soc. Hist. Norm.), p. 8. Mr. Loyd notes that in view of the conservative nature of tenure in France this is practically decisive.
5 *Bk. of Fees*, p. 33. The honour of Tickhill had been held by Roger de Busli.
6 *Ibid.*, p. 517.
7 F. M. Stenton, *Danelaw Charters*, no. 495.
8 *Ibid.*, no. 471.
9 *Ibid.*, no. 325.
10 *Cal. Docs. France*, nos. 409, 410.
11 Du Buisson-Aubenay, *Itinéraire de Normandie* (Soc. Hist. Norm.), p. 187. In the charter as printed Leicester is represented by 'le Guere,' but its substance establishes the true reading.

held by the earls of Leicester in the twelfth century, but was held of the *comté* of Evreux.[1] Adam de Cierrey, its lord in the second half of the twelfth century, was brother of Garin bishop of Evreux and founded a prebend in the cathedral.[2] This same Adam held Bois-Normand (Eure, arr. Evreux, cant. Rugles) of the earl of Leicester,[3] and between 1193 and 1201 gave a rent there to the abbey of Lyre, the charter being witnessed by his brother the bishop and his son and heir Theobald.[4] The Leicestershire under-tenant was clearly a member of this family, although his exact relationship has not been ascertained.

CHOKES.

Chocques: Pas de Calais, west of Béthune.

The details given by Farrer in his account of the honour of Chokes[5] place the identity beyond doubt.

CLAVILLA.

Claville-en-Caux: Seine-Inf., arr. Yvetot, cant. Cany.

In 1086 Robert de Clavilla was an under-tenant of Robert Malet in Suffolk.[6] In the Registers of Philip Augustus Matthew de Buletot held one fee in Claville and elsewhere of the lord of Graville (Malet).[7] The prior of Graville, a Malet foundation, was patron of the church of Claville.[8]

CLERE, CLERA.

Clères: Seine-Inf., arr. Rouen, cant. Clères.

A family of this name held an under-tenancy of Tosny in Normandy before 1066[9]; and a branch is found in Yorkshire on lands which had been held by Berenger de Tosny or Todeni of Belvoir.[10] A pre-conquest charter shows that Roger de Clere gave lands at Blainville in the vicinity of Clères to the abbey of St. Ouen.[11] In 1172 Matthew de Clere (*Clara*) held six or seven knights' fees of Tosny in Normandy,[12] and he made a gift from the mill of Le Tôt in the parish of Clères to Bondeville abbey.[13] There are remains of a castle at Clères.[14]

1 Blosseville, *Dict. topogr. de l'Eure*, p. 56.

2 A. Le Prévost, *Mém. et Notes . . . . de l'Eure*, i, 510.

3 *Ibid.*, i, 356; Charpillon et Caresme, *Dict. hist. de l'Eure*, i, 397. Much information as to the family is contained in these two works *sub* ' Bois-Normand ' and ' Cierrey.'

4 Archives de l'Eure, *Inventaire sommaire, Série H*, p. 87; H. 490.

5 *Honors and Knights' Fees*, i, 20 *et seq.*

6 *D.B.*, ii, 314b.

7 *Rec. Hist. France*, xxiii, 642c.

8 *Ibid.*, p. 288e.

9 *Ord. Vit.*, ed. Le Prévost, iii, 426–7; *Gall. Christ.*, xi, Instr. 132b; and cf. *Cal. Docs. France*, no. 625; and for a further reference D. C. Douglas, *The Rise of Normandy* (Raleigh Lecture, 1947), p. 31.

10 *Early Yorks. Charters*, i, 466 *et seq.*

11 A. Le Prévost, *Mém. et Notes . . . . de l'Eure*, iii, 467.

12 *Red Bk. Exch.*, p. 642.

13 Delisle et Berger, *Rec. des Actes de Henri II*, ii, 390.

14 Cochet, *Rép. arch. . . . . de la Seine-Inf.*, col. 281.

CLINTON.

Saint-Pierre-de-Semilly: Manche, arr. St-Lô, cant. St-Clair.

For this identification as the place of origin of Geoffrey de Clinton, chamberlain of Henry I, and for the remains of the castle there, see J. H. Round in *Ancestor*, xi, 156.

COLEVILLE, of Suffolk.

Colleville: Seine-Inf., arr. Yvetot, cant. Valmont.

In 1086 Gilbert de Colavilla was an under-tenant of Robert Malet in Suffolk.[1] In the 1166 return of the knights of the honour of Eye William de Colevill held four fees.[2] In the Registers of Philip Augustus Eustace de Colevilla held one fee in Coleville of the lord of Graville (Malet).[3] In the thirteenth century the abbot of Le Bec was patron of the church of Colleville[4]; and the Malets were benefactors of Le Bec.[5] In 1503 Colleville was part of the lands of Louis Malet, sieur de Graville, admiral of France.[6]

COLUMBIERS, COLUMBERS.

Colombières: Calvados, arr. Bayeux, cant. Trévières; *or* Colombières: Calvados, arr. Bayeux, cant. Ryes.

Although a considerable amount is known about the family, the evidence as a whole seems consistent with either as their place of origin.[7]

COLUNCES.

Coulances: Calvados, arr. and cant. Vire.

The early history of the family is given by Orderic.[8] Thomas de Colunces witnessed charters of Henry II, *c.* 1170–72.[9] Between 1180 and 1189 Henry II confirmed to the abbey of St-Lô the church of St-Jean-des-Baisants near Torigny, previously confirmed by Thomas de Colunces and Hugh his son.[10] Hugh the son is almost certainly identical with Hugh de Colunces who adhered to Philip Augustus in 1204. He was one of the Norman barons who on 13 Nov. 1205 at Rouen certified the rights which the late kings of England had over the clergy in the duchy.[11] His lands in England had included interests in Stebbing and Woodham Ferrers, Essex.[12]

1 *D.B.*, ii, 315b, 319, 324, 326.

2 *Lib. Niger*, i, 301; this and another entry are omitted in the Red Bk. list (*Red Bk. Exch.*, p. 411*n*).

3 *Rec. Hist. France*, xxiii, 642c.

4 *Ibid.*, p. 287f.

5 Porée, *Hist. de l'Abbaye du Bec*, i, 179, 334.

6 Beaucousin, *Reg. des fiefs . . . . de Caux* (Soc. Hist. Norm.), p. 246.

7 A. de Caumont in *Statistique monumentale du Calvados*, iii, 714, suggests the former of the two.

8 *Ord. Vit.*, ed. Le Prévost, iii, 17.

9 Delisle et Berger, *Rec. des Actes de Henri II*, i, 446, 580.

10 *Ibid.*, ii, 366. A charter of Thomas lord of Coulances for the abbey of Montmorel, twelfth cent., was witnessed by Hugh de Collunces (*Cartulaire de Montmorel*, ed. Dubosc, p. 74).

11 *Cal. Docs. France*, no. 1318. For the holding in Normandy in 1210–20 see *Rec. Hist. France*, xxiii, 611j.

12 *Bk. of Fees*, pp. 488, 615; *Rot. Norm.*, p. 129.

CONTEVILLE, of Somerset.

Conteville: Eure, arr. Pont-Audemer, cant. Beuzeville.

Herluin *vicomte* of Conteville after the death of his first wife, Herleve the mother of William the Conqueror, married Fredesendis, by whom he had a son Ralf.[1] As ' Rodulfus filius Herluini ' he witnessed a charter of the Conqueror for Marmoutier *c.* 1173.[2] Orderic states that king William bestowed lands in England on him, as well as on his half-brothers, Odo bishop of Bayeux and Robert count of Mortain.[3] In 1086 Ralf de Conteville held land of Walter de Douai in Huish (in Burnham), Chapel Allerton, and Admer (in Trent)[4]; and of the abbot of Glastonbury in Brent.[5] The provenance of Walter de Douai, Ralf's overlord, is unknown, but Orderic's statement makes the identification reasonably certain. It is perhaps not without significance that Ralf's half-brother, the count of Mortain, was the largest lay tenant-in-chief in Somerset. The family continued at Allerton until the fourteenth century.[6]

CONTEVILLE, CUNCTEVILLE, of Suffolk.

Conteville: Seine-Inf., arr. Neufchâtel, cant. Aumale.

In a charter *temp.* William I Robert Malet at the request of Osbert de Cuncteville gave to Eye priory all the land which Osbert held in Occold (*Acolte*), Suffolk.[7] In 1121 William Malet, Robert's successor in Normandy, gave Conteville to the abbey of Le Bec,[8] and it appears from a confirmation of Henry II that the gift included the manor and the church with all pertaining to them.[9] The *pouillés* show two Contevilles, the churches of which were in the patronage of Le Bec[10]—Conteville (cant. Aumale) as above, and Conteville (Eure, arr. Pont-Audemer, cant. Beuzeville), the home of Herluin the Conqueror's step-father. In 1195, however, Richard I gave this latter Conteville to the abbey of Jumièges,[11] and the fact that William Malet's gift to

[1] Both Fredesendis (a form to be preferred to Fredefeudis) and Ralf occur as benefactors of the abbey of Grestain, founded by Herluin, in Richard I's charter of confirmation (C. Bréard, *L'Abbaye . . . de Grestain,* p. 203). Although the contrary has often been assumed, Fredesendis was the second wife (*Complete Peerage,* new ed., vii, 125*n*); see also *Ord. Vit.*, ed. Le Prévost, iii, 246; and D. C. Douglas, *Domesday Monachorum,* pp. 33-6, for Herluin's wives and descendants.

[2] *Cal. Docs. France,* no. 1174.

[3] *Loc. cit.*

[4] *V.C.H. Somerset,* i, 500, 497, 501. These are references to the Exchequer Domesday, but they are corroborated by the Exon Domesday.

[5] *Ibid.*, i, 467.

[6] *Proc. Som. Arch. Soc.*, vol. xlv, part ii, pp. 25 *et seq.*

[7] *Mon. Ang.*, iii, 405; confirmed by Henry II (*Cal. Chart. Rolls,* 1341-1417, p. 364).

[8] *Cal. Docs. France,* no. 372.

[9] Delisle et Berger, *Rec. des Actes de Henri II,* ii, 379.

[10] Mr. Loyd gives no reference here; but this was presumably A. Longnon, *Pouillés de la province de Rouen,* pp. 38, 255. He adds in pencil that there was a third Conteville, also in the patronage of Le Bec (*ibid.*, p. 116)—dept. Calvados, arr. Caen, cant. Bourguébus.

[11] Vernier, *Chartes de Jumièges,* ii, 120. A Jumièges document of 1238 connects this Conteville with Grestain and so identifies it (Charpillon et Caresme, *Dict. hist. de l'Eure,* i, 835).

Le Bec included the manor and its appurtenances shows that it cannot have been this Conteville, which no doubt came to the king in 1106 on the forfeiture of Herluin's grandson, William count of Mortain. A slight difficulty in identifying Conteville (cant. Aumale) with the subject of William Malet's gift seems to arise from the fact that in the same charter Henry II confirms various gifts by Odo son of Turold and Eustachia his wife which include a moiety of the church of Conteville,[1] and the other places mentioned as given by them show this to be Conteville (cant. Aumale). The explanation is probably that William Malet's 'gift' was really the confirmation of an overlord, at any rate so far as this moiety is concerned.

The complexities of the case do not end here, for there is a third[2] Conteville to be considered. It is a hamlet of Paluel (Seine-Inf., arr. Yvetot, cant. Cany) and lies 6 kil. N of Claville-en-Caux, a Malet fief, and 8 kil. NW of Crasville-la-Malet which was possibly, but not certainly, another. Since there was no church it cannot be the subject of William Malet's gift, and it belonged in its entirety to the abbey of Fécamp, having been so confirmed to it by duke Richard II in 1025,[3] which renders it unlikely that an under-tenant of Robert Malet came from it.

The case for Conteville (cant. Aumale) is further strengthened by the facts that there was a motte there,[4] and that Robert Malet's charter for Eye shows him to have had an under-tenant, Hugh de Avilers, who seems to have taken his name from Auvilliers, 11 kil. NW of Conteville.[5]

CORBUN.

Corbon: Calvados, arr. Pont-l'Evêque, cant. Cambremer.

In 1086 Hugh de Corbun held in Osmondiston (now Scholes), Norfolk, and in Strickland in Yoxford, Suffolk, of Roger Bigot.[6] Corbon lies at the south end of the Val d'Auge, and the Registers of Philip Augustus contain a list of fees of the period 1204–1208 in which under the heading 'Feoda de Valle Augiae' is the entry, 'Johannes de Roboreto debet servicium duorum militum pro terra Rogeri Bigot ad sumptus suos.'[7] These lands had been given him by king Philip in May 1204.[8] In the list of summonses to the host of Foix in 1272 is the entry, 'Johannes de Rouvray, miles, comparuit pro se dicens se debere unum militem pro feodo de Corbone et pertinenciis.'[9] These entries, taken in conjunction with the occurrence of a Hugh de Corbun as an under-tenant of Roger Bigot in 1086, show that Corbon was held by Roger in the eleventh century, and that it was from this place that Hugh derived his name.

[1] Delisle et Berger, *op. cit.*, ii, 377.
[2] Or fourth (see note above).
[3] Bonnin, *Cartulaire de Louviers*, i, 4.
[4] Cochet, *Rép. arch. . . . . de la Seine-Inf.*, col. 168.
[5] See AVILERS.
[6] *D.B.*, ii, 176b, 278, 335.
[7] *Rec. Hist. France*, xxiii, 709j.
[8] Delisle, *Cat. des Actes de Philippe-Auguste*, no. 819.
[9] *Rec. Hist. France*, xxiii, 754d.

Corcelle, Curcella.

Courseulles-sur-Mer: Calvados, arr. Caen, cant. Creully.

A charter of William duke of Normandy, which may be dated 1060–66, confirmed to Odo bishop of Bayeux land in Bernières (*Brenerias*) which the bishop had bought of William de Curcella.[1] Bernières-sur-Mer is the next commune to Courseulles. Lanfranc, when abbot of Caen, bought some meadow land of William de Corcellis[2]; this was confirmed by Henry II.[3] In 1084 Roger de Corcella witnessed a gift of Roger d'Aubigny to the abbey of Lessay[4]; and between 1087 and 1094 Roger de Curcella witnessed a charter of duke Robert for Holy Trinity, Caen.[5] In his charter of confirmation for the abbey of Troarn, 1155–57, Henry II confirmed lands in Bernières of the gift of Roger de Curcella, his heirs and men[6]; the mention of heirs shows Roger to have been dead some time,[7] and that of Bernières that he was William's successor. In the Bayeux Inquest of 1133 Walklin (*Vacellinus*) de Corcella is shown as holding of the bishop a fief of five knights in Courseulles, Bernières, 'Maisnill' and elsewhere.[8]

There is no express evidence showing that Roger de Curcelle, a tenant-in-chief in Somerset, was the same man as the Roger mentioned above; but the attestations of charters show the Norman family moving in the ducal and royal circle, and the chronology is consistent with the identification, which was accepted by Round.[9]

The evidence suggests that the original feoffee in England may well have been William, and his overlord bishop Odo may have assisted his advancement.

Cormeilles, de Cormeliis.

Cormeilles: Eure, arr. Pont Audemer, cant. Cormeilles.

In 1086 the abbey of Cormeilles held the church of 'Anne,' in Andover hundred, Hampshire, the manor of which was held by Goslin de Cormelies in chief.[10] The abbey was founded by William FitzOsbern; and it seems clear that Goslin had been a follower and tenant of his, his tenure becoming one in chief after the forfeiture of William's son,

[1] *Antiq. cartul. Baioc.* (Soc. Hist. Norm.), i, 1, 10.

[2] E. Deville, *Analyse d'un ancien cartulaire . . . . de Saint-Etienne de Caen*, p. 12.

[3] *Cal. Docs. France*, no. 453. [4] *Ibid.*, no. 920.

[5] *Ibid.*, no. 423.

[6] *Ibid.*, no. 480; Delisle et Berger, *Rec. des Actes de Henri II*, i, 126.

[7] This is consistent with Gaudric son of Roger de Curcella witnessing a charter of Henry I for St. Vincent, Le Mans, of 1103–06 (*Cal. Docs. France*, no. 1048).

[8] *Rec. Hist. France*, xxiii, 700h. An undated writ of Geoffrey duke of Normandy and count of Anjou ordered an inquest to say whether Walklin de Corceliis was seised in the time of king Henry of Cramesnil (arr. Caen, cant. Bourguébus) and Rocquancourt (same cant.), and if so to give him seisin (Haskins, *Norman Institutions*, p. 210). Cramesnil, held of the bishop of Bayeux (C. Hippeau, *Dict. topogr. du Calvados*, p. 90), is presumably the 'Maisnill' of the Bayeux Inquest.

[9] *V.C.H. Somerset*, i, 412.

[10] *D.B.*, i, 49; *V.C.H. Hants.*, i, 501.

Roger earl of Hereford, in 1075. It can be deduced, therefore, that he took his name from this Cormeilles and not from Cormeilles-en-Vexin.

The same deduction can be made for Ansfrid de Cormeliis, a tenant-in-chief in Herefordshire in 1086.[1]

COSTENTIN.

The Cotentin: Manche.

William d'Aubigny 'pincerna,' who died in 1139, enfeoffed Richard de Costentin of half a knight's fee in Kent, which with other fees was given by his son the earl of Arundel to John count of Eu in marriage with his daughter Alice.[2] Aubigny itself and William's Norman lands lay in the Cotentin.

CRAON, CREUN, DE CREDONIO.

There can be no doubt that this was a branch of the family of the barons of Craon in Anjou. The Angevin and English lines were distinct, but in the reign of Henry II the head of each line was named Maurice, and they have been confused both by French and English writers, though they had different parents and different offspring. For the Angevin house see Bertrand de Broussillon, *La Maison de Craon.*

CRASMESNIL.

Saint-Vincent-Craménil: Seine-Inf., arr. Le Havre, cant. Saint-Romain-de-Colbosc.

Ursel de Crasmesnil gave land in Denton, co. Lincoln, to Belvoir priory, *temp.* Stephen; his gift was confirmed by Luke de Crasmesnil, and by William and Ralf, successively chamberlains of Tancarville.[3] Henry I confirmed to the abbey of St-Georges-de-Boscherville, a Tancarville foundation, a rent from the land of Walter de Crasmaisnil in England.[4] St-Vincent-Craménil is *c.* 7 kil. W of Tancarville. In the feodary of 1204–1208 Luke de Crasso Mesnillo held a quarter of a fee of the honour of the earl of Clare in Normandy.[5]

LA CRESSIMERA.

La Cressonière: Calvados, arr. Lisieux, cant. Orbec.

A charter of Theobald, archbishop of Canterbury, for the priory of Stoke-by-Clare includes a gift of Ralf de la Cressimera among gifts made by the men of the lords of Clare[6]; and Ralf de la Cressimere witnessed a charter of Gilbert Fitz Richard dated 1099 for the priory, recited by archbishop Theobald in another charter.[7] La Cressonière is 3 kil. W of Orbec, the *caput* of Richard Fitz Gilbert's Norman lands,

[1] *D.B.*, i, 186.

[2] *Red Bk. Exch.*, p. 399; *Complete Peerage*, new ed., v, 157.

[3] Hist. MSS. Comm., *Duke of Rutland*, iv, pp. 98–9, 134.

[4] *Cal. Docs. France*, no. 197.

[5] *Rec. Hist. France*, xxiii, 708c.

[6] *Mon. Ang.*, vi, 1659.

[7] *Ibid.*, p. 1660.

and in later times was a dependency of the *vicomté* of Orbec.[1] The earliest recorded spelling in Normandy is 'Cressoniera,' and the sixth and seventh letters are invariably 'on' and not 'im.' It is possible that the latter is a misreading, for it is difficult to doubt the identity. In both spellings the definite article occurs.

CRESSY, CREISSI.

Cressy: Seine-Inf., arr. Dieppe, cant. Bellencombre.

Hugh de Creissi was a royal official in the reign of Henry II, and an outline of his activities has been given by Delisle.[2] He married Margaret daughter and coheir of William de Chesney, through whom he obtained Blythburgh, Suffolk, Rottingdean, Sussex, and other lands held of Warenne.[3] In 1166 he was holding one knight's fee of the old feoffment of the honour of Giffard.[4] He died about Easter 1189.[5] Between 1186 and 1189 Hugh de Cressy gave the church of Cressy to the priory of St-Lô at Rouen[6]: among the seven witnesses to the charter were the archbishops of Rouen and Canterbury, St. Hugh bishop of Lincoln and the earls of Essex and Arundel, which identifies the grantor with the royal official. The feodary of 1204–1208 shows Cressy to have been held of Warenne as of the honour of Bellencombre.[7] It lies 4 kil. NW of Bellencombre, and 8 kil. S of Longueville, the *caput* of the Norman honour of the Giffards.

CREVEQUER, CREVECORT, CREVECUIR.

Crèvecœur: Calvados, arr. Lisieux, cant. Mézidon.

The barony of Crevequer was responsible for one of the wards of Dover castle[8]; and a comparison of the fees whose service of castle-guard is specified with the list of fees held by Hamo de Crevequer in 1242–43[9] establishes the connexion of the family with the castle.[10] Hugh de Crevecuir was one of the jurors on the Bayeux Inquest of 1133, and was then holding five knights' fees of the bishopric.[11] Two letters of Eugenius III show that *c.* 1150 there was a dispute between Hugh de Crevecort and his son William of the one part and the church of Bayeux because they had established a market to the prejudice of an

1 C. Hippeau, *Dict. topogr. du Calvados*, p. 91.

2 Delisle, *Rec. des Actes de Henri II, Introduction*, p. 388.

3 Farrer, *Honors and Knights' Fees*, iii, pp. 314, 317, 321; *cf.* Stapleton, *Rot. Scacc. Norm.*, ii, pp. cxvii *et seq.*

4 *Red Bk. Exch.*, p. 312. That the Warenne and Giffard under-tenant was the same man is shown by the fact that in 1173 scutage on both fees was pardoned to Hugh de Creissi (*Pipe Roll* 19 *Hen. II*, pp. 28, 79), which suggests the royal official.

5 In 1188 under 'terræ datæ' the sheriff accounted for Blythburgh, held by Hugh de Cressi (*Pipe Roll* 34 *Hen. II*, p. 53); in 1189 there is a similar entry, but for the half-year only (*Pipe Roll* 1 *Ric. I*, p. 39).

6 L. de Glanville, *Prieuré de Saint-Lô de Rouen*, ii, 337.

7 *Rec. Hist. France*, xxiii, 708j. It was then in the king's hand, the heir being in England.

8 *Red Bk. Exch.*, pp. 615, 711, 722.

9 *Bk. of Fees*, pp. 655, 660.

10 As in the case of Maminot (*q.v.*) the Crevequer service to the castle evidently dates back to the time when Odo bishop of Bayeux held the earldom of Kent.

11 *Rec. Hist. France*, xxiii, 699h, 700h.

ancient market belonging to the church.[1] A mandate of Henry duke of Normandy to the bailiffs of Exmes and Auge ordered them to prevent the men of their bailiwicks from attending the fair of Crèvecœur.[2] This shows that Crèvecœur, which is in Auge, was the scene of the dispute, and that it was held by Hugh.

CRIKETOT.

[?] Criquetot-sur-Longueville: Seine-Inf., arr. Dieppe, cant. Longueville.

In 1166 Hubert de Criketot held two knights' fees of the old feoffment of Geoffrey de Mandeville, earl of Essex.[3] A charter of the earl's father, the elder Geoffrey, was witnessed by Ralf de Crichtote, 1140–44.[4] Criquetot-sur-Longueville is 9 kil. SE of Manneville. Jordan de Criketot gave 10 acres of land at Bois-Hulin, cant. Longueville (which is 6 kil. NNE of Criquetot-sur-Longueville) to Longueville priory.[5] The identification is not perhaps certain, as there are two other Criquetots, in the arrondissement of Yvetot, but the nearest of these to Manneville is 22 kil. distant.

CRUEL.

Criel-sur-Mer: Seine-Inf., arr. Dieppe, cant. Eu.

In 1086 Robert de Cruel held Ashburnham (*Esseborne*), Sussex, of the count of Eu.[6] Criel is 8½ kil. W of Eu. Near the bourg was the castle; in 1870 the walls were still imposing, and there were traces of ditches, but both were being gradually destroyed.[7]

CUELAI.

Cully-le-Patry: Calvados, arr. Falaise, cant. Thury-Harcourt.

In 1086 Humphrey de Cuelai held land in Great Massingham and Burnham Thorpe, Norfolk, of Roger Bigot.[8] Cully is 9 kil. S of Courvaudon in which was situate the fief of Savenay, held by Roger Bigot of the bishop of Bayeux.[9] There is no evidence that Roger had any interest in Cully, but there is nothing impossible in his enfeoffing in England one who was his near neighbour in Normandy.

CURCY, COURCY.

Courcy: Calvados, arr. Falaise, cant. Coulibœuf.

For the family see Farrer, *Honors and Knights' Fees*, vol. i, pp. 103 *et seq.*; and for the castle *Mém. Soc. des Antiquaires de Normandie* (1826), vol. iii, pp. 102 *et seq.*

1 *Antiq. cartul. Baioc.* (Soc. Hist. Norm.), i, pp. 233, 247.

2 *Ibid.*, i, 48.

3 *Red Bk. Exch.*, p. 346.

4 Round, *Commune of London*, p. 101.

5 Delisle et Berger, *Rec. des Actes de Henri II*, ii, 424, in a confirmation by Henry II, 1188–89. Charters of Robert and Ralf de Criquetot or Criketot to Longueville are given in P. Le Cacheux, *Chartes du Prieuré de Longueville*, nos. 64–6, 12th cent. date. For another example of Giffard and Mandeville lands being intermixed in this region see GWERES.

6 *D.B.*, i, 18.

7 Cochet, *Rép. arch. . . . de la Seine-Inf.*, col. 36.

8 *D.B.*, ii, 173, 179.

9 See BIGOT.

CURZON.

Notre-Dame-de-Courson: Calvados, arr. Lisieux, cant. Livarot.

In 1086 Hubert[1] held West Lockinge, Berkshire, of Henry de Ferrers. In 1135 a Hubert de Curcun held three knights' fees of the honour of Ferrers, of which his 'nepos' Stephen held two in 1166; and Richard de Curcun held four fees of the same honour in 1135, which were held by Robert his son in 1166.[2] Courson was a fief of the Norman barony of Ferrières according to an 'aveu' of 1604.[3] In 1223 Hubert de Courson was seigneur of Courson.[4]

DAIVILE, DAIVILLA, DAVIDIS VILLA, ETC.

Déville: Seine-Inf., arr. Neufchâtel, cant. Londinières, comm. Grandcourt.[5]

Robert de Daivile gave to Robertsbridge abbey a tenement in Pelsham[6] [in Peasmarsh, Sussex], *c.* 1200[7]; and Henry count of Eu confirmed to St. Mary in the castle of Hastings several churches given by his father or his grandfather, Robert count of Eu, among which was the church of Peasmarsh.[8] In 1107 Henry count of Eu confirmed to the abbey of Le Tréport a gift of Walter de Davidisvilla.[9] In a charter addressed to Hugh archbishop of Rouen, and therefore before 1164, Robert de David Villa is described as a baron of John count of Eu.[10] The tenure of the family under the counts of Eu, certainly in Normandy and apparently in England, makes it possible to trace it to Déville in the *comté* of Eu.

DIVE, DIVA, of Sussex and co. Northampton.

Dives-sur-Mer: Calvados, arr. Pont-l'Evêque, cant. Dozulé.

Buselin de Diva occurs among the knights of archbishop Lanfranc in the Domesday Monachorum of Christ Church, Canterbury. Robert de Belfou granted to St. Stephen's abbey, Caen, all the land in or around Dives which Hugh de Diva held of him; and Hugh de Diva and Boselin his brother gave land at Moult (*Modol*) to the abbey.[11] An account of the early generations of the family is given by Professor D. C. Douglas in his edition of the *Domesday Monachorum*, pp. 37–8.

DOL.

Dol: Ille-et-Vilaine, arr. Saint-Malo, cant. Dol.

In 1086 Walter de Dol was an under-tenant of Hugh earl of Chester

[1] Identified as Hubert de Curson by Round in *V.C.H. Berks.*, i, 348*n.*

[2] *Red Bk. Exch.*, pp. 337–8; *Lib. Niger*, p. 220.

[3] A. Le Prévost, *Mém. et Notes . . . de l'Eure*, ii, 100.

[4] A. de Caumont, *Statistique monumentale du Calvados*, v, 732.

[5] Grandcourt (*q.v.*) was a fief of the count of Eu.

[6] *Place-Names of Sussex* (Eng. Place-Name Soc.), ii, 532.

[7] Hist. MSS. Comm., *Lord De L'Isle and Dudley*, i, 55.

[8] P.R.O. Anc. Deed D. 1073; *Cat. Anc. Deeds*, iii, 532.

[9] *Cartulaire . . . du Tréport*, ed. L. de Kermaingant, p. 26.

[10] *Ibid.*, p. 55.

[11] *Cal. Docs. France*, no. 453, p. 159. Moult lies to the SE of Caen.

in Norfolk and Suffolk.[1] The name by itself is practically sufficient to establish the identity; and the proximity of Dol to the Avranchin shows that Walter must have been a Breton follower of earl Hugh.

DUMARD, DUMART, DE DOMNOMEDARDO.

Dumart-en-Ponthieu : Somme, arr. Doullens.

By a charter of *c.* 1150 Bernard de Baliol[2] gave Faxton, co. Northampton, to Gerold de Domnomedardo in exchange for all the land which Gerold's father and afterwards Gerold himself had held overseas of Bernard.[3]

DUN.

Le Bourg-Dun : Seine-Inf., arr. Dieppe, cant. Offranville.

In 1166 Godfrey de Dun held four knights' fees of the new feoffment of William de Roumare.[4] In an exchange of lands between William de Roumare and Robert le Calceis of apparently the same period the former excepted from a transfer of what he held in La Chapelle the service of Walter de Cantelou and Richard de Dun.[5] La Chapelle is 3 kil. W of Le Bourg-Dun, and Richard, William de Roumare's Norman tenant, clearly derived his name from the latter place. It can be supposed that Godfrey de Dun, his tenant in England, derived his name from the same.

Robert, who held Dalbury, co. Derby, of Henry de Ferrers in 1086,[6] can be identified as Robert de Dun whose gift of tithe in Dalbury to Tutbury priory was confirmed at a later date by Robert de Ferrers, the second earl.[7] The Ferrers *carta* of 1166 shows that a Robert de Dun held two knights' fees in 1135 and that his son James held them in 1166.[8] Although the bulk of the Norman honour of Ferrières lay in the Eure near Bernay and in the parts of Calvados near by, there was a detached part at and near St-Aubin-sur-Mer (Seine-Inf., arr. Yvetot, cant. Fontaine-de-Dun).[9] Le Bourg-Dun is 3½ kil. SE of St-Aubin ; and an 'aveu' for the barony of Ferrières in 1604 shows that its member of St-Aubin extended into the parish of Le Bourg-Dun.[10]

DUNSTANVILLE.

Dénestanville : Seine-Inf., arr. Dieppe, cant. Longueville.

Walter de Dunstanville occurs on the Pipe Rolls from 1156 onwards. Between 1156 and 1164 Walter de Donestanvilla gave the church of

[1] *D.B.*, ii, 152–3, 299.

[2] Of the family (*q.v.*) which derived its name from Bailleul, dept. Somme.

[3] *Sir Christopher Hatton's Book of Seals*, no. 302.

[4] *Red Bk. Exch.*, p. 377.

[5] Delisle et Berger, *Rec. des Actes de Henri II*, i, 559.

[6] *D.B.*, i, 276.

[7] *Mon. Ang.*, iii, 392; cf. *V.C.H. Derby*, i, 301.

[8] *Red Bk. Exch.*, p. 337.

[9] A. Le Prévost, *Mém. et Notes . . . de l'Eure*, ii, 100.

[10] *Ibid.*, ii, 83 *et seq.*

Vaudreville to Longueville priory.[1] An account of his family is given by Farrer.[2] Vaudreville, now amalgamated with Longueville, and Dénestanville are contiguous. In 1861 there was a large motte on the banks of the Seie, then in course of demolition.[3]

ENVERMOU.

Envermeu : Seine-Inf., arr. Dieppe, cant. Envermeu.

Hugh de Euremou was a knight of the abbot of Peterborough, *temp.* Henry I.[4] Between 1098 and 1105 Turold bishop of Bayeux and Hugh de Euvremou his brother gave the church of St. Laurence at Envermeu to the abbey of Le Bec.[5] Henry I confirmed to the priory of St. Laurence of Envermeu, subject to Le Bec, all its possessions in England, namely what Baldwin son of Gilbert gave of the land which belonged to Hugh de Envremou, *c.* 1130.[6] The English lands of Hugh de Euremou, the Peterborough knight, passed to Baldwin son of Gilbert.[7]

On the banks of the Eaulne there is a motte called Le Câtel, remains of the castle of the lords.[8]

ESCHETOT, ESKETOT.

Ectot : Calvados, arr. Caen, cant. Villers-Bocage, comm. Epinay-sur-Odon.

Richard de Eschetot witnessed as one of the men of Roger son of Walter de Lacy in 1085 a charter of Robert bishop of Hereford granting Holme Lacy to Roger.[9] In 1100 Gilbert de Esketot, his wife and Robert his son, gave to St. Peter's, Gloucester, his land in Duntisbourne, co. Gloucester, for the soul of his lord Walter de Lacy.[10] In the *carta* of Hugh de Lacy in 1166 Richard de Esketot held three knights' fees of the old feoffment and three men of the name held a knight's fee and land of the new feoffment.[11] Ectot, in medieval times Esketot, is *c.* 18 kil. N of Lassy; this is some distance, but the fact that another Lacy tenant who witnessed the charter of 1085 took his name from Le Saussey, also in Epinay-sur-Odon, reinforces the identification.[12]

ESCOIS, SCOHIES, ETC.

Ecouis : Eure, arr. Les Andelys, cant. Fleury-sur-Andelle.

In 1086 William de Scohies was a tenant-in-chief in several counties, principally in Norfolk. He gave the church of Moreton, Essex, and

[1] P. Le Cacheux, *Chartes du Prieuré de Longueville*, no. 12.

[2] *Honors and Knights' Fees*, iii, 37 *et seq.*; and cf. *Ancestor*, xi, 56.

[3] Cochet, *Rép. arch. . . . de la Seine-Inf.*, col. 50.

[4] Round, *Feudal England*, pp. 159 *et seq.*

[5] *Cal. Docs. France*, no. 392.

[6] *Ibid.*, no. 396.

[7] *Feudal England*, p. 161.

[8] Cochet, *Rép. arch. . . . . de la Seine-Inf.*, col. 30.

[9] Text with facsimile in ' An Episcopal Land-Grant of 1085 ' by Prof. Galbraith in *Eng. Hist. Rev.*, xliv, 353 *et seq.*

[10] *Mon. Ang.*, i, 546.

[11] *Red Bk. Exch.*, pp. 282–3.

[12] See SALCEIT.

Wells, Norfolk, with its church to St. Stephen's, Caen.[1] In 1086 Huard de Vernon held of him Market Weston, Suffolk; and Roger de Ebrois [Evreux] held of him Great Bircham, Little Ringstead and Old Buckenham, Norfolk.[2] Vernon is 26 kil. S of Ecouis, and Evreux 38 kil. SSW of it, the distance between Evreux and Vernon being 26 kil. These are substantial distances, but the ancient forms of Ecouis are well attested and do not seem to be applicable to any other known place in Normandy.

ESMALEVILLA, MALAVILLA, SMALAVILLA.

Emalleville : Seine-Inf., arr. Le Havre, cant. Goderville, comm. Saint-Sauveur d'Emalleville.

In 1086 William de Malavill' or Smalavill' was an under-tenant of Robert Malet in Suffolk.[3] In the Registers of Philip Augustus William de Esmalevilla held one fee at 'Esmalevilla' of the lord of 'Gerarvilla.'[4] The latter place is Graville-Sainte-Honorine by Le Havre, the *caput* of the Malet barony in Normandy; and in 1503 Emalleville was held of the lord of Graville as a 'fief de haubert.'[5]

ESTOUTEVILLE.

Etoutteville-sur-Mer : Seine-Inf., arr. Yvetot, cant. Yerville.

In spite of its name it lies inland. The earth-works in the 'bois aux mottes' seem to be the castle of the Estoutevilles.[6] The *caput* of the barony was later at Valmont.

ESTRE.

Etre : Calvados, arr. and cant. Falaise, comm. Saint-Germain-Langot.

In 1166 Thomas de Estre held one knight's fee of the old feoffment of Henry de la Pommeraye.[7] Etre is a farm about 7 kil. E of La Pommeraye.[8]

EU, AUGUM, OU, the count of.

Eu : Seine-Inf., arr. Dieppe, cant. Eu.

There are remains of a castle.

EUDO DAPIFER.

Ryes : Calvados, arr. Bayeux, cant. Ryes.

That Eudo was son of Hubert de Ryes is well known, and the circumstance that certain of his knights came from places close to Ryes brings Eudo himself into connexion with his paternal home; see the entries under AMBLIE, BERNERS, SACHEVILLE.

[1] *Cal. Docs. France*, no. 452; Delisle et Berger, *Rec. des Actes de Henri II*, i, 263; and *cf.* i, 265 and 272.

[2] *D.B.*, ii, 353b, 222b, 223.

[3] *D.B.*, ii, 306b, 307.

[4] *Rec. Hist. France*, xxiii, 642a.

[5] Beaucousin, *Reg. des fiefs . . . de Caux* (Soc. Hist. Norm.), p. 248; and *cf.* p. 275.

[6] Cochet, *Rép. arch. . . . de la Seine-Inf.*, col. 551.

[7] *Red Bk. Exch.*, p. 260.

[8] C. Hippeau, *Dict. topogr. du Calvados*, p. 109.

EVREUX.

Evreux : Eure.

William, who in the following year succeeded his father as count of Evreux, was present at the battle of Hastings.[1] In 1086 he held lands in Hampshire, Berkshire and Oxfordshire.[2]

Roger de Evreux was a tenant of William de Escois (*q.v.*) in Norfolk in 1086.

FANECURT, FANUCURT, FANENCORT.

Fallencourt : Seine-Inf., arr. Neufchâtel, cant. Blangy.

In 1166 Helias de Fanucurt held of Walter de Aincurt one knight's fee of the old feoffment and half a knight's fee of the new.[3] These holdings had been restored to him (Eliseus de Fanecurt) by Walter de Aincurt, of whom they had been held by Gerard de Fanecurt, his father.[4] Gerard de Fanecurt (*Phanecurt*) was a benefactor of Thurgarton priory, an Aincurt foundation.[5] Fallencourt[6] is 30 kil. E of Ancourt[7]; it was probably a fee of the count of Eu. In the absence of any other place of a similar name the identification, if not certain, is highly probable.[8] A motte exists there.[9]

FAVARCHES.

Fervaques : Calvados, arr. Lisieux, cant. Livarot.

This place is 13 kil. WNW of Orbec, the *caput* of the Norman barony of Richard FitzGilbert, lord of Clare. Geoffrey de Favarchis witnessed an agreement between Herbert bishop of Norwich and Peter de Valognes in 1108.[10] He was dead by 1130 when William de Houghton (the chamberlain) made a render in Norfolk for the widow and her land and the wardship of the son.[11] A younger Geoffrey founded the priory of Walsingham, his charter being confirmed by Roger earl of Clare.[12]

DE FERITATE.

La Ferté-Macé : Orne, arr. Alençon, cant. La Ferté-Macé.

Matthew de Feritate, lord of La Ferté-Macé, married Gundreda daughter of Fulk Paynel (probably) of Bampton, who had Holsworthy, Devon, as her 'maritagium'; their son William adhered to John and lost his

[1] D. C. Douglas in *History*, xxviii, 134. [2] *D.B.*, i, 52, 56b, 154.

[3] *Red Bk. Exch.*, pp. 380–1.

[4] F. M. Stenton, *English Feudalism*, p. 106; text, p. 272; and the location of the holdings, p. 107 *n*.

[5] *Mon. Ang.*, vi, 192. As Gerard de Fanacuria he witnessed charters of William count of Aumale, 1138–42 (*Early Yorks. Charters*, iii, nos. 1313–4; and *cf.* nos. 1340, 1380, 1400).

[6] Delisle et Berger, *Rec. des Actes de Henri II*, i, 309, for the form Fanencort.

[7] See AINCOURT. [8] See WALTERVILLA.

[9] Cochet, *Rép. arch. . . . . de la Seine-Inf.*, col. 181.

[10] D. C. Douglas, *East Anglia*, p. 242; spelling Fanarchis.

[11] *Pipe Roll* 31 *Hen. I*, p. 94.

[12] *Mon. Ang.*, vi, 73; and *cf.* p. 1659 for the under-tenancy in Walsingham.

Norman lands.[1] In 1205 Philip Augustus gave La Ferté-Macé to Warin de Glapion.[2] The family had descended from a sister of Odo bishop of Bayeux.[3]

FERRERS, earls of Derby.

Ferrières-Saint-Hilaire : Eure, arr. Bernay, cant. Broglie.

The Norman branch of the family continued in the male line until the early years of the sixteenth century.[4] The fact that Boscherville, Curzon and Livet,[5] all of whom were Ferrers under-tenants of the old feoffment in England, derived their names from places which were members of the barony of Ferrières in Normandy puts the identification beyond doubt.

FERRERS, of Bere Ferrers and Newton Ferrers, Devon.

Ferrières : Manche, arr. Mortain, cant. Le Tilleul.

In 1086 Bere Ferrers (*Birland*) and Newton Ferrers (*Niwetona*) were both held by Reginald de Valletorte of Robert count of Mortain.[6] At a later date both were held by Ferrers of Valletorte as of the barony of Trematon. The earliest recorded occurrence of this family in Devon was Ralf de Ferrers in 1168.[7] Ferrières is 12 kil. S of Mortain and 26 kil. N of Vautorte (dept. and arr. Mayenne, cant. Ernée). In 1112 Roger de Ferrariis occurs among the witnesses 'de valle Moritonii' to Henry I's charter of confirmation for the abbey of Savigny.[8] Ferrers of Churston Ferrers, Devon, appear to have been cadets of this family, and it is probable that all those of the name in Devon and Cornwall were of the same stock.

FEUGERES, DE FULGERIIS.

Feugères : Calvados, arr. Bayeux, cant. and comm. Isigny.

In 1166 Henry de Fulgeriis held of Walkelin Maminot three knights' fees of the old feoffment.[9] This cannot be Henry de Fougères, the Breton baron (who derived his name from Fougères, dept. Ille-et-Vilaine), who became a monk at Savigny in 1150.[10] 'Filgeriæ juxta Nulleyam' appears in the Bayeux Inquest of 1133 as one of the fees held by Maminot of the bishop of Bayeux[11]; and this is the Feugères mentioned above.

It does not follow that a Yorkshire family of Feugers or 'de Filgeriis' came from this place. Of that family the earliest mention is that of

1 *Early Yorks. Charters*, vi, pp. 53–5, and the authorities there cited.

2 Delisle, *Cat. des Actes de Philippe-Auguste*, no. 933A.

3 D. C. Douglas, *Domesday Monachorum*, pp. 35–6.

4 *Complete Peerage*, new ed., iv, 191 *n*.

5 See the details under those families.

6 *D.B.*, i, 105.

7 *Pipe Roll* 14 *Hen. II*, p. 137.

8 *Cal. Docs. France*, no. 792; for the date see Haskins, *Norman Institutions*, p. 311.

9 *Red Bk. Exch.*, p. 194.

10 L. Delisle in *Journal of Brit. Arch. Assoc.*, vii, 126.

11 *Rec. Hist. France*, xxiii, 700h.

a member who witnessed charters of Robert de Brus I *ante* 1135.[1] Although it is not certain that Robert de Brus derived his name from Brix, dept. Manche, arr. Valognes, and a Feugères, dept. Manche, arr. Coutances, cant. Périers, lies as much as 65 kil. S of Brix, it is more likely that it was from this place that the Yorkshire family came, rather than from Feugères, dept. Calvados, mentioned above.

Fitz Osbern.

Breteuil : Eure, arr. Evreux, cant. Breteuil.

This was the *caput* of the Norman honour of William FitzOsbern, earl of Hereford. His elder son, who inherited the Norman lands, was known as William de Breteuil, Roger his younger son receiving the English lands and the earldom.[2]

Floc.

Flocques : Seine-Inf., arr. Dieppe, cant. Eu.

At the Domesday survey Geoffrey de Floc held Guestling, Sussex, of the count of Eu.[3] That Flocques is adjacent to Eu is a sufficient reason for the identification.

Folie.

La Folie : Calvados, arr. Bayeux, cant. Isigny.

In 1166 Beatrix, late the wife of Roger de la Folie, held one knight's fee and Richard de la Folie two, all of the old feoffment, of Adam de Port of Mapledurwell.[4] Enguerrand de Port was one of the jurors on the Bayeux Inquest of 1133[5]; when dying he granted the churches of St-Manvieu and La Folie to the church of Bayeux, a grant afterwards confirmed not later than 1150 by Jordan Tesson who had succeeded to his lands by marriage with his daughter and heir.[6] In 1166 Adam de Sancto Manevo was holding one fee of Port of Basing.[7] Enguerrand was clearly a collateral relation of the Ports of Basing and Mapledurwell, and this shows these under-tenants of the latter to have come from La Folie.

Foliot.

This family seems to have originated in the Cotentin and Western Normandy. Gilbert Foliot 'consilio patrui mei domini Gileberti Lundonensis episcopi' gave the church of Vauville, Manche, arr. Cherbourg, cant. Beaumont, to the abbey of Cerisy.[8] A Sampson Foliot was *seigneur* of Montfarville near Cherbourg, and gave two houses in Barfleur to Quarr abbey.[9] In England a branch of the family were tenants of the earls of Devon.[10] So far back as the middle of the eleventh

1 *Early Yorks. Charters*, v, 320 *n*, where several details about the family are given.

2 *Complete Peerage*, new ed., vi, 449.

3 *D.B.*, i, 19b.

4 *Red Bk. Exch.*, p. 279.

5 *Rec. Hist. France*, xxiii, 699.

6 *Antiq. cartul. Baioc.* (Soc. Hist. Norm.), ii, pp. 11–12.

7 See Sancto Manevo.

8 Delisle, *Rec. des Actes de Henri II*, *Introduction*, p. 376 *n*.

9 Madox, *Formulare*, no. 419; and see L. Couppey, *L'Abbaye de Notre Dame du Voeu de Cherbourg*, pp. 11, 22.

10 *Bk. of Fees*, p. 447.

century a Rainald Foliot witnessed a charter of Neel de St-Sauveur, *vicomte* of the Cotentin.[1] It does not of course follow that there was only one family of the name.

FONTENAY.

Fontenay-le-Marmion : Calvados, arr. Caen, cant. Bourguébus.

In 1253 a Lincolnshire jury found that John de Funtenay, a Norman, held 1½ carucates in Willingham, co. Lincoln, of Robert Marmion the elder; John killed himself and the king's escheator seized the land; later the king restored it to Robert the elder, who was succeeded by Robert Marmion the younger; the latter gave part of the land to one Ridel who was then holding it, William Marmion son and heir of Robert the younger holding the remainder.[2] John de Funtenay evidently took his name from Fontenay-le-Marmion, the *caput* of the Marmion barony in Normandy. In the Lindsey survey, 1115–18, Roger Marmion held 1 carucate 6 bovates in Cherry Willingham.[3]

FRAELVILLA.

Freulleville : Seine-Inf., arr. Dieppe, cant. Envermeu.

Ancel de Fraelvilla, brother of Osbern abbot of Le Tréport, gave to the abbey 65*s*. at Playden, Sussex, *c*. 1107.[4] His family were under-tenants of the counts of Eu in Normandy.[5]

FRESNE.

Le Fresne : Calvados, arr. Bayeux, cant. Trévières, comm. Russy.

In 1166 the under-tenants of Adam de Port of Mapledurwell included Walter del Fresne one fee, Ralf del Fresne three fees, and Thomas del Fresne one fee, all of the old feoffment; and also Alvred de Fresne a third of a fee of the new feoffment.[6] Le Fresne is *c*. 5 kil. W of Port-en-Bessin.

FRESSENVILLE.

Fressenville : Somme, arr. Abbeville, cant. Ault.

Rainald de Meiniers and Maud his wife gave to Robertsbridge abbey land in the rape of Hastings, held of the count of Eu, which Ingelram de Fressenvile gave to Maud his daughter in marriage; which Maud was the wife of Rainald de Meiniers.[7] Engeran de Fressenevilla witnessed charters of the counts of Eu to the abbey of Le Tréport.[8] Ault is at no great distance from Eu and Le Tréport.

FRIARDEL.

Friardel : Calvados, arr. Lisieux, cant. Orbec.

Picot de Friardel was among the men of Gilbert Fitz Richard of Clare who witnessed a charter of Gilbert for Bury St. Edmunds, 1090–1098,

[1] Delisle, *Château de St-Sauveur*, Preuves, p. 24.

[2] *Cal. Inq. Misc.*, i, no. 186. For these members of the Marmion family see *Complete Peerage*, new ed., viii, 507.

[3] Linc. Rec. Soc., vol. xix, p. 241.

[4] *Cal. Docs. France*, no. 233. [5] *Ibid.*, no. 230. [6] *Red Bk. Exch.*, pp. 279–80.

[7] Hist. MSS. Comm., *Lord De L'Isle and Dudley*, i, pp. 36, 71.

[8] *Cartulaire . . . du Tréport*, ed. L. de Kermaingant, pp. 38, 60, 65.

which was clearly issued at Bury.[1] Friardel is 3 kil. SW of Orbec, the *caput* of the Norman honour of Richard Fitz Gilbert, Gilbert's father.

GAMAGES.

Gamaches : Eure, arr. Les Andelys, cant. Etrepagny.

It is stated in an inquest of 1251–52 that Godfrey de Gamages, a Norman, held Mansell Gamage, co. Hereford, of Walter de Lacy in the time of Richard I; that Matthew his elder son remained in Normandy at the separation, and that Godfrey gave Mansell Gamage to William his younger son, whose son, another Godfrey, held it in 1251–52.[2] A charter dated 1184 shows that Hugh de Vals gave to the abbey of Lyre tithe in Flipou, arr. Les Andelys, cant. Fleury-sur-Andelle[3]; and about the same time Matthew de Gamaches gave to the abbey a grange in Flipou, a gift which was confirmed by his brother William de Gamaches.[4] Flipou is about 24 kil. W of Gamaches. If we allow for a slight mistake in the chronology in the inquest of 1251–52 by making Godfrey de Gamages survive to the reign of Richard I, it is permissible to identify Matthew and his brother William, the benefactors of Lyre, with the brothers mentioned in the inquest. It follows that the family came from Gamaches named above, and not from the better known Gamaches, dept. Somme, arr. Abbeville, which incidentally was not in Normandy. An account of the family is given in Eyton's *Antiquities of Shropshire*, iv, pp. 143–50.

GIFFARD, earls of Buckingham.

Longueville-la-Gifart (now Longueville-sur-Scie): Seine-Inf., arr. Dieppe, cant. Longueville.

This place with its castle formed the *caput* of the honour of Giffard in Normandy.[5] The priory of Longueville was a Giffard foundation.[6]

GIRON, GIRUNDE.

Gueron : Calvados, arr. and cant. Bayeux.

In 1086 Turstin de Giron or Girunde was an under-tenant of Odo bishop of Bayeux in Buckinghamshire and Kent.[7] In the Bayeux Inquest of 1133 Gueron occurs as a ' vavassoria ' of the bishop of Bayeux.[8]

GISORS.

Gisors : Eure, arr. Les Andelys, cant. Gisors.

In 1210–12 William de Cresek held Birling in East Dean, Sussex, formerly held by John de Gisors[9]; in 1237 Hugh de Gournay held it, John being

[1] D. C. Douglas, *Feudal Documents from Bury St. Edmunds*, p. 153.

[2] *Bk. of Fees*, p. 1270.

[3] A. Le Prévost, *Mém. et Notes . . . de l'Eure*, ii, 111.

[4] Archives de l'Eure, *Inventaire sommaire, Série H*, p. 83; H. 465.

[5] Stapleton, *Rot. Scacc. Norm.*, i, p. civ.

[6] P. Le Cacheux, *Chartes du Prieuré de Longueville*.

[7] *D.B.*, i, 144b, 10b. [8] *Rec. Hist. France*, xxiii, 701c. [9] *Red Bk. Exch.*, p. 555.

described as 'extraneus.'[1] In 1228 the king granted to Hubert de Burgh the manor of Titchfield, Hampshire, late of John de Gisors.[2] It is clear that John was a Norman who lost his lands in England at the separation. In 1204–8 he was holding Besu in the Norman Vexin by the service of three knights[3]; and in 1212–20 there is a long extent of the lands which he held of the king of France, showing many places in the vicinity of Gisors.[4] He was head of a family which had first appeared in the time of William Rufus.[5]

Glanville.

Glanville : Calvados, arr. Pont-l'Evêque, cant. Dozulé.

In the Registers of Philip Augustus (1204–1208) among the fees of the Val d'Auge is the entry 'Feodum Ricardi de Glanvilla terciam partem militis; rex habet.'[6] In 1213 Philip Augustus gave to Stephen de Longchamp Glanville and other land in the Val d'Auge which Richard de Glanville had held.[7] In the *Querimoniæ Normannorum* of 1247 a Richard de Glanville complained that the king was detaining various lands including 17 librates in Glanville which were the inheritance of his elder brother and himself after the death of his uncle who died overseas; and another complaint by William Maloi shows that the uncle must have died in England.[8] This uncle can be identified as the Richard de Glanville who made a journey to Normandy on the king's service before 1204.[9]

Members of a family of this name held fees of Hugh Bigod, earl of Norfolk, in 1166[10]; but there is no reason to suppose that Glanville itself was held of Bigod.

Glapion.

Glapion : Orne, arr. Alençon, cant. Courtomer, comm. Sainte-Scolasse-sur-Sarthe.

Warin de Glapion succeeded William Fitz Ralf as seneschal of Normandy in 1200, and held office until 1201. Later he deserted John for Philip Augustus. In the latter's Registers Glapion is entered as a fief held of the barony of Ste-Scolasse by the service of half a knight.[11] Among the *Querimoniæ Normannorum* of 1247 is one by Robert Burneth claiming the lands of Warin de Glapion his kinsman, in which he described the 'manerium' of Glapion as situate in the parish of Ste-Scolasse.[12]

1 *Bk. of Fees*, p. 618.

2 *Cal. Chart. Rolls*, 1226–57, p. 71.

3 *Rec. Hist. France*, xxiii, 713h.

4 *Ibid.*, pp. 630–1.

5 See Duchesne, *Hist. . . . . de Montmorency*, pp. 667–8, and Preuves, p. 414; *Cartulaire de St-Martin-de-Pontoise*, ed. Depoin, i, 84; and V. Patte, *Hist. de Gisors*, p. 41.

6 *Rec. Hist. France*, xxiii, 709g.

7 Delisle, *Cartulaire Normand*, no. 1109.

8 *Rec. Hist. France*, xxiv, 8g and j.

9 *Curia Regis Rolls*, iii, 117; *Pipe Roll 6 John*, p. 15.

10 *Red Bk. Exch.*, pp. 395–7.

11 *Rec. Hist. France*, xxiii, 618e.

12 *Ibid.*, xxiv, 70 (§ 530); and *cf.* p. 71 (§ 532).

The chapel of Glapion, founded by Warin,[1] was in the parish of Ste-Scolasse.[2]

In England Warin held a moiety of the manor of Cottesmore, Rutland, and 100 solidates of land in Seaford, Sussex.[3]

GOURNAY.

Gournay-en-Bray : Seine-Inf., arr. Neufchâtel.

This was a fortified town. The family is so well known that it is sufficient to refer to the documents in Daniel Gurney, *Record of the House of Gournai*.

GRANDCOURT, GRANCURT.

Grandcourt : Seine-Inf., arr. Neufchâtel, cant. Londinières.

A family of this name held land in Norfolk of the honour of Warenne.[4] Grandcourt lies somewhat apart from most of the Warenne fees, and is *c*. 30 kil. from Bellencombre, the *caput* of the honour in Normandy. The chartulary of St-Michel du Tréport shows that Grandcourt was held of the counts of Eu, and not of Warenne; and the same is true of Pierrepont which lies adjacent to it. The evidence as to Pierrepont (*q.v.*), however, shows that the Pierreponts, also tenants of the honour of Warenne in England, came from that place; and there seems no reason to doubt that it was from that locality that the Grandcourts also came.

There is a motte near the church of Grandcourt.[5]

GRENTEMAISNIL.

Le Grand-Mesnil: Calvados, arr. Lisieux, cant. St-Pierre-sur-Dives.

The Norman honour of Hugh de Grentemaisnil, the Domesday tenant-in-chief, descended to his great-granddaughter Parnel, who married Robert earl of Leicester *ante* 1155–59; of this honour Le Grand-Mesnil was the *caput*.[6]

GRENVILLE, GRAINVILLE, GREINVILLE, ultimately dukes of Buckingham.

Grainville-la-Teinturière : Seine-Inf., arr. Yvetot, cant. Cany.

In 1166 Gerard de Grainville held three knights' fees of the old feoffment of the Giffard honour of Buckingham.[7] In the Conqueror's reign Ralph de Granvilla witnessed a charter of Walter Giffard for the abbey of Cerisy-la-Forêt[8]; and the family split into two branches, Norman and English, both under-tenants of Giffard. Charters for Longueville priory show that successive heads of the Norman branch were named Eustace.[9] Eustace *seigneur* of Grainville's gift of the church of that

[1] Particulars in Delisle, *Cartulaire Normand*, no. 705.

[2] *Pouillé de Séez* (Soc. Hist. de l'Orne), ii, 199.

[3] *Bk. of Fees*, pp. 619, 1151; *Red Bk. Exch.*, pp. 555, 805.

[4] Farrer, *Honors and Knights' Fees*, iii, 389.

[5] Cochet, *Rép. arch. . . . . de la Seine-Inf.*, col. 227.

[6] *Complete Peerage*, new ed., vii, 532, and note with the authorities cited.

[7] *Red Bk. Exch.*, p. 312.

[8] *Mon. Ang.*, vi, 1074.

[9] P. Le Cacheux, *Chartes du Prieuré de Longueville*, nos. 11, 22-3

place was confirmed by Hugh archbishop of Rouen to the abbey of St-Wandrille between 1142 and 1146[1]; and the fact that thereafter the abbey had the church of Grainville-la-Teinturière[2] proves the identification. That the Norman and English families were of the same stock is shown by a charter of Louis VIII of 1225 allowing Robert de Grainville to succeed to Grainville on the extinction of the Norman branch, notwithstanding that his father Gerard had died in England.[3]

The West country Granvilles are quite distinct from the above family. As they first appear as tenants of the honour of Gloucester it is probable that they came from Western Normandy, but their place of origin has not been determined.[4]

GRINCURT.

Graincourt : Seine-Inf., arr. Dieppe, cant. Offranville, comm. Derchigny.

In 1166 Ralf de Waltervilla (*q.v.*) and Ralf de Grincurt held half a knight's fee of the new feoffment of Walter de Aincurt.[5] Graincourt is 3 kil. N of Ancourt.

GRINNOSAVILLA.

Grigneuzeville : Seine-Inf., arr. Dieppe, cant. Bellencombre.

A family of the name occurs in the Lewes Chartulary as holding land of the honour of Warenne in Norfolk.[6] Grigneuzeville being only 4 miles from Bellencombre, the *caput* of the honour of Warenne in Normandy, there can be no doubt of their provenance. In 1204–1208 in the register of the fees of Normandy there is the entry 'Militum de Belemcombre . . . . Hugo de Grenosevilla 1 militem.'[7]

GWERES, DE GUERRIS.

Gueures : Seine-Inf., arr. Dieppe, cant. Bacqueville.

In 1166 Roger, Manasser and William de Gweres were under-tenants of Geoffrey de Mandeville, earl of Essex.[8] Adelard de Guerr' witnessed a charter of the latter's father for Walden abbey[9]; and in 1130 Manasser de Guerres accounted for having his father's land as a tenancy of Geoffrey de Mandeville in Essex.[10] Guerres is shown in the Registers of Philip Augustus as a fief of Manneville,[11] from which it lies 3 kil. WNW. A confirmation charter of Henry II to Longueville priory included a messuage 'apud Guerras' which had been the subject of a gift by Audulf de Guerris[12]; and Audulf and Peter de Guerris were

[1] F. Lot, *St-Wandrille*, pp. 137–8.
[2] *Ibid.*, pp. lxxviii–lxxix.
[3] Delisle, *Cartulaire Normand*, no. 351.
[4] Round, *Family Origins*, pp. 130 *et seq.*
[5] *Red Bk. Exch.*, p. 381.
[6] Sussex Rec. Soc., vol. xxxviii, pp. 35, 62.
[7] *Rec. Hist. France*, xxiii, 708j.
[8] *Red Bk. Exch.*, pp. 345–7.
[9] *Mon. Ang.*, iv, 149.
[10] *Pipe Roll* 31 *Hen. I*, p. 55.
[11] *Rec. Hist. France*, xxiii, 640k.
[12] Delisle et Berger, *Rec. des Actes de Henri II*, ii, 424.

commemorated at Longueville.[1] In another charter of Henry II there is mentioned a gift of Walter Giffard 'quicquid ex feodo ejus erat in ecclesia de Guerris tam in decimis quam in terris'[2]; and this suggests that the lands of Giffard and Mandeville were intermixed in this region.

HAIG, DE LA HAGA, DE HAGA.

The district of La Hague: Manche, arr. Cherbourg.

Hugh de Moreville witnessed charters of David earl of Huntingdon, afterwards king of Scotland, for St. Cuthbert's Durham, *c.* 1118, and the abbey of Selkirk (afterwards Kelso), *c.* 1120.[3] He subsequently became constable of Scotland and founded Dryburgh abbey.[4] He died in 1162, and was succeeded by his son Richard who died in 1189. Richard married Avice daughter of William de Lancaster, and is the Richard de Moreville who in 1166 held five knights' fees of Roger de Mowbray,[5] since Nigel de Mowbray confirmed to Furness abbey the land in Selside and Birkwith, co. York, W.R., given by Richard de Moreville and Avice (of Lancaster) his wife.[6] The family held lands in Northamptonshire, Huntingdonshire and Rutland of the honour of Huntingdon.[7]

Bemersyde, held by the Haigs as early as the twelfth century, lies on the Tweed close to Dryburgh. Between 1162 and 1190 Peter de la Haga witnessed several charters of Richard de Moreville and his son William, notably for the abbeys of Melrose and Kelso, and this Peter or his son witnessed charters of Roland and Alan of Galloway, constables of Scotland, the heirs and successors of the Morevilles.[8] No satisfactory evidence as to the tenure of Bemersyde seems to be forthcoming, but the contiguity of Bemersyde to Dryburgh, combined with the persistent attestation of Moreville charters by Peter de la Haga, suggests somewhat strongly that it was held of Moreville.

In Normandy La Hague (*Haga*, *Hagua*) was a district lying to the west of Cherbourg, and in the middle ages a rural deanery. The name survives in the Cap de la Hague, the north-westernmost point of Normandy. Morville, arr. Valognes, cant. Bricquebec, lies *c.* 16 kil. S of the southern limit of the deanery of La Hague. In the thirteenth-century *pouillé* of the diocese of Coutances it is stated that the prior of St-Germain 'de Hagua'—now St-Germain-des-Vaux—had a right to four sheaves 'in feodo de Morevilla' in the neighbouring parish of Jobourg.[9] These two parishes lie in the extreme NW corner of

1 *Rec. Hist. France*, xxiii, 437h.

2 Delisle et Berger, *op. cit.*, ii, 389; a charter for the abbey of Bondeville.

3 Lawrie, *Early Scottish Charters*, nos. 32, 35.

4 See additional note below.

5 *Red Bk. Exch.*, p. 419.

6 *Furness Coucher*, Chetham Soc., vol. 76. p. 338.

7 Farrer, *Honors and Knights' Fees*, ii, 356–8.

8 A list of these attestations is given in J. Russell, *The Haigs of Bemersyde* (1881), pp. 41–3, 46–7.

9 *Rec. Hist. France*, xxiii, 528f.

Normandy, within a short distance of Cap de la Hague. To this must be added the fact that a charter of William de Moreville of Dorset was witnessed by a William de Haga.[1] There does not appear to be any other Morville in Normandy; and the occurrence of the definite article in the early forms of Haig is significant.

The cumulative effect of the connexion of the Haigs and Morevilles in Berwickshire, the territorial interest of Moreville in the deanery of La Hague, and finally the attestation of a Moreville charter in Dorset by a William de Haga, seem to establish that

(i) the Morevilles, constables of Scotland, derive from Morville in the Cotentin and were akin to the Moreville under-tenants of the earls of Devon;

(ii) Haig derives from the district of La Hague and probably from that part of it which is adjacent to the Cap de la Hague.

Additional Note.

The author of *The Haigs of Bemersyde,* already cited, argued that David I and not Hugh de Moreville founded Dryburgh abbey, and that there is no evidence that the Morevilles ever held any land in the immediate neighbourhood of Dryburgh, inferring from this that there was no connexion between the Morevilles and the Haigs beyond attestation of a certain number of charters.[2] The evidence for the foundation by Hugh de Moreville, however, seems to be conclusive. A charter of Robert, bishop of St. Andrews, who died in 1159 and therefore in Hugh's lifetime, states that he was the founder; and this statement is repeated in a charter of Richard, bishop of St. Andrews (1165–78).[3] A charter of Malcolm IV (1153–65) mentions among the gifts of Hugh and his wife Beatrix de Beauchamp 'ipsam Driburgh et terras et aquas ei adjacentes.'[4] Finally the Melrose chronicle, in recording Hugh's death in 1162, describes him as the founder of Dryburgh.[5]

HAMO DAPIFER.

Torigny-sur-Vire : Manche, arr. St-Lô, cant. Torigny.

An account of Hamo, who was son of Hamo Dentatus (slain at Val-es-Dunes in 1047), and who was dapifer both to the Conqueror and William Rufus and sheriff of Kent in 1086, is given, together with an account of his sons Hamo and Robert, by D. C. Douglas in *The Domesday Monachorum of Christ Church Canterbury*, pp. 55–6, where the relevant authorities are cited. That Hamo *dapifer* and Hamo the sheriff were undoubtedly one and the same person is proved by the Kentish returns of 1242–43 in *The Book of Fees*, pp. 654 *et seq.*, when the lands held by the sheriff in 1086 were held by the earl of Gloucester, who was the heir of Hamo *dapifer* through the marriage of Robert earl of Gloucester with the daughter and heir of Robert, son of Hamo *dapifer*.

[1] See MOREVILLE.

[2] Mr. Russell, the author, derived the Haigs from La Hague, but apparently relied solely on the similarity of name.

[3] *Liber de Dryburgh*, Bannatyne Club, no. 14, p. 9; no. 236, p. 174.

[4] *Ibid.*, no. 240, p. 178.

[5] *Chron. of Melrose*, facsimile ed., p. 36.

HARCOURT.

Harcourt : Eure, arr. Bernay, cant. Brionne.

The tenure which the family had of the honour of Beaumont in Normandy and of the earls of Leicester and Warwick in England make the identity clear. The remains of a castle were existing in 1879.[1]

HAYE, HAIA.

La Haye-du-Puits : Manche, arr. Coutances, cant. La Haye-du-Puits.

In 1123 Robert de Haia issued a charter, mentioning Muriel his wife and Richard and Ralf his sons, and recording his earlier gift of the church of Boxgrove, Sussex, to the abbey of Lessay.[2] Later Richard de Haia gave the church of St. John of Haye to the same abbey.[3] The church of La Haye-du-Puits is dedicated in honour of St. John the Evangelist,[4] and the abbot of Lessay was patron.[5] The priory of Boxgrove founded by Robert de Haia was a cell of Lessay.[6]

HELION.

Helléan : Morbihan, arr. Pontivy, cant. Josselin.

An account of the family has been given by Round,[7] who, however, gave no evidence for the identification beyond the name and the fact that the family was of Breton origin.

HESDIN.

Hesdin : Pas de Calais, arr. Montreuil, cant. Hesdin.

At the Domesday survey Arnulf de Hesdin was a tenant-in-chief in several counties. The gifts which he made to the priory of St. George, Hesdin, of land in Hesdin and churches in England[8] clearly show that it was from this Hesdin, where the priory was situate,[9] that he took his name.

DE HISPANIA, HISPANIENSIS.

Epaignes : Eure, arr. Pont-Audemer, cant. Cormeilles.

In 1086 Alvredus de Hispania or Hispaniensis was a tenant-in-chief in Herefordshire, Dorset, and other counties.[10] Epaignes, occurring in the twelfth century and later as Hispania and Yspania, is 5½ kil. NE of Cormeilles, held by William FitzOsbern who founded the abbey there.[11] As Round points out in his introduction to the Hereford

[1] Charpillon et Caresme, *Dict. hist. de l'Eure*, ii, 333.
[2] *Cal. Docs. France*, no. 922; and *cf.* no. 921.
[3] *Ibid.*, no. 927.
[4] Lecanu, *Hist. du diocèse de Coutances*, ii, 333.
[5] A. Longnon, *Pouillés de la province de Rouen*, p. 322.
[6] *Mon. Ang.*, iv, 641.
[7] 'Helion of Helion's Bumpstead' in *Essex Arch. Soc. Trans.*, viii, pp. 187–91.
[8] *Cal. Docs. France*, no. 1326.
[9] Cottineau, *Rép. Topo-bibl. des Abbayes et Prieurés*, i, col. 1412.
[10] *D.B.*, i, 82b, 186.
[11] *Mon. Ang.*, vi, 1075.

Domesday,[1] William FitzOsbern's position in Herefordshire was palatine, and the Norman settlement on the lands there was controlled by him. As Alveredus de Hispania he gave two thirds of the tithe of his manor called ' Forneguerde quod situm est juxta Guartiam in territorio comitatus Dorsaetae ' to St. Stephen's, Caen, for the health of king William his lord and of the souls of his parents, a witness being ' filius Golberti de Ponte Aldomari.'[2] Pont-Audemer is only 9 kil. N of Epaignes. ' Forneguerde ' seems to be a scribal corruption of ' Torneworde,' *i.e.* Turnworth, Dorset, which was held by Alvred in chief in 1086.

It is doubtful if Hervey de Ispania, a considerable under-tenant of count Alan in Essex in 1086, was connected with Epaignes.[3] Hervey is a distinctly Breton name, and the Breton overlord points the same way.[4]

LE HOMMET.

Le Hommet : Manche, arr. St-Lô, cant. Saint-Jean-de-Daye.

This well-known derivation has been established by Stapleton[5] and Delisle,[6] and is further illustrated in charters in the Livre Noir of Bayeux.[7] There were very slight remains of the motte at Le Hommet in 1830.[8]

IVRY.

Ivry-la-Bataille : Eure, arr. Evreux, cant. Saint-André.

Roger d'Ivry, butler to the Conqueror,[9] was a tenant-in-chief in several counties at the Survey. He founded the abbey of Ivry, but the exact nature of his connexion with the place is obscure.[10] The Hugh d'Ivry who was a tenant-in-chief of less importance at the Survey appears to have been Roger's uncle, for Roger restored (*reddidit*) to the abbey of St. Stephen, Caen, the land at Cheux which Hugh his *avunculus* had held.[11] A charter *c.* 1066–7 describes Hugh as ' pincerna de Ivry.'[12]

KEYNES, CAHAGNES.

Cahagnes : Calvados, arr. Vire, cant. Aunay-sur-Odon.

Evidence is given in Stapleton, *Rotuli Scaccarii Normanniæ*, vol. ii, p. ccli *n*.

LAIGLE, L'AIGLE, DE AQUILA.

Laigle : Orne, arr. Mortagne-sur-Huine.

Laigle was held of the count of Evreux by the service of three knights and castle-guard at Evreux.[13]

1 *V.C.H. Hereford*, i, 270.
2 E. Deville, *Analyse d'un ancien cartulaire . . . . de Saint-Etienne de Caen*, pp. 38–9.
3 *Early Yorks. Charters*, v, p. 230 *n*.
4 Mr. Loyd has a pencil note : ' ? Espinay, a few kil. W of Vitré.'
5 *Rot. Scacc. Norm.*, i, p. lxxix.
6 *Chron. Robert de Torigni*, i, 97.
7 *Antiq. cartul. Baioc.* (Soc. Hist. Norm.), i, 110–2.
8 *Mém. Soc. Ant. Norm.*, v, 284.
9 Davis, *Regesta*, introd., p. xxvii.
10 *Complete Peerage*, new ed., viii, 208 *n*.
11 E. Deville, *Analyse d'un ancien cartulaire . . . de Saint-Etienne de Caen*, p. 27.
12 *Cartulaire de la Sainte-Trinité de Rouen*, ed. A. Deville, no. 47; and see Davis, *loc. cit.*
13 *Rec. Hist. France*, xxiii, 618b.

LANGETOT.

Lanquetot : Seine-Inf., arr. Le Havre, cant. Bolbec.

In 1086 Ralf de Langetot was an under-tenant of Walter Giffard in Bedfordshire and Suffolk.[1] He witnessed a gift by Walter Giffard to the abbey of Le Bec of Blakenham, Suffolk, *temp.* William I.[2] A Ralf de Langetot witnessed a charter of Walter Giffard, earl of Buckingham, to Longueville priory, 1152–58.[3]

LASCY, LACEY.

Lassy: Calvados, arr. Vire, cant. Condé-sur-Noireau.

In the Bayeux Inquest of 1133 the fief of the bishop included 'feodum de Lacey in Campellis duorum militum.'[4] Robert earl of Gloucester by a charter dated 1146 quitclaimed to Philip bishop of Bayeux *inter alia* 'tota feoda Ilberti et Gilberti de Laceio que de Baiocensi ecclesia et de episcopo tenebant apud Laceium et apud Campels vel alibi.'[5] The latter place is Campeaux, dept. Calvados, arr. Vire, cant. Le Beny-Bocage, about 20 kil. W of Lassy. In 1219 Philip Augustus gave land which Gilbert de Lassi had held at Lassy and Campeaux.[6] The identification of Lassy is confirmed by the details given under CAMPEAUX, RAINEVILLE and SCORCHEBOFE.

LAVAL.

Laval : Mayenne.

It is reasonably certain that the Hugh de Laval to whom Henry I gave the honour of Pontefract after the forfeiture of Robert de Lascy, and who was dead by Michaelmas 1130,[7] was of this family. According to Bertrand de Broussillon[8] he was a son of Hamo de Laval, but the English Lavals are somewhat hard to place.

LESTRE.

Lestre: Manche, arr. Valognes, cant. Montebourg.

Roger de Lestra witnessed a charter of Richard de Reviers (who died in 1107) for the priory of Christchurch, Hampshire.[9] In 1107 Henry I issued a confirmation charter to the abbey of Montebourg which included 30 acres of land that Richard de Lestre had held in 'Coeres'—a place which Delisle identified as a hamlet of St-Floxel in cant. Montebourg.[10] A charter of Baldwin de Reviers to Christchurch priory, recording a gift by Roger del Estre of Apse (in Wroxall, Isle of Wight), was witnessed by Jordan del Estre[11] ; and as Jordan de Lestra he

1 *D.B.*, i, 211b; ii, 430.

2 *Mon. Ang.*, vi, 1002.

3 *Newington Longueville Charters* (Oxfords. Rec. Soc.), p. 2.

4 *Rec. Hist. France*, xxiii, 700k.

5 *Antiq. cartul. Baioc.* (Soc. Hist. Norm.), i, 49. This reference illustrates the connexion between the families of Lascy of co. Hereford and Lascy of Pontefract.

6 Delisle, *Cat. des Actes de Philippe-Auguste*, no. 1912.

7 *Early Yorks. Charters*, iii, pp. 143, 148.

8 *La Maison de Laval*, i, pp. 44–5.

9 *Mon. Ang.*, vi, 304.

10 *Cal. Chart. Rolls*, 1327–41, p. 158; Delisle, *Cartulaire Normand*, no. 737 and p. 165 *n.*

11 *Mon. Ang.*, vi, 304–5.

witnessed Baldwin earl of Devon's foundation charter of Quarr abbey, 1141–44,[1] and a charter of his for Montebourg.[2] Lestre is 22 kil. NE of Néhou, the *caput* of the Reviers honour in the Cotentin, 6 kil. NNE of Montebourg, and 6½ kil. NE of St-Floxel.

LIMESI.

Limésy : Seine-Inf., arr. Rouen, cant. Pavilly.

In 1086 Ralf de Limesi was a considerable tenant-in-chief. He founded Hertford priory as a cell of St. Albans; and among the witnesses to his foundation charter was Fulk de Mustervell,[3] who seems to have taken his name from Montreuil-en-Caux, 18 kil. NE of Limésy, which at the beginning of the thirteenth century occurs as 'Mosterol.'[4] Another charter of Ralf for the same house was witnessed by .... de Flamentvilla.[3] Flamanville is 7½ kil. NW of Limésy. A charter of Alan de Limesi, Ralf's son and heir, for Hertford priory was witnessed by Ralf de Boskervilla.[3] The commune of St-Martin-de-Boscherville is 18 kil. S of Limésy, and in it is the abbey of St-Georges-de-Boscherville. Henry I confirmed to the abbey a rent from the land of Geoffrey de Limesi[5]; and William the chamberlain of Tancarville, the founder, confirmed the tithes in Limésy which Geoffrey and Alan his knights had given.[6] Taken singly these are but slight pieces of evidence, but cumulatively, in conjunction with the fact that there does not seem to be any other place of the name of Limésy in Normandy, they seem to put the identification beyond any reasonable doubt.

LINGIEURE.

Lingèvres : Calvados, arr. Bayeux, cant. Balleroy.

In 1166 Ralf de Lingieure held one knight's fee of the old feoffment of John de Port.[7] Lingèvres lies 19 kil. S of Port-en-Bessin and 12 kil. W of St-Manvieu.[8] In the eleventh and twelfth centuries it was held by a family taking its name from the place, and there is no reason to suppose that it was held of Port. In 1204–8 Philip Augustus had half a fee in Lingèvres as an escheat[9]; and in 1242–3 Albreda de Lingyvre was holding half a fee in East Parley, Hants, of William de la Falese, who held of Robert de St. John, the heir and successor of Hugh de Port.[10] This suggests the possibility that on the separation of England and Normandy the successor of Ralf remained in England and forfeited land held by him in Lingèvres. This seems to be a case of the Ports of Basing enfeoffing a man from the Bessin, with whom they had no feudal link: see the remarks under PORT of Basing.

1 *Cambridge Hist. Journal*, iv, 298.
2 *Complete Peerage*, new ed., iv, 769.
3 *Mon. Ang.*, iii, 300.
4 *Rec. Hist. France*, xxiii, 613k.
5 *Cal. Docs. France*, no. 197.
6 *Mon. Ang.*, vi, 1066.
7 *Red Bk. Exch.*, p. 208.
8 See SANCTO MANEVEVO.
9 *Rec. Hist. France*, xxiii, 709b.
10 *Bk. of Fees*, p. 693.

LIVET.

Livet-en-Ouche : Eure, arr. Bernay, cant. Beaumesnil.

In 1135 Robert de Livet held two knights' fees of Ferrers; and in 1166 William Pantulf held them by the service of one knight.[1] According to the 'aveu' of 1604 Livet-en-Ouche, which is close to Ferrières-St-Hilaire, was a fief of the Norman barony of Ferrières.[2]

LOCELS.

Loucelles : Calvados, arr. Caen, cant. Tilly-sur-Seulles.

William de Locels occurs as a Domesday under-tenant of Beauchamp of Bedford. For the evidence of identification see under BROILG.

LONGCHAMP, LONGUS CAMPUS.

Longchamps : Eure, arr. Les Andelys, cant. Etrépagny.

The account of William de Longchamp, bishop of Ely and chancellor of Richard I, given by Stubbs, makes it clear that the family took its name from this place.[3] Members of the family appear to have been 'novi homines,' and the castle was a royal one.

LONGVILLERS.

Longvillers : Calvados, arr. Caen, cant. Villers-Bocage.

In 1166 Eudo de Longvilliers held one knight's fee of the old feoffment of Henry de Lascy of Pontefract.[4] Longvillers is 6 kil. S of Villy-Bocage, whence the family of Veilly (*q.v.*), under-tenants of Lascy of Pontefract, derived their name; and 4 kil. S of Epinay-sur-Odon, the commune in which lie Ectot and Le Saussey, places which gave their name to Eschetot (*q.v.*) and Salceit (*q.v.*), under-tenants of Lascy of Hereford.

LOVEL, of Titchmarsh.

Ivry-la-Bataille : Eure, arr. Evreux, cant. Saint-André.

The pedigree of the family showing its descent from the lords of Ivry is worked out in *The Complete Peerage*, new ed., viii, pp. 208–14. There is no evidence that the family was related to Roger the butler of Ivry (*q.v.*).

LUCY.

Lucé : Orne, in the bailiwick of Le Passeis, near Domfront.

The evidence cited in *The Complete Peerage*, new ed., viii, 257*n.*, establishes the identification. The rise of the family appears to have been due to king Henry I.

LUVETOT.

Louvetot : Seine-Inf., arr. Yvetot, cant. Caudebec.

An agreement between the abbey of St-Wandrille and Richard de Luvetot settling rights as to certain assarts near Ecclesfield, co. York,

[1] *Red Bk. Exch.*, p. 337.

[2] A. Le Prévost, *Mém. et Notes . . . . . de l'Eure*, ii, 84.

[3] *Roger of Howden* (Rolls Ser.), iii, pp. xxxvii *et seq.*, and *cf.* Stapleton, *Rot. Scacc. Norm.* i, 74.

[4] *Red Bk. Exch.*, p. 423. For the family see *Early Yorks. Charters*, iii, 304.

and including a grant by Richard of the tithe of his venison of Hallamshire, was executed in 1161 at St-Wandrille.[1] Louvetot is *c.* 6 kil. from St-Wandrille.

MALET.

Graville-Sainte-Honorine : Seine-Inf., arr. and cant. Le Havre. That Graville was the *caput* of the Malet barony in Normandy is well established. The facts given under CLAVILLA, COLEVILLE and ESMALEVILLA show that William Malet and his son Robert Malet, the Domesday tenant-in-chief, held this barony. In 1066–78 William Malet consented to the gift to the abbey of Préaux of land held of him at Buletoth.[2] In 1212–20 Matthew de Buletot held land in Buletot of the lord of Graville.[3] The ditches of the castle of the Malets below the priory of Graville were visible in 1870.[4]

MALORY.

[?] Tessancourt : Seine-et-Oise, arr. Versailles, cant. Meulan. That this family held an under-tenancy of the earls of Leicester in England in the twelfth century is shown by the fact that Robert earl of Leicester included gifts to Nun Eaton priory made by Richard Mallore in Swinford, co. Leicester, and Nun Eaton, co. Warwick, in his confirmation charter to that house, 1155–59.[5] An entry in the feodary of Philip Augustus, 1204–1208, mentions the 'feodum Anquetini Malore de Tessencurt.'[6] Tessancourt is the next parish to Meulan, the *caput* of the French *comté* of Robert count of Meulan, the first earl of Leicester. Anquetin was a name borne by the Leicestershire family of Malory. The evidence is slight, but it possibly indicates the original home of the family.

MALQUENCI.

Mauquenchy : Seine-Inf., arr. Neufchâtel, cant. Forges. In 1204, when he adhered to Philip Augustus, Gerard de Malquenci was dispossessed of land in Stoke Bruern and Shutlanger, co. Northampton, which he had held of the honour of Warenne.[7] In 1212–20 he held one fee at Blainville, arr. Rouen, cant. Buchy, and at Héron, arr. Rouen, cant. Darnetal, 'de ducatu,' and half a fee at Fontaines-sous-Préaux, arr. Rouen, cant. Darnetal, of the fee of Bellencombre, *i.e.* the *caput* of the Warenne honour in Normandy.[8] Mauquenchy is 17½ kil. S of the Warenne castle of Mortemer-sur-Eaulne, and 17½ kil. NE of Blainville. It is true that Mauquenchy itself was then in

[1] *Early Yorks. Charters*, iii, no. 1268.

[2] *Cal. Docs. France*, no. 319.

[3] *Rec. Hist. France*, xxiii, 642d.

[4] Cochet, *Rép. arch. . . . . de la Seine-Inf.*, col. 123; and *cf.* Ch. de Beaurepaire, *Notes historiques* (1883), pp. 98 *et seq.*

[5] *Cal. Docs. France*, no. 1062.

[6] *Rec. Hist. France*, xxiii, 713c.

[7] Farrer, *Honors and Knights' Fees*, iii, 413.

[8] *Rec. Hist. France*, xxiii, 613a.

other hands,[1] but in view of the above facts and the absence of any other place of the same name there can be no doubt that it was from there that the family originated.

MAMINOT.

Dept. Calvados.

In 1086 Gilbert Maminot was an under-tenant of Odo bishop of Bayeux in Kent.[2] One of the wards of Dover castle was that of Maminot.[3] In the Bayeux Inquest of 1133 the 'feodum Maminoth,' held of the bishop, rendered a service of five knights from fiefs in the following places, all in dept. Calvados: Surrain (arr. Bayeux, cant. Trévières), Bazenville (arr. Bayeux, cant. Ryes), Feugères (arr. Bayeux, cant. and comm. Isigny), Thaon (arr. Caen, cant. Creully), Noyers (arr. Caen, cant. Villers-Bocage), and 'Froigneium' or 'Floeneium' juxta Laceyam (*i.e.* Lacey, arr. Vire, cant. Condé-sur-Noireau).[4] As Maminot is a nickname and not territorial it is impossible to identify the exact place of origin, but the above facts leave no doubt that the family came from Calvados.

MANDEVILLE, MAGNAVILLA, MANNEVILLA, earls of Essex.

Manneville: Seine-Inf., arr. Dieppe, cant. Bacqueville.

It is now in the combined commune of Le Thil-Manneville. The *Historia Cœnobii Mortui-maris* states that earl William de Mandeville gave to the abbey the church of 'Magnavilla' of which he was the patron and that he was buried in the abbey.[5] The place is identified by an entry in the *pouillé* of 1337: 'Tilia et Magnavilla—patronus abbas de Mortuomari.'[6] The above facts are of themselves sufficient, but the identification is confirmed by the fact that the Mandeville *carta* of 1166 shows no less than five under-tenants coming from the immediate neighbourhood of Manneville, four of whom held land of its lord: see OSEVILLE, GWERES, SAINT-OUEN, CRIKETOT, MARTEL.

MANDEVILLE, MAGNEVILLA, of Earl's Stoke, Wilts., and of Devon.

Magneville: Manche, arr. Valognes, cant. Briquebec.

An account of this family in Normandy and England is given by Stapleton.[7] The charters from the chartularies of St-Sauveur-le-Vicomte and Montebourg which he cites show the family in possession of a considerable estate in the Cotentin. Stephen de Mandeville gave to St-Sauveur a rent in Orlande (arr. Coutances, cant. La Haie-du-Puits, comm. Canville), and to Montebourg the church of Catz (arr.

[1] *Ibid.*, pp. 612k, 613a, 614g. [2] *D.B.*, i, 7. [3] *Red Bk. Exch.*, p. 617.

[4] *Rec. Hist. France*, xxiii, 700h; and, for the distribution of service in the places named, *ibid.*, 633g, 634b, e.

[5] *Rec. Hist. France*, xiv, 514. He is called 'comes Willelmus Mortuimaris,' an obvious scribal error for 'Magnaevillae.' There was no such person as earl William de Mortemer, and moreover William de Mandeville was in fact buried at Mortemer (*Complete Peerage*, new ed., v, 119).

[6] A. Longnon, *Pouillés de la Province de Rouen*, p. 32.

[7] *Rot. Scacc. Norm.*, ii, pp. clxxxviii *et seq.*

St-Lô, cant. Carentan); his son Roger confirmed to St-Sauveur his father's gift of the church of Grosville (arr. Cherbourg, cant. Les Pieux) and of the church of Fresville (arr. Valognes, cant. Montebourg), and he himself gave to Montebourg the churches of Besneville, adjacent to Orlande, and of Earl's Stoke, Wilts. He also sold to the empress Maud all his rights in the church and fee of 'Octevilla,' evidently for her foundation of the abbey of Cherbourg.[1] In 1172 Roger de Mannevilla was a tenant by knight-service of the honour of Mortain in the Cotentin[2]; and he was dead by 1195, when his son William owed 30*li*. for his relief.[3] William was dead by 1198, leaving an heir under age, to have whom, a daughter to wife, Thierry Teutonicus offered 300 marks in 1200.[4] In that year, however, in a plea relating to the church of Stokenham, Devon, Mabel Patrick (William de Mandeville's widow) stated that her daughter was married to Matthew son of Herbert[5]; and in 1202 the latter made a fine with the king for the land of Orlande (*Hurland'*), which had belonged to William de Mandeville.[6] Matthew son of Herbert, who confirmed to the abbey of Montebourg land previously confirmed by Roger de Mandeville,[7] adhered to king John; and in 1205 Philip Augustus gave Orlande to Robert de Argences.[8] In 1203 Matthew son of Herbert owed 300 marks in Devon for land which had belonged to William de Mandeville.[9]

Stapleton derives the family from Mandeville, dept. Calvados, arr. Bayeux, cant. Trévières, giving as the sole reason that it was known as Mandeville-Hollande from the fief of Ollande [Orlande] in the Cotentin; but this receives no countenance from Hippeau's *Dictionnaire topographique du Calvados*. Stapleton appears to have relied on the mistaken belief that this family was a branch of that of the earls of Essex, and on the belief, equally mistaken, that the latter came from that Mandeville in the Bessin. But in view of the geographical position of Magneville, dept. Manche, lying in the midst of the churches and lands given by the family to the abbeys of St-Sauveur and Montebourg, and the essential connexion of the family with that district and not with the Bessin,[10] there can be no reasonable doubt of the place of origin. At Magneville there is a motte with its ditches not far from the existing and later château.[11]

1 *Cal. Docs. France*, no. 934.
2 *Rec. Hist. France*, xxiii, 696f.
3 *Rot. Scacc. Norm.*, i, 277.
4 *Ibid.*, ii, 477; *Rot. de Obl.*, p. 87 (Wilts.).
5 *Curia Regis Rolls*, i, 201.
6 *Rot. Norm.*, p. 51.
7 *Cal. Docs. France*, no. 886.
8 Delisle, *Cartulaire Normand*, no. 121.
9 *Pipe Roll 5 John*, p. 75.
10 Mr. Loyd adds a note that Stephen de Mandeville and his son Roger held Montchauvet (Calvados, arr. Vire, cant. Le Beny-Bocage), the church and tithe of which they gave to the priory of Le Plessis-Grimould (*Mém. Soc. Ant. Norm.*, viii, 95; and, for one of the charters, *Cal. Docs. France*, no. 546). The occurrence of Nicholas Folin as a witness to *ibid.*, nos. 546, 934, 990, shows the identity of Stephen and Roger. The place, however, is not in the Bessin, but in the extreme south of dept. Calvados (A. de Caumont, *Statistique monumentale du Calvados*, iii, 200).
11 *Mém. Soc. Ant. Norm.*, i, pp. 268–9.

MANDEVILLE, MANNEVILLE, MAGNEVILLE, under-tenants of Montfort and of the counts of Meulan.

Manneville-sur-Risle : Eure, arr. and cant. Pont-Audemer.

Manneville lies between Pont-Audemer and Montfort-sur-Risle, 3½ kil. from the former and 9½ kil. from the latter. Before 1067 Osbern de Magnivilla gave a man in Manneville to the abbey of St. Peter de Préaux, and also a mill on the Risle to Jumièges with the consent of Roger de Beaumont, lord of Pont-Audemer.[1] In 1141 Ralf de Mannevilla witnessed a charter of Waleran count of Meulan for Bordesley abbey,[2] and at an uncertain date another of the same for St-Nicaise of Meulan.[3] Between 1163 and 1166 he or a later Ralf witnessed a charter of Rotrou archbishop of Rouen for St-Nicaise.[4] The Norman Exchequer roll of 1203 shows a Ralf de Magneville holding one knight's fee of the honour of Montfort,[5] and 'aveus' of 1473 and 1572 show Manneville as a fief of the barony of Montfort.[6] These Mandevilles were men both of the count of Meulan and of the lord of Montfort.

In 1086 Hugh de Manneville was holding Court-at-Street (*Estraites*), Kent, of Hugh de Montfort.[7] At some date before the death of Waleran count of Meulan his son, as 'Robertus filius comitis Mellenti,' confirmed the gift by Ralf de Manneville of a rent in Charlton Marshal (*Carlentonum*), Dorset, to the priory of the Holy Trinity at Beaumont-le-Roger.[8] Charlton was a member of the honour of Sturminster, held in 1086 by Roger de Beaumont, Waleran's grandfather. Although the pedigree of this family of Mandeville has not been worked out, the above facts show both Hugh and Ralf to have come from Manneville-sur-Risle.

MARINNI.

Marigny : Calvados, arr. Bayeux, cant. Ryes.

In 1166 Gwerri de Marinni held half a knight's fee of the old feoffment of Adam de Port of Mapledurwell.[9] Marigny is 4 kil. E of Port-en-Bessin.

[1] A. Le Prévost, *Mém. et Notes . . . . de l'Eure*, ii, 371.

[2] Warner and Ellis, *British Museum Facsimiles*, no. 15. R. de Mannevilla witnessed two charters of Roger earl of Warwick, Waleran's cousin, one of them dated 1123 (*Mon. Ang.*, vi, 1327).

[3] E. Houth, *Rec. des chartes de St-Nicaise de Meulan* (Soc. Hist. de Pontoise et du Vexin), no. 17.

[4] *Ibid.*, no. 23.

[5] *Rot. Scacc. Norm.*, ii, 559. The feodary of 1204–1208 confirms this (*Rec. Hist. France*, xxiii, 710).

[6] A. Le Prévost, *op. cit.*, ii, 374.

[7] *D.B.*, i, 13b.

[8] *Cartulaire de la Sainte-Trinité de Beaumont-le-Roger*, ed. E. Deville, no. 38; *cf.* no. 37. Charlton is identified by Round in *Cal. Docs. France*, no. 248. The hospital of St-Gilles at Pont-Audemer held a small manor in Charlton (Hutchins, *Dorset*, iii, 138).

[9] *Red Bk. Exch.*, p. 280. The Red Book reads 'Guerri de Mairinnis'; the reading of the Black Book is the better and has been followed here.

MARMION.

Fontenay-le-Marmion : Calvados, arr. Caen, cant. Bourguébus. This identification is beyond question.[1] An account of the castle is given by A. de Caumont.[2]

MARSTON.

Damblainville : Calvados, arr. and cant. Falaise. In 1086 Robert of Rhuddlan held four hides in Marston St. Lawrence, co. Northampton, of Hugh earl of Chester[3]; and in 1081 William the Conqueror confirmed to the abbey of St-Evroul the church of Marston given by Robert of Rhuddlan with the consent of Hugh earl of Chester.[4] Robert of Rhuddlan also held Byfield, co. Northampton, of earl Hugh[3]; and he gave that church and his interest in the church of Damblainville to St-Evroul.[5] Humphrey de Merestona gave to St-Evroul all his land in the demesne of Damblainville and land at Byfield.[6]

MARTEL.

Bacqueville-en-Caux : Seine-Inf., arr. Dieppe, cant. Bacqueville. In 1086 Geoffrey Martel was the under-tenant of Geoffrey de Mandeville in Abbess Roding, Essex.[7] In 1085 he was one of the judges in a plea between the abbey of Fécamp and Gulbert de Auffay.[8] He was dead by 1130 when his son William occurs on the Pipe Roll under Dorset, Essex, and Bedfordshire.[9] On 15 May 1134 William Martel executed a charter giving the church of Bacqueville to the abbey of Tiron with the assent of his mother Albreda, of his wife also Albreda, and of his brother Eudo; it was witnessed by his sons Geoffrey and Roger.[10] Between 1146 and 1166 in conjunction with his wife Albreda and his son and heir Geoffrey he executed a charter for St. John's abbey at Colchester, mentioning his father Geoffrey and his mother Albreda[11]: this establishes the identity of the Essex landowner with the lord of Bacqueville. By 1166 he had been succeeded by his son Geoffrey, who in his *carta* of that year mentioned his brother Roger.[12] In 1172 the service due to the duchy for his Norman lands was two knights and he himself had the service of eight and three quarters.[13] William, Geoffrey's son, adhered to the French king in 1204 and lost his English lands, though other members of the family seem to have remained in England. There is no evidence that Martel held land of Mandeville

[1] See, *e.g.*, *Rot. Scacc. Norm.*, ii, p. xcvi, and *Cartulaire de Fontenay-le-Marmion*, ed. G. Saige (Monaco, 1895).

[2] *Statistique monumentale du Calvados*, ii, 166.

[3] *D.B.*, i, 224b.

[4] *Ord. Vit.*, ed. A. Le Prévost, iii, 26.

[5] *Cal. Docs. France*, nos. 631–2.

[6] *Ibid.*, no. 633.

[7] *D.B.*, ii, 57b.

[8] *Cal. Docs. France*, no. 116.

[9] *Pipe Roll* 31 *Hen. I*, pp. 13, 15, 56, 104.

[10] L'Abbé Sauvage, *Chartes du Prieuré de Bacqueville-en-Caux*, p. 17; *Cal. Docs. France*, no. 1009.

[11] *Cartularium Monasterii . . . . de Colecestria* (Roxburghe Club), p. 168.

[12] *Red Bk. Exch.*, p. 217.

[13] *Ibid.*, p. 629.

in Normandy, but Bacqueville is only 6½ kil. S of Manneville, which explains the English under-tenancy. The castle of the Martels at Bacqueville was on the banks of the Vienne; there is now no trace of it.[1]

MARTIGNY.

Pays de Caux, between the forest of Eawy and the Seine : dept. Seine-Inf.

In 1204 Elyas de Marteny gave 5 marks to have seisin of his lands in Wiltshire and Nottinghamshire, of which he had been disseised 'occasione Normannorum.'[2] In the early part of the thirteenth century Elyas de Martingni gave land in Fittleton, Wilts., to Thomas Makerel.[3] By a charter dated at Pont-de-l'Arche in 1206 Philip Augustus gave to William Havart and the heirs male of his body whatever Michael de Ponnengues and Helias de Martigneio used to have in Caux between the forest of Eawy and the river Seine.[4] This shows that Elyas, holding land in both countries, had wavered, but ultimately threw in his lot with England and lost his Norman lands. He may have derived his name either from Martigny (Seine-Inf., arr. Dieppe, cant. Offranville), or from Martagny, formerly *Martiniacum* (Eure, arr. Les Andelys, cant. Gisors). Geographically the former is perhaps somewhat the more likely, but evidence is entirely lacking. The land here in question could not have been situated at either of these places. *Cf.* POYNINGS.

MARTINWAST.

Martinvast : Manche, arr. Cherbourg, cant. Octeville.

Among the fees of the old feoffment in the *carta* of Ralf Ansel in 1166 is the entry ' Ricardus de Martinwast et Willelmus de Sefriwast et Peverellus de Bello Campo tenent feoda iij militum.'[5] The return of knights' fees in Normandy in 1172 among the bailiwicks of the Cotentin includes ' In ballia Regnaudi de Cornelun . . . . Guillelmus de Siffrewast terciam partem militis; Guillelmus filius Estulti dimidium militem; Ricardus de Martinwasto cum equis et armis cum communia de Cesaris Burgo.'[6] The association of Martinwast and Sifrewast (*q.v.*) both in England and Normandy at the same period, together with the exceptional name, puts the identification beyond doubt. Martinvast is 16 kil. NW from Chiffrevast.

MASSEY, MACI, MASCI.

Macey : Manche, arr. Avranches, cant. Pontorson.

In 1086 members of this family, from which the place Dunham Massey, Cheshire, took its name, held under-tenancies of the earl of Chester

1 Cochet, *Rép. arch. . . . de la Seine-Inf.*, cols. 2–3.
2 *Rot. de Obl. et Fin.*, p. 204.
3 *Sir Christopher Hatton's Book of Seals*, no. 378.
4 Delisle, *Cartulaire Normand*, no. 1084.
5 *Red Bk. Exch.*, p. 340.
6 *Rec. Hist. France*, xxiii, 696e.

in several counties.[1] In the twelfth century Macey is shown as a fief of the abbey of Le Mont-Saint-Michel.[2] Its geographical position among the earl of Chester's fees in the Avranchin points very strongly to its being the place of origin of the family.

MATUEN.

Mathieu : Calvados, arr. Caen, cant. Douvres.

Not later than 1104 Henry I confirmed to St. John's, Colchester, a gift of the tithe of Fimborough, Suffolk, made by Serlo de Matuen, a man of Eudo Dapifer.[3] In 1142–47 Robert earl of Gloucester quitclaimed to Philip bishop of Bayeux 'totum feodum quod Eudo dapifer tenuit apud Mattonum.'[4] In the Bayeux Inquest of 1133 Mathieu occurs as 'Mathonium,'[5] and in 1155 as 'Matoen.'[6] It is 23 kil. SE of Ryes.[7]

MAUDUIT, MALDUIT.

Saint-Martin-du-Bosc : Eure, arr. Les Andelys, cant. and comm. Etrepagny.

In 1193 there were enrolled on the Pipe Roll for Northamptonshire the terms of a charter by which John son of John Malduit quitclaimed to William Malduit the chamberlain (of the Exchequer), his lord, all the tenement which he held of the said William at St-Martin 'juxta Strepeigni'[8]; and the terms show that this tenure between two branches of the family was of old standing, and so carry the Mauduit interest at St-Martin back to an early date. The land of W. Mauduit in this place is noted as an escheat to the king of France, *c.* 1204[9]: in 1207 the king gave to John son of Athon the land of William Mauduit at St-Martin[10]; and in 1207–08 he gave to Baldwin de Lihus the land which John and Robert Mauduit had held there.[11]

MAYENNE, MEDUANA.

Mayenne : dept. Mayenne.

Walter de Meduana was a tenant-in-chief in 1166, returning his *carta* from Kent.[12] A letter of Stephen, seneschal of Anjou, shows that he was a son of Juhel lord of Mayenne.[13]

[1] Farrer, *Honors and Knights' Fees*, ii, pp. 288, 292.
[2] *Rec. Hist. France*, xxiii, 703j.
[3] Farrer, *Honors and Knights' Fees*, iii, 167.
[4] *Antiq. cartul. Baioc.* (Soc. Hist. Norm.), i, 49 (no. 49).
[5] *Rec. Hist. France*, xxiii, 702g.
[6] C. Hippeau, *Dict. topogr. du Calvados*, p. 185.
[7] See EUDO DAPIFER.
[8] *Pipe Roll 5 Ric. I*, p. 99.
[9] Delisle, *Cartulaire Normand*, no. 1079.
[10] Delisle, *Cat. des Actes de Philippe-Auguste*, no. 1051A.
[11] Delisle, *Cartulaire Normand*, no. 1088.
[12] *Red Bk. Exch.*, p. 195.
[13] Delisle et Berger, *Rec. des Actes de Henri II*, ii, 135.

Henry I gave the manor of South Peterton, Somerset, to Hamelin de Meduana in exchange for Ambrières and Gorron, both dept. Mayenne[1]; and in 1212 it was recorded that he also gave Black Torrington and King's Nympton, Devon, to the ancestors of Johel de Meduana in exchange for the same two places.[2]

MEINIERS, DE MAINERIIS, MANERIIS.

Mesnières : Seine-Inf., arr. and cant. Neufchâtel.

Before 1066 Robert de Maineriis witnessed a charter of Robert count of Eu for the abbey of Le Tréport.[3] In 1106 Tirel de Maneriis witnessed a charter of Henry count of Eu, giving the manor of Hooe, Sussex, to the priory of St-Martin-du-Bosc[4]; and in 1170 Roger de Maneriis witnessed a charter of John count of Eu, confirming this.[5] In 1107 Henry count of Eu confirmed to the abbey of Le Tréport a gift of Ramelinus de Mesnils of land in Sept Meules 'concessu Walterii Tirelli de Maisneriis domini sui.'[6] About 1180 Reginald de Meiniers and Maud his wife gave to Robertsbridge abbey lands in the rape of Hastings, held of the count of Eu, which her father Ingelran de Fressenvile gave her as a 'maritagium,' and in exchange Reginald gave to Maud a rent of 12*li*. angevin from his mill of Meiniers.[7] In the thirteenth century Mesnières occurs as 'de Maneriis,' and in the fourteenth century as 'Mainieres.'[8]

This place can also be considered in connexion with Sommery and Normanville (*q.v.*). Families of those names held tenancies of the counts of Eu. The three places lie south of the *comté* of Eu and of the district from which it would appear most likely that the count of Eu would draw his English under-tenants; but their proximity to each other strengthens the probability that the count's influence and interest was extended in this direction. Indeed there is a charter, *c.* 1040–*c.* 1050, which shows that William, younger brother of Robert count of Eu, had a contingent interest in Drincourt,[9] the present Neufchâtel-en-Bray, from which Mesnières is 3 kil. to the N.

MEINNIL MALGERI.

Le Mesnil-Mauger : Calvados, arr. Lisieux, cant. Mézidon.

William the chamberlain of Tancarville confirmed to Bruton priory, Somerset, a virgate of land given by Theodoric de Meinnil Malgeri.[10] Le Mesnil-Mauger is 6 kil. E of Mézidon, the *caput* of the Tancarville barony in Western Normandy.[11]

1 *Bk. of Fees*, p. 86.
2 *Ibid.*, p. 97.
3 *Cartulaire . . . du Tréport*, ed. L. de Kermaingant, p. 15; *Cal. Docs. France*, no. 230.
4 *Cal. Docs. France*, no. 399.
5 *Ibid.*, no. 400.
6 *Cartulaire . . . du Tréport*, p. 25.
7 Hist. MSS. Comm., *Lord De L'Isle and Dudley*, i, 36; on Reginald's seal is . . . . MANERIIS; and on Maud's seal . . . MEINIERS (*ibid.*, p. 71).
8 *Rec. Hist. France*, xxiii, 274e; A. Longnon, *Pouillés de la Province de Rouen*, p. 82.
9 *Cartulaire de la Sainte-Trinité de Rouen*, ed. A. Deville, no. 2.
10 *Cal. Docs. France*, no. 486.
11 *Cf.* CANTELU.

MEISI.

[?] Maizet[1] : Calvados, arr. Caen, cant. Evrecy.

In 1166 Elias de Meisi held half a knight's fee of the old feoffment of Robert Marmion.[2] Maizet, of which thirteenth-century forms are Maiset and Meset, is 6 kil. W of Fontenay-le-Marmion.

MILLEVILLE.

Mirville : Seine-Inf., arr. Le Havre, cant. Goderville.

In 1166 Hugh de Milleville held half a knight's fee of the new feoffment of the English honour of Giffard.[3] Mirville is *c.* 5 kil. N of Bolbec, and occurs as Milevilla in charters of Henry II.[4] In 1140 Adam de Milevilla witnessed a charter of Wakelin du Bec giving land in Normandy to the Giffard foundation of Longueville priory.[5]

MILLIERES, MILERS.

Millières : Manche, arr. Coutances, cant. Lessay.

William d'Aubigny, *pincerna,* enfeoffed William de Milers of half a knight's fee in Kent.[6] Millières lies 5 kil. NW of St-Martin d'Aubigny.[7] An account of the family is given in Farrer, *Honors and Knights' Fees,* vol. iii, pp. 97, 153.

MINERS, DE MINERIIS.

Minières : Eure, arr. Evreux, cant. Damville.

In 1204 Gilbert de Mineres, a Norman, lost his lands in Girton and Barton, co. Cambridge, and also unnamed land in Buckinghamshire.[8] On the Norman Exchequer Roll of 1198 Gilbert de Mineriis paid 100*li.* for having right against Roger de Tosny respecting the land of Richard de Romilly.[9] In the feodary of 1204-08 Gilbert was holding a quarter of a fee at Romilly (Eure, arr. Les Andelys, cant. Fleury-sur-Andelle) of the honour of Breteuil.[10] In 1190–1204 he witnessed two charters of Robert earl of Leicester, lord of Breteuil,[11] to whom at one time he was seneschal.[12] In the feodary of 1212–20 the quarter fee at Romilly was held by William de Mineriis,[13] presumably his son, who was then holding a fee in Corneuil (Eure, arr. Evreux, cant. Damville), also of the honour of Breteuil.[14] Corneuil is 5 kil. NE of Minières. In the *Querimoniæ Normannorum* of 1247 William de Mineriis, knt, of Corneuil mentions his son William, a knight, and his son's wife; and there is a

1 Mr. Loyd subsequently queried this, considering that the evidence was insufficient.

2 *Red Bk. Exch.*, p. 327.

3 *Ibid.*, p. 313.

4 Delisle et Berger, *Rec. des Actes de Henri II*, i, 548; ii, 88, 98.

5 P. Le Cacheux, *Chartes du Prieuré de Longueville*, no. 2.

6 *Red Bk. Exch.*, p. 399.

7 See also AVRANCHES.

8 *Red Bk. Exch.*, pp. 537, 800; *Bk. of Fees*, p. 616.

9 *Mém. Soc. Ant. Norm.*, xvi, 10.

10 *Rec. Hist. France*, xxiii, 714j.

11 *Cal. Docs. France*, nos. 607, 653.

12 Delisle, *Cartulaire Normand*, no. 791*n*.

13 *Rec. Hist. France*, xxiii, 614f.

14 *Ibid.*, p. 617f. The correct reading is *Cornulium*, which is Corneuil, not Cormeilles (*ibid.*, xxiv, 33a and note).

complaint by William de Mineriis 'juvenis, miles, de Mineriis.'[1] This shows that Minières itself was in the possession of the family. Though there is no express evidence that Gilbert had held Corneuil, this is a justifiable inference from the facts.

There was also a family of Miners in Gloucestershire and Herefordshire. In 1130 Gilbert de Mineriis was pardoned danegeld in Gloucestershire,[2] and there are several mentions of him in the Chartulary of St. Peter's, Gloucester. Henry de Telmbrugge sold land in Cubberley, co. Gloucester, to the abbey with the consent of his lord Gilbert de Miners; and as the abbey was to make a yearly payment to the lord of Foxcote, this must have been held by Gilbert.[3] Gilbert confirmed to the abbey land in Brookthorp and Ridge (in Standish) in the time of abbot Hamelin,[4] who was consecrated on 5 Dec. 1148.[5] A Hereford inquest of 1251–52 shows a William de Miners as having held Burghill, co. Hereford, being succeeded there by his only son Henry, who was succeeded by his three daughters.[6] A Henry de Miners held Foxcote in 1214[7]; and in 1219 he had been succeeded by three ladies and their husbands, the ladies being identical with the three daughters of the Burghill inquisition.[8] This shows that Henry and his father William were the successors of Gilbert de Miners, mentioned above. William de Miners occurs in Gloucestershire in 1162 and in 1176–77,[9] and it is likely that William was the son as well as the successor of Gilbert. In 1086 Burghill was held in chief by Alvred de Merleberge[10]; and it is known that his tenure and the settlement of Herefordshire were largely due to William FitzOsbern, the then lord of Breteuil.[11] It is possible, therefore, that this Miners family also came from Minières, though the gap between the death of William FitzOsbern and the first appearance of Gilbert de Mineriis in 1130 is too great, in the absence of other evidence, to make the deduction more than a conjecture.

MOELS, MOLES, MOLIS.

Meules : Calvados, arr. Lisieux, cant. Orbec.

In 1086 Roger de Moles was an under-tenant of Baldwin FitzGilbert, sheriff of Devon.[12] Meules was the *caput* of Baldwin's Norman barony, whence he himself was often known as Baldwin de Meulles.[13] Roger de Moles may well have been the ancestor of the later family of Moels, of which an account is given in *The Complete Peerage*, new ed., vol. ix, p. 1.

[1] *Ibid.*, xxiv, 33a, 48a.
[2] *Pipe Roll* 31 *Hen. I*, p. 80.
[3] *Hist. and Chartulary of St. Peter's, Gloucester* (Rolls Ser.), i, 233.
[4] *Ibid.*, p. 62.
[5] *Ibid.*, p. 19.
[6] *Bk. of Fees*, p. 1270.
[7] *Curia Regis Rolls*, vii, 252.
[8] *Ibid.*, viii, 45.
[9] *Pipe Roll* 8 *Hen. II*, p. 60; 23 *Hen. II*, p. 55.
[10] *D.B.*, i, 186.
[11] *V.C.H. Hereford*, i, 270.
[12] *D.B.*, i, 106.
[13] Round in *Dict. Nat. Biog.*, s.n. Clare, x, 375.

MOHUN, MOION, MOYON.

Moyon : Manche, arr. St-Lô, cant. Tessy-sur-Vire.

Towards the end of the twelfth century William de Moyon gave to Bruton priory, to hold after the death of Thomas his brother, his rights in the churches of Moyon, Tessy-sur-Vire and Beaucoudray.[1] The last two places are 5 kil. SE and 5 kil. S of Moyon respectively. There was a castle at Moyon.[2] In 1208–12 the barony of Moion, an escheat in the hand of Philip Augustus, owed the service of five knights, castle-guard being apparently due at Moyon.[3] An account of the family is given in *The Complete Peerage*, new ed., vol. ix, pp. 17 *et seq.*, largely based on Sir Henry Maxwell-Lyte's *History of Dunster*.

MONCEAUX, MONCEUS, MOUNCELS, DE MONCELLIS, ETC.

Monchaux (-Soreng) : Seine-Inf., arr. Neufchâtel, cant. Blangy.

As early as 1130 Ralf de Moncellis occurs in Sussex, being pardoned 20*s.* 6*d.* of danegeld.[4] Between 1176 and 1180 Idonea de Herste gave land to Robertsbridge abbey, a gift afterwards confirmed by her son Waleran de Herste, who is described on his seal as Waleran de Munceaus.[5] Another charter of Waleran de Herste, similarly described on his seal, giving land to the same house, is at Penshurst, and his gift was confirmed by ' William de Munceus son of Waleran de Herste.'[6] Herste, *i.e.* Hurstmonceaux, was held of the count of Eu. In 1199 William de Werbinton [Warbleton, Sussex] and Ingram de Monceaus gave 500 marks for the inheritance of Juliane wife of William FitzAldelin, whose heirs they were; and in 1205 Waleran de Monceus gave 100 marks for his share of this same inheritance.[7] Ingram and Waleran were clearly of the same family. Ingram can be identified as the Engelram son of Alan de Munceus who confirmed a carucate in Ugthorpe, co. York, to Guisborough priory, and gave land there to Meaux abbey, 1182–1205[8]; and probably with the Engueran de Moncellis who occurs on the Norman Exchequer Roll of 1184 in the *prévôté* of Drincourt (mod. Neufchâtel).[9] In 1147–53 Alan de Muncell and Ingram his son and heir made gifts to the nuns of Nun Coton, co. Lincoln[10]; and before 1127 Stephen count of Aumale had given the land of Boynton, co. York, to Alan de Mouncels.[11] In 1242–43 William de Munceus and Thomas de Warblinton each held $2\frac{1}{2}$ fees in Sussex of the countess of Eu,[12] clearly moieties of the inheritance of Juliane mentioned above.

[1] *Cal. Docs. France*, no. 505.

[2] Gerville in *Mém. Soc. Ant. Norm.*, v, 214.

[3] *Rec. Hist. France*, xxiii, 611g.

[4] *Pipe Roll* 31 *Hen. I*, p. 72.

[5] Warner and Ellis, *British Museum Facsimiles*, no. 61 and note.

[6] Hist. MSS. Comm., *Lord De L'Isle and Dudley*, i, pp. 45, 82.

[7] Farrer, *Honors and Knights' Fees*, iii, 376, for these and several other references to the family; and *cf.* Round, *The King's Serjeants*, pp. 92–8.

[8] *Early Yorks. Charters*, ii, no. 1062 and note.

[9] *Rot. Scacc. Norm.*, i, 116.

[10] *Early Yorks. Charters*, iii, no. 1329.

[11] *Ibid.*, no. 1326.

[12] *Bk. of Fees*, p. 692.

Monchaux lies not far to the N of Blangy within the limits of the *comté* of Eu, of which it was a fief. In 1107 Anscher de Moncellis witnessed a charter of Henry count of Eu for the abbey of Le Tréport[1]; and in 1109, with his brothers William and Ralf, another of the same for the abbey of St-Lucien, Beauvais.[2] In 1175 Ralf de Moncellis confirmed to Le Tréport whatever right he or his ancestors had in the church of Monchaux (*de Moncellis*).[3] Monchaux also lies *c.* 23 kil. N of Aumale; and the tenures of the family in England under the counts of Eu and Aumale thus leave no doubt as to its place of origin. There is a motte with its ditches at Monchaux.[4]

MONCEAUX, MONCELS, DE MUNCELLIS, under-tenants of Tracy; and COVERT, CUVERT, under-tenants of Briouze.

Monceaux : Calvados, arr. and cant. Bayeux.

Couvert : Calvados, arr. Bayeux, cant. Balleroy, comm. Juaye-Mondaye.

Although there is no direct connexion between these families it will be convenient for historical purposes to treat them together. In the Exon Domesday William de Moncels occurs as an extensive under-tenant of Geoffrey bishop of Coutances in Devon and Somerset; and in 1166 William de Muncellis held a knight's fee of the old feoffment of Oliver de Tracy.[5] In 1086 the honour of Barnstaple formed part of the vast possessions of bishop Geoffrey; and at a later date, when in the king's hand, it was granted to Juhel son of Alvred of Totnes, who was living in 1123, when as Johel de Berdestaple he witnessed a charter of Henry I.[6] In 1130 his son Alvred paid a relief for his father's lands.[7] In 1166 one moiety of the honour of Barnstaple was held by William de Briouze,[8] whose father Philip married a daughter of Juhel,[9] and the other moiety by Oliver de Tracy, who was probably descended from another daughter of Juhel.[10]

In the Norman *Infeudationes militum* of 1172[11] are the entries 'Willelmus de Braiosa, iij milites de Braiosa. Idem, servitium j militis de Couvert.' The form of the entries, combined with the fact that Couvert lies *c.* 65 kil. N of Briouze, suggests very strongly that it formed no part of the original Briouze lands; and, as a William de Cuvert witnessed a charter of Juhel of Totnes for Barnstaple priory,[12] it is reasonably certain that Couvert came to the Briouze family by inheritance from Juhel. In 1157–60 Richard de Cuvert witnessed the charter of William de Briouze mentioned above.[13]

[1] *Cartulaire . . . . du Tréport*, ed. L. de Kermaingant, p. 22.

[2] Mabillon, *De re diplomatica* (1681), p. 594.

[3] *Cartulaire*, p. 67.

[4] Cochet, *Rép. arch. . . . de la Seine-Inf.*, col. 185.

[5] *Red Bk. Exch.*, p. 255.

[6] Round, *Feudal England*, p. 483.

[7] *Pipe Roll* 31 *Hen. I*, p. 153.

[8] *Red Bk. Exch.*, p. 258.

[9] *Cal. Docs. France*, no. 1272—William referring to Juhel as his grandfather.

[10] See further under TRACY.

[11] *Red Bk. Exch.*, p. 631.

[12] *Mon. Ang.*, v, 198.

[13] *Cal. Docs. France*, no. 1272.

Monceaux is only 5 kil. N of Couvert; and this proximity, combined with the connexion of the two families with the lords of the honour of Barnstaple, establishes their places of origin. Moreover, since the William de Moncels of 1086 was the tenant of bishop Geoffrey, and Couvert was held in the twelfth century by Briouze, it is possible that both places were held by or of the bishop in the eleventh, thus carrying back their feudal history to an early date.

In 1242–43 William le (*sic*) Covert was holding Sullington and Broadbridge (in Bosham), Sussex, of the honour of Briouze for two knights' fees.[1] This is the earliest record of the family's tenure of land in England which has come to notice; but the appearance of members of the family as witnesses to charters, noted above, suggests an early settlement in England.

MONTFICHET.

Montfiquet : Calvados, arr. Bayeux, cant. Balleroy.

The facts collected under BACON establish this identification.

MONTFORT.

Montfort-sur-Risle : Eure, arr. Pont-Audemer, cant. Montfort.

Hugh de Montfort, the Domesday tenant-in-chief of the lands which became known as the honour of Haughley or *honor constabularie,*[2] took his name from Montfort-sur-Risle. An account of the early lords of the honour of Montfort-sur-Risle, based on English and Norman sources, is given in D. C. Douglas, *The Domesday Monachorum of Christ Church, Canterbury*, pp. 65–70. There is a reference to the castle there in the middle of the eleventh century.[3]

The Montforts of Beaudesert, co. Warwick, were probably a younger branch of the same family.[4]

MONTGOMERY.

Saint-Germain-de-Montgomery :
Sainte-Foy-de-Montgomery : } Calvados, arr. Lisieux, cant. Livarot.

Roger de Montgomery, earl of Shrewsbury, succeeded Roger his father as *seigneur* of Montgomery.[5] There are traces of an early castle in each commune.[6]

With regard to other families of the name, Walter de Montgomery held four knights' fees of earl Ferrers *temp.* Henry I.[7] The communes named above lie 31 kil. W of Ferrières-St-Hilaire, but only 14 kil. S of Auquainville and 7 kil. SW of Courson, both of which were fiefs of the barony of Ferrières; see AUKENVILLA and CURZON. The

[1] *Bk. of Fees*, p. 690.

[2] Round, *Geoffrey de Mandeville*, pp. 326–7.

[3] *Complete Peerage*, new ed., ix, 120 *n*.

[4] *Ibid.*

[5] *Ibid.*, xi, 682–3.

[6] *Ibid.*, p. 682*n*, citing the opinion of A. de Caumont (*Statistique monumentale du Calvados*, v, pp. 646, 650–1) that the castle at St-Germain, which is the larger, was the earlier.

[7] *Red Bk. Exch.*, p. 337.

proximity of these Ferrers fiefs, combined with the fact that there is no other place of the name in Normandy, shows that Walter's family must have derived its name therefrom. There is, however, no evidence, and little likelihood, that they were related in blood to earl Roger.

Another holder of the name, clearly derived from the place, is mentioned in a charter of Roger ' comes Pictavencis ' (son of earl Roger) who gave to the abbey of St-Martin, Sées, among other gifts in Lancashire, Amfrid de Monte gomerii and whatever he held of him.[1] As Ansfrid de Montegommerio he witnessed another charter of count Roger in 1094.[2]

MONTPINÇON, MUNPINCUN, ETC.

Montpinçon : Calvados, arr. Lisieux, cant. Saint-Pierre-sur-Dives. Ralf de Montpinçon the dapifer was the Ralf dapifer of the Domesday survey.[3] Orderic gives an account of the family and of Ralf's benefactions to the abbey of St-Evroul[4]: these lie in the same district as Montpinçon and prove the identification. There was a castle at Montpinçon.[5] In 1172 Hugh de Monte Pincon held the honour of Montpinçon by a service of three knights.[6] In May 1204 Philip Augustus gave it to Garin de Glapion.[7]

MONVILLE, MONTVILLA.

Monville : Seine-Inf., arr. Rouen, cant. Clères.

Nigel de Monville succeeded his father-in-law William of Arques[8] as lord of Folkestone.[9] The charters of Holy Trinity, Rouen, show that William of Arques held Monville.[10]

Evidence is lacking to prove the identity of this Nigel with the Nigel de Monville who in 1086 held a burgage tenement in York.[11]

MORERS.

Morières : Calvados, arr. Lisieux, cant. Saint-Pierre-sur-Dives. In 1175 William de Morers held two knights' fees of the Percy barony.[12] Later records show that the lands lay in Lincolnshire and Yorkshire.[13] Morières is 8 kil. distant from Percy-en-Auge; and it is this fact which was among the reasons for assigning Percy-en-Auge as the place of origin of William de Percy, the Domesday tenant-in-chief: see PERCY.

1 Farrer, *Lancs. Pipe Rolls and Early Charters*, p. 289; and *Cal. Docs. France*, no. 664, from another source.

2 *Cal. Docs. France*, no. 665.

3 Davis, *Regesta*, p. xxiv.

4 *Ord. Vit.*, ii, 435.

5 A. de Caumont, *Statistique monumentale du Calvados*, v, 604.

6 *Rec. Hist. France*, xxiii, 694j.

7 Delisle, *Cat. des Actes de Philippe-Auguste*, no. 817B, and cf. *Rec. Hist. France*, xxiii, 707b.

8 See ARQUES.

9 Stapleton in *Archæologia*, xxxi, 216 *et seq.*

10 *Cartulaire de la Sainte-Trinité de Rouen*, ed. A. Deville, nos. 25–6.

11 *D.B.*, i, 298.

12 *Percy Chartulary* (Surtees Soc.), no. 1092.

13 *Bk. of Fees*, pp. 154, 171, 1019; *Feudal Aids*, vi, pp. 79, 83. Some 13th-cent. Morers charters in Lincolnshire are given in *Reg. Antiquissimum* (Linc. Rec. Soc.), v, pp. 41–4.

MOREVILLE.

Morville : Manche, arr. Valognes, cant. Bricquebec.

In the Registers of Philip Augustus (1212–20) Herbert de Morevilla held a sixth of a knight's fee in Morevilla of Richard de Vernon.[1] Richard de Vernon was head of the Norman branch of a family represented in England by the Reviers earls of Devon; and Morville is 7 kil. N of Néhou, the *caput* of the Vernon honour in the Cotentin.

A mutilated entry on the Pipe Roll of 1130 under Devon shows William de Morevilla as holding land.[2] A charter of Baldwin de Reviers, not yet an earl, which places it before 1142, for Christchurch, Hants, was witnessed by William de Morvill,[3] who also witnessed charters of Baldwin as earl for the abbeys of Quarr[4] and Montebourg.[5] With his son Ivo he witnessed a charter of Richard de Reviers, earl of Devon, for Christchurch, dated 1161.[3] By a charter, shown by the witnesses to have been executed in Dorset, William de Moreville gave a chapel in Bradpole, Dorset, to Montebourg, mentioning Maud his wife and Eudo (Ivo) his son; it was witnessed by William de Haga.[6] At Mich. 1204 the sheriff accounted for 50*s*. from the land of Herbert de Moreville in Portbury, Somerset, among the lands of the Normans.[7] This must be the Herbert noted above who held Morville in 1212–20. Portbury was a manor of the earl of Devon.[8] Members of the family, however, continued in Dorset, for Bradpole was held in serjeanty by William de Moreville in 1212, 1219 and 1226–28[9]; but Herbert the Norman must have been the head of the family.

Another branch of the family, for which see HAIG, settled in Scotland before 1120 and became constables of Scotland.

MORTIMER, of Attleborough, Norfolk.

Mortemer-sur-Eaulne : Seine-Inf., arr. and cant. Neufchâtel.

This family, of whom accounts are given in Farrer, *Honors and Knights' Fees*, vol. iii, p. 385, and *The Complete Peerage*, new ed., vol. ix, p. 243, held under-tenancies of Warenne in Norfolk from an early date in the twelfth century, and there can be no doubt that they derived their name and came from Mortemer-sur-Eaulne, which was given with its castle to William de Warenne by duke William after the forfeiture of Roger de Mortemer in 1054. There is, however, no reason to believe that they were connected in blood with the original lords of Mortemer, from whom descended the Mortimers of Wigmore.

MORTIMER, of Wigmore.

Mortemer-sur-Eaulne : Seine-Inf., arr. and cant. Neufchâtel.

After the restoration of some of his lands to Roger de Mortemer, which did not include Mortemer-sur-Eaulne, the *caput* of his honour became

[1] *Rec. Hist. France*, xxiii, 609h.
[2] *Pipe Roll* 31 *Hen. I*, p. 157.
[3] *Cal. Chart. Rolls*, 1300–26, p. 229.
[4] *Camb. Hist. Journal*, iv, 297.
[5] *Complete Peerage*, new ed., iv, 769, no xiv, and *cf*. no. xv.
[6] *Cal. Docs. France*, no. 885.
[7] *Pipe Roll* 6 *John*, p. 186.
[8] *Bk. of Fees*, p. 1265.
[9] *Ibid*., pp. 92, 261, 378.

St-Victor-l'Abbaye, dept. Seine-Inf., arr. Dieppe, cant. Tôtes,[1] where the motte is close by the abbey church.[2] From his son Ralph descended the Mortimers of Wigmore.[3]

MOWBRAY.

Montbrai : Manche, arr. St-Lô, cant. Percy.

The second family of Mowbray was descended from Nigel d'Aubigny who married the former wife of Robert de Mowbray, earl of Northumberland, and who was granted the lands in Normandy which the earl had forfeited.[4] In the second half of the twelfth century Nigel de Mowbray was holding Montbrai.[5] A description of the castle was given by Gerville.[6]

MUCHEGROS.

Mussegros : Eure, arr. Les Andelys, cant. Fleury-sur-Andelle, comm. Ecouis.

Roger de Mucegros witnessed a charter of Ralf de Conchis son of Roger de Toneio (*i.e.* Ralf de Tosny) for the abbey of St-Evroul, *c.* 1080.[7] In 1086 Roger was an under-tenant of Ralf de Tosny in Monnington, co. Hereford[8]; and Round[9] identified him as Roger de Muchegros, pointing out that in 1242–43 Walter de Muchegros was holding Monnington of the honour of Tosny.[10] Mussegros is 11 kil. NE of Tosny.

NAZANDA.

Nassandres : Eure, arr. Bernay, cant. Beaumont-le-Roger.

Theobald archbishop of Canterbury confirmed to the priory of Stoke-by-Clare the gift by Ernald de Nazanda of two-thirds of his tithe in 'Hamstedia,' and he also recited a charter of Gilbert FitzRichard of Clare dated 1099 which was witnessed by Ernald de Nazanda.[11] Nassandres is 27 kil. E of Orbec, the *caput* of the Norman honour of Richard FitzGilbert, Gilbert's father; but it is only 8 kil. S of Brionne which had been held by Gilbert count of Brionne, Richard's father. The earliest recorded form of the name in Normandy is 'Nacande' in 1179.[12] The patron of the church was the abbot of Le Bec, a house of which the family of Clare were notable benefactors.[13]

1 *Complete Peerage*, new ed., ix, 266.

2 Cochet, *Rép. arch. . . . de la Seine-Inf.*, col. 89.

3 *Complete Peerage*, ix, 267 *et seq.*

4 *Ibid.*, ix, 368. The family descended from Nigel d'Aubigny's second wife.

5 *Cal. Docs. France*, no. 599.

6 *Mém. Soc. Ant. Norm.*, v, 202. The true medieval form of the name is Molbrai or Monbrai, the 't' being a modern intrusion.

7 *Cal. Docs. France*, no. 625.

8 *D.B.*, i, 183.

9 *V.C.H. Hereford*, i, 327*n*.

10 *Bk. of Fees*, p. 802.

11 *Mon. Ang.*, vi, 1659–60.

12 Blosseville, *Dict. topogr. de l'Eure*, p. 152.

13 A. Longnon, *Pouillés de la Province de Rouen*, p. 183.

NEUBOURG, DE NOVO BURGO.

Neubourg : Eure, arr. Louviers, cant. Neubourg.

In 1166 Henry de Novo Burgo held half a knight's fee of the old feoffment of the earl of Warwick.[1] He was son and heir of Robert de Neubourg, seneschal of Normandy, a younger son of Henry, first earl of Warwick. Neubourg was held of the honour of Beaumont-le-Roger, and Robert must have been enfeoffed of it before 1118 by Robert count of Meulan, the lord of Beaumont and elder brother of Henry earl of Warwick.[2]

NEUFMARCHE, DE NOVO MERCATO.

Neufmarché : Seine-Inf., arr. Neufchâtel, cant. Gournay.

Orderic (ii, 112, and iii, 43) clearly establishes this place as the original home of Bernard de Neufmarché, lord of Brecknock. Bernard's father Geoffrey was deprived of it before 1066, and the castle was thereafter in ducal hands.

Neufmarché can also be assigned as the place of origin of the family of Reginald de Neufmarché who held land in Lincolnshire, though there is no ground for supposing that he was related in blood to the lord of Brecknock. *Temp.* Henry II William de Roumare gave a bovate of land in East Kirkby and another in Mavis Enderby, both co. Lincoln, to Reinold de Novo Mercato.[3] Gerold the seneschal, grandfather of the first William de Roumare, became castellan of Neufmarché *c.* 1064[4]; and the custody of the castle continued in his descendants, being held in 1172 by William de Roumare who owed the service of twelve or fourteen knights for castle-guard.[5]

No connexion has been traced between these families and the family of Neufmarché, under-tenants of the honour of Tickhill, whose place of origin is unknown.[6]

NEVILLE.

Néville : Seine-Inf., arr. Yvetot, cant. Saint-Valery.

The history of the family of Neville of Raby is carefully worked out in *The Complete Peerage*, new ed., vol. ix, pp. 491 *et seq.* The descent through Isabel de Neville, heiress of the first line and wife of Robert FitzMaldred, is proved from Gilbert de Neville who in 1166 held five knights' fees of the bishop of Lincoln and four of the honour of Manasser Arsic. The tenure of Scothern and Reepham, held of the bishop at the Lindsey survey, and of Walcot, co. Lincoln, held of the abbot of Peterborough, shows that this Gilbert was the successor of Geoffrey de Neville who had succeeded an earlier Gilbert de Neville; and the tenure of Walcot shows that this earlier Gilbert was either identical with or the successor of the tenant named Gilbert of the abbot of Peterborough at Walcot in 1086.

1 *Red Bk. Exch.*, p. 326.

2 Orderic (iv, 327) records that Robert de Neubourg rebelled against Henry I in 1118 (before the death of his father earl Henry), who thereupon took and burnt Neubourg.

3 F. M. Stenton, *Danelaw Charters*, no. 519.

4 *Complete Peerage*, new ed., vii, 667*n*.

5 *Rec. Hist. France*, xxiii, pp. 694j, 707h.

6 *Complete Peerage*, ix, 542–3; *Early Yorks. Charters*, viii, 142.

From 1070 onwards the abbot of Peterborough was Turold, who had been a monk at Fécamp.[1] Two supposed original charters of duke Robert I for Fécamp, enumerating his grants of land to the abbey, have been printed by Haskins.[2] Both have the same list of witnesses, and from the photographs both appear to be in an eleventh-century hand. Haskins regarded the first as genuine, but rejected the second on account of its wide exemption clause. The second has the clause 'dedi quoque Nevillam et omne alodum filiorum Audoeni ubicumque tenere videbantur de me.' Accepting Haskins's opinion, this is nevertheless sound evidence that when the charter was written the abbey was in possession of Néville, since a document of this nature when dealing with possession of land as contrasted with a claim to exemption could in practice only be of use as a defence of possession. Indeed, though it is unnecessary to go so far for present purposes, there seems no reason to doubt the fact of duke Robert's gift. 'Nevilla' can be identified as above, since Ermenouville, just previously mentioned in the document, lies 6 kil. SE of Néville, and Anglesqueville, mentioned immediately afterwards, lies 7½ kil. SSE. The possession of Néville by the abbey of Fécamp is confirmed by the feodary of 1212–20 in the Registers of Philip Augustus, where Nevilla occurs as a knight's fee among the military tenancies of the abbey; and its identity is confirmed by its being immediately preceded by Anglesqueville and immediately followed by Ermenouville.[3] It seems justifiable to infer that Gilbert of the Domesday survey came from Néville and was enfeoffed of Walcot by abbot Turold in view of the latter's previous connexion with Fécamp. There was a castle at Néville of which there are now no traces.[4]

The relationship of Gilbert to Ralph, the ancestor of the Nevilles of Scotton, has not been determined[5]; but as Ralph was also a tenant of the abbot of Peterborough in 1086 it is likely that his place of origin can be similarly deduced.

NORMANVILLE.

Normanville[6] : Seine-Inf., arr. Neufchâtel, cant. Argueil, comm. Mesnil-Lieubray.

Between 1107 and 1120 Henry I confirmed to Battle abbey land in Sussex bought of Gerold de Normanville, which had already been confirmed by Henry count of Eu[7]; and in 1106 Gerold de Normanville witnessed a charter of Henry count of Eu giving the manor of Hooe, Sussex, to the priory of St-Martin-du-Bosc.[8] In 1212–20 a Hugh de Normanville was a joint holder of a fee in this Normanville and places

[1] William of Malmesbury, *De gestis pontificum* (Rolls Ser.), p. 420.

[2] *Norman Institutions*, pp. 260–3.

[3] *Rec. Hist. France*, xxiii, 645j.

[4] Cochet, *Rép. arch. . . . de la Seine-Inf.*, col. 535.

[5] The descent of Neville of Scotton is given in *Complete Peerage*, new ed., ix, 476.

[6] Mr. Loyd has questioned this, but his doubt was probably made earlier than his notes on MEINIERS.

[7] *Mon. Ang.*, iii, 247.

[8] *Cal. Docs. France*, no. 399.

near by.[1] For reasons given under MEINIERS, coupled with the fact that there is no other place of the name nearer thereto than in the canton of Evreux, dept. Eure, it can be suggested that the family which held of the counts of Eu originated from this Normanville, arr. Neufchâtel.

NOWERS, NOERS.

Noyers : Calvados, arr. Caen, cant. Villers-Bocage.

In 1086 Robert de Nouuers held Gayhurst, co. Buckingham, of the bishop of Lisieux (Gilbert Maminot), who held of the bishop of Bayeux; and also Crafton (in Wing) of the bishop of Lisieux.[2] In 1166 Ralf de Noers held a knight's fee of the old feoffment of Walkelin Maminot; and this fee owed the service of castle-guard at Dover for the Maminot ward.[3] In the Bayeux Inquest of 1133 the 'feodum Maminoth,' held of the bishop of Bayeux, owed the service of five knights, one fief being at Noyers.[4] In 1174–89 Henry bishop of Bayeux confirmed to the priory of Plessis-Grimould the church of Noyers and tithes and lands given by Ralf de Noers and his sons Hugh and Henry and other members of the family.[5]

Some account of the family of Nowers of Gayhurst has been given by Mr. E. St. John Brooks in *Beds. Hist. Rec. Soc.*, vol. xiv, pp. 51–2.

NOYERS, DE NUERIIS.

Noyers : Eure, arr. Les Andelys, cant. Gisors.

In his confirmation charter for Belvoir priory Henry I included a gift made by William de Nueriis of the church of Hose, co. Leicester, with land and tithe there[6]; and the charter shows that William was a tenant of Robert de Todeni, who held Hose in chief.[7] Noyers is 2 kil. E of Vesly and 2½ kil. N of Guerny. Vesly was the 'maritagium' of Bertha wife of Guy de Laval[8]; and Guerny was held by Robert de 'Toeniaco,' who was Bertha's brother.[9] In 1063 Robert de Toeniaco and his son Berenger confirmed to the abbey of Marmoutier its rights in Guerny.[10] There is, independently of the above, abundant evidence that this Robert de Toeniaco was the tenant of Belvoir at the Domesday survey.

OGLANDER, ORGLANDRES.

Orglandes: Manche, arr. Valognes, cant. Saint-Sauveur-sur-Douve (or le-Vicomte).

A charter of Henry II, 1174–82, confirmed a gift of William son of Roger de Orglandres to the abbey of Montebourg of land at Orglandes, and

[1] *Rec. Hist. France*, xxiii, 639j.

[2] *D.B.*, i, 145, 145b.

[3] *Red Bk. Exch.*, pp. 194, 617.

[4] *Rec. Hist. France*, xxiii, pp. 634e, 700h; and see MAMINOT *supra*.

[5] *Cal. Docs. France*, no. 553.

[6] *Cal. Chart. Rolls*, 1327–41, p. 295.

[7] See Nichols, *Leicestershire*, ii, 218.

[8] *Cal. Docs. France*, no. 1167.

[9] *Ibid.*, no. 1171.

[10] *Ibid.* Round in his index wrongly identifies it with Gournay.

other gifts by members of the family.[1] Herbert de Oglandris witnessed a gift of Adeliz wife of Richard de Reviers to the same house, 1141–55[2]; and Jordan de Oglandres witnessed a confirmation of William de Vernon for the abbey of St-Sauveur-le-Vicomte, *c.* 1150.[3] Robert de Oglandris witnessed the foundation charter of Quarr abbey, Isle of Wight, by Baldwin de Reviers, earl of Devon (brother of William de Vernon) in 1141–44.[4] Henry Doggelondr' held tenancies of the countess of Devon in 1287–90.[5] Orglandes is 7 kil. from Néhou, the *caput* of the honour held by the family of Reviers-Vernon in the Cotentin.

Orbec.

Orbec: Calvados, arr. Lisieux, cant. Orbec.

In 1086 Roger de Orbec was an under-tenant in Suffolk of Richard FitzGilbert of Clare.[6] Between 1138 and 1149 a Richard de Orbet (*sic*) witnessed a charter of Gilbert earl of Pembroke for Thierry son of Deorman (of London).[7] Both the subject matter and the witnesses strongly suggest that the charter was executed in the eastern counties. Orbec was the *caput* of the Norman honour of Richard FitzGilbert.

Oseville.

Auzouville-sur-Saane: Seine-Inf., arr. Dieppe, cant. Bacqueville.

In 1166 Sewale de Oseville held four knights' fees of the old feoffment of Geoffrey de Mandeville, earl of Essex.[8] As Sawil de Osonvilla he witnessed a charter of William de Mandeville, earl of Essex, for Hurley priory.[9] In the Registers of Philip Augustus Osunvilla, held by William de Lindebouf for a quarter of a knight's fee, is entered as a fief of the barony of Manneville[10]; and in the thirteenth-century *pouillé* of the diocese of Rouen it occurs as Osovilla.[11] Auzouville lies 12 kil. S of Manneville.

Pacy, Pasci, de Paceio.

Pacy-sur-Eure: Eure, arr. Evreux, cant. Pacy.

By a charter of 1153 Henry duke of Normandy and count of Anjou gave to Robert son of Robert earl of Leicester ' Pasci cum toto honore et totam terram quam Willelmus de Pasci in Anglia et in Normannia

1 Delisle et Berger, *Rec. des Actes de Henri II*, ii, pp. 153–5.

2 *Complete Peerage*, new ed., iv, 768.

3 *Cartulaire des Iles Normandes* (Soc. Jersiaise), p. 291.

4 *Camb. Hist. Journal*, iv, 298. A charter of Richard de Reviers (d. 1107) for Christchurch, Hants, mentions his clerk Peter de Oglandes (*Mon. Ang.*, vi, 304).

5 *Bk. of Fees*, p. 1306.

6 *D.B.*, ii, 393b, 447. A Landri de Orbec died in 1093 (Douglas, *Domesday Monachorum*, p. 39*n*).

7 *Cal. Chart. Rolls*, 1257–1300, p. 72.

8 *Red Bk. Exch.*, p. 345.

9 Madox, *Formulare*, no. 412.

10 *Rec. Hist. France*, xxiii, 640l.

11 *Ibid.*, 285h.

tenuit.'[1] William de Pacy died in 1153.[2] His lands in England have not been identified, but the charter proves his Norman provenance.

PANTULF.

Noron: Calvados, arr. and cant. Falaise.

William Pantulf was a knight of Roger de Montgomery. Orderic[3] recounts his benefactions to the abbey of St-Evroul, the particulars showing that Noron was the *caput* of his Norman possessions; and as he gave churches and tithe in England he is identified with Roger's knight. The family continued in England to the thirteenth century.

PATRIC.

La Lande-Patri: Orne, arr. Domfront, cant. Flers.

In 1166 in the return of knights' fees in Kent the heirs of Ingeram Patrik held fifteen knights' fees[4]; and in 1172 in Normandy William Patric held one fee of the honour ' de Loanda ' and three knights ' ad servitium suum.'[5] William Patric and his elder son William both died in 1174.[6] The second son Engueran succeeded, who completed the payment of relief for his father's land in Normandy in 1180[7], and in 1186 rendered account in Kent for the land of his brother's widow, which she had held in dower[8] and were therefore Patric lands. Engueran died between Michaelmas 1190 and 1191,[9] when he was still in debt on this account; and in 1196 the balance was paid by Ralph Tesson and John de Préaux.[10] Reference to Engueran's daughter Maud is made in the certification of a seal as ' sigillum proprium domine Matillis de Landa Patricii filie Enguerrandi Patric militis prius Radulfi Tesson militis postea uxoris Willelmi de Milleio militis quod videlicet sigillum habebat in viduitate sua.'[11] This shows that the family came from La Lande-Patri; and the assumption that John de Préaux married another daughter of Engueran is supported by the fact that he and Ralph Tesson, both adherents of Philip Augustus, occur in a list of lands of the Normans as each holding 9 *li*. of land in Ryarsh, Kent.[12] In 1210–12 Geoffrey de Say the younger held seven fees ' de honore Patricii.'[13] He had been granted a moiety of Patrixbourne, Kent, by king John as the escheat of Ralph Tesson[14]; and it is recorded that Patrixbourne was held *temp*. Stephen by William Patric.[15]

[1] Delisle et Berger, *Rec. des Actes de Henri II*, i, 52; *cf*. Vernon Harcourt, *His Grace the Steward*, pp. 58–9.

[2] *Chron. Rob. de Torigni* (Rolls Ser.), p. 175.

[3] *Ord. Vit.*, ed. Le Prévost, ii, 427 *et seq*.

[4] *Red Bk. Exch.*, p. 197.

[5] *Ibid.*, p. 631.

[6] *Chron. Rob. de Torigni* (Rolls Ser.), p. 262.

[7] Stapleton, *Rot. Scacc. Norm.*, i, 54.

[8] *Pipe Roll* 32 *Hen. II*, p. 188.

[9] *Pipe Roll* 2 *Ric. I*, p. 147; 3 *Ric. I*, p. 143.

[10] *Chancellor's Roll*, 8 *Ric. I*, p. 283.

[11] Delisle, *Château de St-Sauveur-le-Vicomte*, preuves, p. 82.

[12] *Rot. Norm.*, p. 140.

[13] *Red Bk. Exch.*, p. 475.

[14] *Bk. of Fees*, pp. 270, 1346.

[15] *Oxford Dict. of Place-names*, p. 342.

PAVILLY.

Pavilly: Seine-Inf., arr. Rouen, cant. Pavilly.

In 1172 Roger de Pavillio or Pavelli owed the service of two knights in Normandy; and in the period 1211–20 Thomas de Pavilli held two knights' fees at Pavelli; there is no doubt that these men were the *seigneurs* of Pavilly.[1] In a case of 1204–05 Tiffany widow of Roger de Pavelli was plaintiff for her dower in Hillington, Norfolk, her son Thomas de Pavelli, who had adhered to the king of France, being vouched to warranty.[2]

By a charter of 1184–88 Henry II confirmed to the abbey of l'Isle-Dieu (Eure, arr. Les. Andelys, cant. Fleury-sur-Andelle, comm. Pernel) a moiety of the vill of Charlton Marshall, Dorset, given by Reginald de Paveilli.[3] L'Isle-Dieu is *c.* 34 kil. E of Pavilly; and this suggests that the West country family also came from there.

PAYNEL, PAGANEL.

Les Moutiers-Hubert: Calvados, arr. Lisieux, cant. Livarot; and Hambye: Manche, arr. Coutances, cant. Gavray.

These places were in the possession of descendants of Ralph Paynel, the Domesday tenant-in-chief. In 1204 Hugh Paynel of Les Moutiers-Hubert and of West Rasen, co. Lincoln, adhered to king John, losing the former place; and his cousin Fulk Paynel of Hambye and of Drax, co. York, adhered to the king of France, Drax being then given to Hugh Paynel to compensate him for the loss of his Norman lands. An account of the family is given in *Early Yorkshire Charters*, vol. vi. Although Les Moutiers-Hubert was probably the original home of the family, and Hambye may have been acquired by marriage, it is impossible to speak with certainty on the point. It was recorded in 1867 that the site of the castle at Les Moutiers-Hubert could be recognized.[4] The extensive remains of the castle at Hambye are well known.

PERCY.

Percy-en-Auge: Calvados, arr. Lisieux, cant. Mézidon.

The reasons for assigning this place of origin for William de Percy, the Domesday tenant-in-chief and under-tenant of Hugh earl of Chester, and ancestor of the second line of Percy through his great-granddaughter Agnes de Percy, wife of Jocelin of Louvain, are given in detail in *The Complete Peerage*, new ed., vol. x, p. 435 note (b)[5]; and they show that Percy, dept. La Manche, arr. St-Lô, cant. Percy, the traditional place of origin, and one which in view of the connexion with earl Hugh is *prima facie* probable, must be discarded.

1 *Red Bk. Exch.*, p. 632; *Rec. Hist. France*, xxiii, 613c.

2 *Curia Regis Rolls*, iii, pp. 183, 259.

3 Delisle et Berger, *Rec. des Actes de Henri II*, ii, 305.

4 A. de Caumont, *Statistique monumentale du Calvados*, v, 745.

5 These reasons include the association of ' Perci ' with ' Mureres,' the latter place being Morières, 8 kil. from Percy-en-Auge; see MORERS.

PINKENY.

Picquigny: Somme, arr. Amiens.

Ghilo brother of Ansculf de Pinchengi was a Domesday tenant-in-chief in Northamptonshire and other counties[1]; he was probably the father of a younger Ghilo,[2] who founded a priory at Weedon, co. Northampton, as a cell of St-Lucien of Beauvais, 'his choice of that house being clearly due to the fact that its monks had a small priory (Notre Dame du Mont) near Picquigny.'[3]

PIERREPONT, DE PETROPONTE.

Pierrepont: Seine-Inf., arr. Neufchâtel, cant. Londinières.

In 1086 Godfrey and Robert de Petroponte were under-tenants of William de Warenne in Suffolk and Sussex.[4] They gave the tithe of Cuverville-sur-Yère (Seine-Inf., arr. Dieppe, cant. Eu) to the abbey of Le Tréport with the consent of Robert count of Eu[5] (who died 1089–93).

Pierrepont is 7 kil. SE of Cuverville; and it is adjacent to Grandcourt (*q.v.*).

POMERAI, POMERIA, LA POMMERAYE, of Berry Pomeroy, Devon.

La Pommeraye: Calvados, arr. Falaise, cant. Thury-Harcourt.

In 1086 Ralf de Pomaria, in addition to his tenancies-in-chief, held among other under-tenancies lands in Devon and Cornwall of Robert count of Mortain.[6] In 1166 Henry de Pomereia, Ralf's representative, held 30 fees of the old feoffment and $1\frac{11}{12}$ of the new.[7] In the Norman *Infeudationes militum* of 1172 under the heading 'De honore Mortonii in eadem baillia' (*i.e.* Osberti de Hosa) is the entry 'Henricus de Pomaria iij partem militis de feodo de Vado; et tenet castrum de Pomaria cum purpestura de Rege.'[8] As most of the tenants entered under this bailiwick are clearly men of the Cotentin it is tempting to identify 'Pomaria' with St-Sauveur-de-la-Pommeraye (Manche, arr. Coutances, cant. Bréhal). The two entries immediately preceding Henry de Pomaria, however, are John de Botemont 'in Lexoviis' and Robert de Uxeio 'in Falesia,' which suggest Calvados. Le Vey (*Vadum*), of which fee Henry was holding in 1172, is 4 kil. W of La Pommeraye (Calvados), while Ussy (*Uxeium*) is 11 kil. E of it; moreover, in a list of fees of the period 1212–20 in the Registers of Philip Augustus, William, Geblan and Humphrey 'de Vado' each held fractions of a fee by service

[1] *Complete Peerage*, new ed., x, 521. [2] *Ibid.*

[3] *V.C.H. Northants*, i, 291, citing Darsy, *Picquigny et ses seigneurs* (1860), p. 101.

[4] Farrer, *Honors and Knights' Fees*, iii, pp. 322, 331, where there are some notes on the family.

[5] Coquelin, *Hist. de l'Abbaye de St-Michel du Tréport* (Soc. Hist. Norm.), i, pp. 327, 340, 357; *Cal. Docs. France*, no. 230. The former gives them as brothers, and the latter as son and father. The former is probably correct, though in *Cartulaire du Tréport*, ed. L. de Kermaingant, pp. 6, 15, there is a discrepancy on the point. This latter reference was added by Mr. Loyd since his note embodying the substance of the above was printed in *Sussex Notes and Queries*, vol. vii (1939), p. 244.

[6] *D.B.*, iv (Exon Domesday), 197, 459.

[7] *Red Bk. Exch.*, p. 260. [8] *Ibid.*, p. 635.

at Falaise.[1] This all points strongly to La Pommeraye (Calvados) as the place now in question, but the matter is put beyond doubt by a notification of Henry bishop of Bayeux, dated 1167, that Henry de la Pommeraye had in his presence confirmed the gifts of his father Joscelin to the abbey of Le Val-Notre-Dame, and had renounced all rights over the churches of Saint-Omer, Benoeil, Angoville, Le Bô, Cosseville, Saint-Clair, La Pommeraye and Placy[2]; and all these places lie within 8 kil. of La Pommeraye (Calvados). By a charter dated 1125 Goslin de Pomeria gave the church of Le Val to the canons there; he also gave them rents in Berry Pomeroy with the church and tithe.[3] Le Val is in the commune of St-Omer adjacent to La Pommeraye; the abbey was founded on the fee of Richard de Tornebu, who assented to Joscelin's gift[4]; and Tornebu is 9 kil. N of La Pommeraye.

PORT, of Basing.

Port-en-Bessin: Calvados, arr. Bayeux, cant. Ryes.

For this family see Round in *Genealogist,* vol. xvi, p. 1, and *Complete Peerage,* new ed., vol. xi, *sub* ' St. John of Basing.' In 1086 Hugh de Port was the greatest lay tenant-in-chief in Hampshire and an under-tenant of Odo bishop of Bayeux in Hampshire and Kent. The Bayeux Inquest of 1133 shows Henry de Port, Hugh's son and heir, holding three knights' fees of the bishop of Bayeux in Normandy.[5] These three fees seem to have been Fontenelles in Port-en-Bessin, Commes, 1½ kil. to the SE, and Létanville (Calvados, arr. Bayeux, cant. Isigny, comm. Grandcamp), 19 kil. W of Port.[6] When to this is added the fact that in the twelfth century the family of Scures held land in England of Port and obviously took their name from Escures, 2½ kil. S of Port-en-Bessin, the derivation of Port from this place is proved. The evidence suggests that Hugh de Port was a man of very moderate possessions in Normandy who owed his good fortune in England to his own ability, and also perhaps to the bishop of Bayeux his overlord in both countries. In such circumstances it would be natural that men not holding of him in Normandy should be found as under-tenants of him and his heirs in England, *e.g.* St-Manvieu, Lingèvres, and Anisy (*q.v.*).

PORT, of Mapledurwell.

Port-en-Bessin: Calvados, arr. Bayeux, cant. Ryes.

In 1083 Hubert de Port witnessed a charter of William the Conqueror confirming an agreement between the abbeys of St. Stephen and Holy Trinity at Caen.[7] In 1086 he held Mapledurwell, Hants, in chief.

[1] *Rec. Hist. France,* xxiii, 619 b and c.

[2] *Mém. Soc. Ant. Norm.,* viii, 265; summary by Léchaudé d'Anisy.

[3] *Cal. Docs. France,* no. 1455; this is followed in no. 1456 by bishop Henry's charter noted above, though the gifts in Normandy are not there set out.

[4] *Ibid.,* no. 1455.

[5] *Rec. Hist. France,* xxiii, 700j.

[6] *Bulletin Soc. Ant. Norm.,* xlv, 30, note 67.

[7] E. Deville, *Analyse d'un ancien cartulaire . . . de Saint-Etienne de Caen,* p. 19.

An account of the family will be found in two articles by Round in *Genealogist*, vols. xvi and xviii, which establish the pedigrees of Port of Basing and Port of Mapledurwell and clear up the confusion between the two families. Hubert was succeeded by Adam I de Port, probably his son, who *temp.* Henry I had the honour of Kington, co. Hereford. Adam I was succeeded by his son Roger, and Roger by his son Adam II, who in 1172 suffered exile and forfeiture. Adam I gave the tithe of his demesne in Littleton, Wilts, to the priory of Les Deux Jumeaux, which is 15 kil. W of Port-en-Bessin,[1] and the further fact that among the under-tenants of Adam II de Port in 1166 are the families of Arguges, Fresne, and Marinni,[2] coming from places within a few miles of Port-en-Bessin, leaves no doubt as to Hubert's provenance. The exact connexion between the Domesday tenants-in-chief of Basing and Mapledurwell is not known, but it must have been close. It is to be noted that a charter of Roger de Port of Mapledurwell, *c.* 1150, for Andwell priory[3] was witnessed by Walter de Sancto Maneveu, a family who were under-tenants of Port of Basing.

PORTES.

Portes: Eure, arr. Evreux, cant. Conches.

Kirtling, co. Cambridge, was of the fee of Tosny; and in 1177 the sheriff accounted for 40*s.* imposed on the township, which had been pardoned to Roger de Portes.[4] A charter of Ralf de Tosny, *c.* 1115, addressed to the men of the soke of Necton, Norfolk, was witnessed by Roger de Port'.[5] Another charter of the same, *c.* 1115, and one of Roger de Tosny, Ralf's son and heir, *c.* 1125, were witnessed by G. de Port.[6] Another charter of Roger de Tosny, for Wootton Wawen priory, was witnessed by William (*Gulielmus*) de Portis and Richard de Portes.[7] At Michaelmas 1204 the sheriff accounted for 55*s.* 5*d.* of the rent of the land of Roger de Portes in Bromsberrow, co. Gloucester, from Whitsuntide.[8]

Portes lies 8 kil. N of Conches, which rather than Tosny was the effective *caput* of the Tosny honour in Normandy, and 8 kil. NW of the abbey of La Noë, comm. La Bonneville. By a charter in 1203 Philip Augustus gave to Bernard du Plessis the homage (*hominagium*) of Portes and the ' alveus ' beside La Noë and St-Germain, which had belonged to Roger de Portis.[9] The chartulary of La Noë contains charters which include one issued by Roger de Tosny and witnessed by Roger de Portes, *ante* 1160, and one by which Roger de Portes gave to the abbey trees at Villers-sur-la-Roule[10] (6 kil. SW of Tosny).

[1] *Genealogist*, xviii, 138.
[2] *Red Bk. Exch.*, pp. 279–80; for particulars see those names in the present work.
[3] *Cal. Docs. France*, no. 1461.
[4] Farrer, *Feudal Cambridgeshire*, p. 48.
[5] D. C. Douglas, *Medieval East Anglia*, app., no. 56.
[6] *Ibid.*, nos. 57, 59.
[7] *Mon. Ang.*, vi, 995.
[8] *Pipe Roll* 6 *John*, p. 153.
[9] Delisle, *Cartulaire Normand*, no. 70.
[10] Note thereto.

There was a fortress belonging to the lords of Conches at Portes which was demolished by the terms of the treaty between John and Philip Augustus in 1200; traces of the motte and ditches remain.[1]

PORTMORT.

Portmort: Seine-Inf., arr. and cant. Neufchâtel, comm. Flamets-Frétils.

In 1166 Wermund de Portmort held half a knight's fee of the old feoffment of the earl of Gloucester.[2] In a list of fees of the honour of Gloucester, 1201–12, Michael de Portinote (*sic*) held half a fee.[3] In 1242–43 Wermund de Portu Mortuo held Hollacombe, Devon, of the honour of Gloucester for half a knight's fee,[4] which is clearly the half fee of 1166. In an inquest of 1251–52 it is recorded that Wormundus de Portu Mortuo 'qui dictus fuit Normannus' had purchased land in Devon of Juhel de Valletort, and was then dead.[5]

In Normandy Wermund de Portmor witnessed a charter of Hugh de Mortemer for the abbey of St-Victor-en-Caux before 1179.[6] In 1212-20 Michael de Portmort held one knight's fee at Portmort of the honour of Mortemer.[7] Robert archbishop of Rouen (1208–21) instituted a clerk to the church of Graval (*Girardi Vallis*) on the presentation of Michael de Portmort, and archbishop Eudes Rigaud (1248–75) instituted to the same church on the presentation of Wermund de Portmort.[8] Graval is 2 kil. distant from Portmort.

The occurrence and chronology of the names Wermund and Michael both in England and Normandy remove all doubt that it was from this Portmort that the family came.[9]

By a charter of 1156–61 Henry II confirmed to the abbey of Foucarmont 'ex dono Willelmi de Pormort et Girardi filii ejus terram suam de Fraitiz,'[10] a place which is the modern Le Frétils in the commune of Flamets-Frétils.

POTERIA.

La Poterie-Mathieu: Eure, arr. Pont-Audemer, cant. Saint-Georges.

In 1130 .ath's de Potereia rendered account of 10 marks for his land of Wallop, Hampshire, which Roger son-in-law of Albert formerly held.[11] In 1161 Matthew de Pottaria rendered account of 5 marks in Hampshire for his knights,[12] apparently for 2½ fees.[13] In 1204 Baldwin de Winsinton rendered 20 marks for his corn and chattels in the manor

1 A. Le Prévost, *Mém. et Notes . . . . de l'Eure*, ii, 609.

2 *Red Bk. Exch.*, p. 290.

3 *Ibid.*, p. 154.

4 *Bk. of Fees*, p. 778.

5 *Ibid.*, p. 1263.

6 *Mélanges* (Soc. Hist. Norm.), 5me série, p. 412.

7 *Rec. Hist. France*, xxiii, 641a.

8 *Ibid.*, p. 272f.

9 The index in *ibid.* wrongly identifies this Portmort with Portmort, dept. Eure, arr. and cant. Les Andelys.

10 Delisle et Berger, *Rec. des Actes de Henri II*, i, 309.

11 *Pipe Roll* 31 *Hen. I*, p. 39; and amendment in 1929 ed., corrigenda; the name can be suggested as (M)ath's.

12 *Ibid.*, 7 *Hen. II*, p. 58.

13 *Red Bk. Exch.*, p. 28.

of Wallop, which he held at farm from Matthew de Poteria, and also to have the manor at farm.[1] An entry of 1242–43 shows Wallop to have been the land of the Normans[2]; and later evidence shows that as such it had escheated in 1204.[3]

The feodary of 1204–08 in the Registers of Philip Augustus shows that Matthew de Poteria was holding one fee of the honour of Montfort,[4] and a quarter of a fee 'apud Haulam juxta Beccum Heloini' (*i.e.* La Haule-du-Bec) of the honour of Breteuil[5]; and the feodary of 1212–20 shows that he was holding half a fee at Lieurey,[6] which is 4½ kil. SSW of La Poterie-Mathieu. It seems reasonably certain that in 1204 Matthew de Poteria was in Normandy[7] and adhered to Philip Augustus, thus losing his lands in England; and that the family originated from that La Poterie to which the prevalent christian name has become attached as a suffix.

Moreover, a charter of Robert count of Meulan, 1166–87, for the abbey of St-Pierre-des-Préaux (6½ kil. N of La Poterie-Mathieu) was witnessed by Matthew de la Poterie[8]; and Matthew de Poteria had witnessed a charter of count Waleran for the church of Holy Trinity, Beaumont, in Dec. 1142.[9] A charter of Henry II, 1156–61, confirmed a gift of land by Robert 'Potier' 'apud Poteriam' to the hospital of St. Giles at Pont-Audemer,[10] which was a foundation of the counts of Meulan. With regard to the holding in Normandy of the honour of Breteuil, noted above, which was the Norman honour of the earls of Leicester, it is significant that a Matthew de Poteria is shown as holding half a knight's fee in a list of fees of 1210–12 of the honour of the earl of Leicester in England.[11]

POYNINGS.

Pays de Caux, between the forest of Eawy and the Seine: Seine-Inf. By a charter dated at Pont-de-l'Arche in 1206 Philip Augustus gave to William Havart and the heirs male of his body whatever Michael de Ponnengues and Helias de Martigneio used to have in Caux between the forest of Eawy and the river Seine.[12] Poynings, Sussex, was held of the earl de Warenne by a family of that name, and in 1206 the tenant was Michael.[13] Bellencombre, the *caput* of the Norman honour

[1] *Rot. de Fin.*, p. 211; James de Poteria there mentioned is *recte* James de Poterne (*Pipe Roll* 6 *John*, p. 128). There seems to be no sure evidence as to whether Matthew's holding was in Nether Wallop (as in *Bk. of Fees*, index for p. 256) or in Over Wallop (*V.C.H. Hants.*, iv, 531).

[2] *Bk. of Fees*, p. 705.

[3] *V.C.H. Hants.*, iv, 531 *n.*

[4] *Rec. Hist. France*, xxiii, 710d.

[5] *Ibid.*, p. 714e.

[6] *Ibid.*, p. 637d.

[7] He made payments there between 1198 and 1203 (*Mag. Rot. Scacc. Norm.*, pars secunda, ed. Léchaudé D'Anisy et A. Charma, pp. 17, 103).

[8] *Cal. Docs. France*, no. 348.

[9] *Ibid.*, no. 370; witnesses in *Cartulaire de la Sainte-Trinité de Beaumont-le-Roger*, ed. E. Deville, p. 17.

[10] Delisle et Berger, *Rec. des Actes de Henri II*, i, 328.

[11] *Red Bk. Exch.*, p. 553.

[12] Delisle, *Cartulaire Normand*, p. 290.

[13] Farrer, *Honors and Knights' Fees*, iii, 328; *Complete Peerage*, new ed., x, 657.

of Warenne, lies on the edge of the forest of Eawy; and striking south from it towards the Seine one passes through a number of Warenne fiefs, such as Grigneuseville. Although there is no evidence to identify the actual lands held by Poynings in Normandy, the above facts suggest very strongly that the family was Norman in origin and came from this district; *cf.* MARTIGNY.

PRAERES.

Presles: Calvados, arr. Vire, cant. Vassy.

Before the separation of England and Normandy Hasculf de Praeres held land in Adderbury, co. Oxford, and in Chyngton (in Seaford), Sussex.[1] In the Register of Philip Augustus, 1204–1208, John de Livet and Hasculf de Praeriis each held a quarter of a fee in the bailiwick of the castle of Vire[2]; and in the Register of 1212–20 they held together half of a fee ' apud Praerias.'[3]

Farrer has given several notes on members of the family, primarily in connexion with its tenure of Ulceby, co. Lincoln, of the earl of Chester.[4] Presles, which occurs as ' Praelliae ' in 1198 and as ' Praeriae ' in 1269,[5] lies 9 kil. NE of Vire, an important possession of the earls of Chester.

PUNCHARDON, DE PONTE CARDONIS.

Pontchardon: Orne, arr. Argentan, cant. Vimoutiers.

In 1086 Robert de Ponte Cardonis held of Baldwin FitzGilbert, sheriff of Devon, land in Heanton Punchardon, West Haggington (in Ilfracombe), Blakewell (in Marwood), and Charles, all in Devon.[6] In 1166 William de Punchardun held four knights' fees of the old feoffment in Devon of Robert the king's son.[7] In 1213 Agnes widow of Roger de Punchardon claimed the vill of Heanton Punchardon as her dower against William de Punchardon, who pleaded that it was the ' capitale messuagium.'[8] In 1242–43 William de Punchardun held the four Domesday manors named above of the fee of Okehampton, which had been Baldwin's, by the service of four knights.[9]

In Normandy it was stated in the *Querimoniæ Normannorum* of 1247 that at the conquest of Normandy the ' dominus de Pontchardon ' went to England, and that Philip Augustus took his land.[10] It seems clear that from 1086 to the loss of Normandy Pontchardon and Heanton Punchardon were in the same ownership.

Pontchardon is 9 kil. SW of Meules, the *caput* of Baldwin FitzGilbert's Norman barony.

[1] *Bk. of Fees*, pp. 72, 614; *cf. Red Bk. Exch.*, p. 799.
[2] *Rec. Hist. France*, xxiii, 707e. [3] *Ibid.*, p. 619d.
[4] *Honors and Knights' Fees*, ii, 143.
[5] C. Hippeau, *Dict. topogr. du Calvados*, p. 231.
[6] *D.B.*, iv (Exon Domesday), 276–7.
[7] *Red Bk. Exch.*, p. 252. [8] *Curia Regis Rolls*, vii, pp. 41, 48.
[9] *Bk. of Fees*, p. 784.
[10] *Rec. Hist. France*, xxiv, 44f. A footnote gives the reference to a gift by Philip Augustus in 1216 of part of the land of William de Ponte Cardonis; and Mr. Loyd adds with a fuller reference to the terms, that three of the places were in cant. Vimoutiers.

QUILLI.

Quilly: Calvados, arr. Falaise, cant. and comm. Bretteville-sur-Laize.

In 1166 Walter de Quilli held half a knight's fee of the new feoffment of Robert Marmion.[1] A charter of Henry II, 1182–89, confirmed to the abbey of Barbery the gift of the church of Quilly made by Robert Marmion.[2] Quilly is 5 kil. SE of Fontenay-le-Marmion.

QUINCY, earls of Winchester.

Cuinchy: Pas-de-Calais, near Béthune.

In the Northamptonshire survey, *temp.* Henry I, Saher de Quincy, the ancestor of the family,[3] occurs as holding Long Buckby, co. Northampton, of Anselm de Chokes.[4] As Cuinchy is less than 16 kil. from Chocques, the original home of his Northamptonshire overlord, it is in all probability the place from which Saher derived his name.

RAIMES, RAMES.

Rames: Seine-Inf., arr. Le Havre, cant. Saint-Romain de Colbosc, comm. Gommeville.

For the complicated story of the Raimes lands in England see Round, *Geoffrey de Mandeville*, pp. 399–404. Rames itself was inherited by Leonia daughter of Edward of Salisbury, who by her marriage with Robert d'Estouteville brought it to the Norman branch of that family.[5]

RAINEVILLE, REINEVILLE, REINERVILLE.

Reineville: Calvados, arr. Vire, cant. Condé-sur-Noireau, comm. Lassy.

An account of the early generations of the family, tenants of the honour of Pontefract, dating to the closing years of the eleventh century, has been given by Farrer in *Early Yorkshire Charters*, vol. iii, pp. 248–9. In 1166 William de Reinerville held four knights' fees, apparently of the old feoffment, of Henry de Lascy.[6] Reineville is a hamlet of Lassy,[7] the original home of Lascy.

REINES, RAINES, REDNES, RETNES.

[?] Rennes: Ille-et-Vilaine.

Ralph de Raines and his brothers Walter and William gave land to Belvoir priory by a charter, which as being witnessed by Roger Bigot was earlier than Sept. 1107, and which was also witnessed by William d'Aubigny the elder and Cecily his wife.[8] In the Sempringham charters printed by Major Poynton in *Genealogist*, vols. xv *et seq.*, there are

[1] *Red Bk. Exch.*, p. 327. [2] Delisle et Berger, *Rec. des Actes de Henri II*, ii, 393.

[3] For the early generations of the family see Farrer, *Honors and Knights' Fees*, i, 32–3.

[4] *V.C.H. Northants.*, i, 379.

[5] *Cal. Docs. France*, nos. 211–2. Edward of Salisbury married a member of the Raimes family, Leonia's mother being 'de progenie Rogeri de Reimes' (*Rot. de Dominabus*, pp. 69, 70 *n.*).

[6] *Red Bk. Exch.*, p. 422. [7] C. Hippeau, *Dict. topogr. du Calvados*, p. 237.

[8] Nichols, *Leicestershire*, ii, pt. i, app. p. 7.

several *c.* 1150 of William de Reines granting land with the consent of his lord William d'Aubigny of Belvoir. St-Aubin-d'Aubigné is 17 kil. N of Rennes, and the variant spellings above support the identification with Rennes. It is, however, impossible to obtain any Breton evidence for a man taking his name from so large a place as Rennes, and the identification cannot be considered as entirely proved; but in view of the number of other Bretons among William d'Aubigny's under-tenants, it has a high degree of probability.

REVIERS, REDVERS.

Reviers: Calvados, arr. Caen, cant. Creully.

Richard de Reviers, father of Baldwin the first earl of Devon, gave to Montebourg abbey the church of Reviers and also the manor of Loders, Dorset.[1]

RHUDDLAN, ROELENT.

Tilleul-en-Auge: Calvados, arr. Lisieux, cant. Saint-Pierre-sur-Dives, comm. Saint-Georges-en-Auge.

According to Orderic[2] Robert of Rhuddlan was a son of Humphrey son of Amfrid by Adeliza sister of Hugh de Grandmesnil; and this Humphrey can be identified with the Humphrey de Telliolo 'sororius' of Hugh de Grandmesnil, who was the first castellan of Hastings, but who returned to Normandy in 1069.[3] As Robert was a notable benefactor of the abbey of St-Evroul Orderic would be well informed as to the family; and he wrote Robert's epitaph at the request of the latter's brother Ernald, a monk at St-Evroul.[4] Robert gave to St-Evroul the whole church of 'Telliole,' all that he had in the church of Damblainville (arr. and cant. Falaise), and all that he held in the church of 'Torneor.'[5] In later times the abbot of St-Evroul was patron of the church of Damblainville; and so 'Telliole' can be identified with Tilleul-en-Auge,[6] 15 kil. NE of it, although the abbey failed to retain the patronage. 'Torneor' is Le Tourneur (arr. Vire, cant. Beny-Bocage), of which the abbey also failed to retain the patronage. It can be deduced that it was from Tilleul-en-Auge that Robert's father Humphrey derived his name. Charter evidence identifies Robert with Robert of Rhuddlan, the Domesday under-tenant of Hugh earl of Chester, whose wars against the Welsh are a matter of history. Robert de Roelent gave to St-Evroul the church of St. Peter in the market-place in Chester, and other lands including Byfield, co. Northampton[7]; and his gift was confirmed by Ranulf earl of Chester, 1121–29.[8] Byfield was held by Robert of earl Hugh in 1086.[9]

[1] Delisle et Berger, *Rec. des Actes de Henri II*, ii, pp. 150–1.

[2] *Ord. Vit.*, ed. Le Prévost, iii, 280–1. [3] *Ibid.*, ii, 186.

[4] *Ibid.*, iii, 287. [5] *Cal. Docs. France*, no. 631.

[6] The only other possible identification would be Notre-Dame-du-Tilleul (Orne, arr. Argentan, cant. Le Merlerault); but throughout the middle ages this was 'Tilleyum.'

[7] *Cal. Docs. France*, no. 632; *cf. Ord. Vit.*, iii, 281.

[8] *Cal. Docs. France*, no. 636. [9] *D.B.*, i, 224b.

RICARVILLE, RICARDVILE, RICHARDIVILLA.

Ricarville: Seine-Inf., arr. Dieppe, cant. Envermeu.

Walter de Ricardvile, who held the office of sheriff of the honour of Pevensey,[1] was one of archbishop Lanfranc's knights.[2] In 1166 Robert de Ricarville held ten knights' fees of the old feoffment of the count of Eu.[3] The proximity of the count's rape of Hastings to Kent, and of Ricarville to Eu, seems to establish the identity.

In the valley is a motte in part destroyed.[4]

ROLLOS, RULLOS.

Roullours: Calvados, arr. and cant. Vire.

A full account of the family, under-tenants of the honour of Richmond, is given in *Early Yorkshire Charters*, vol. v, pp. 95–99; its origin at Roullours is there clearly established.

It is probable that William de Rollos, lord of Bourne, co. Lincoln, *temp.* Henry I (for whom see Round, *Feudal England*, p. 165), was of the same family; but evidence to establish the connexion has not been discovered.

ROS, of Bedfordshire.

Rots: Calvados, arr. Caen, cant. Tilly-sur-Seulles.

Serlo de Ros was a Domesday under-tenant of Beauchamp of Bedford. For the evidence for his place of origin see BROILG.

ROS, of Kent.

Rots: Calvados, arr. Caen, cant. Tilly-sur-Seulles.

Anschetil de Ros and Geoffrey de Ros were two of archbishop Lanfranc's knights.[5] Rots is 8 kil. WNW of Caen; and a charter of Henry II mentions the place among those to which gifts had been made to the abbey of St. Stephen, Caen.[6]

It must not be supposed that all families of Ros or Roos came from this place; and it can scarcely be doubted that Roos of Helmsley, with its offshoot Roos of Ingmanthorpe, derived the name from Roos in Holderness.[7]

ROSEI, DE ROSETO.

Rosay: Seine-Inf., arr. Dieppe, cant. Bellencombre.

In 1086 Lambert was an under-tenant of William de Warenne in Waterden and West Rudham, Norfolk.[8] Charters of the second earl for

[1] *Cal. Docs. France*, no. 1205.

[2] D. C. Douglas, *Domesday Monachorum*, pp. 41–2, where for the reasons given here the place of origin is regarded as a probability.

[3] *Red Bk. Exch.*, p. 203.

[4] Cochet, *Rép. arch. de la Seine-Inf.*, col. 31.

[5] D. C. Douglas, *Domesday Monachorum*, p. 29, where their connexion with Odo bishop of Bayeux and Lanfranc formerly abbot of St. Stephen's is noted as sufficient evidence for the place of origin.

[6] Delisle et Berger, *Rec. des Actes de Henri II*, i, 269.

[7] W. T. Lancaster, *Ripley and the Ingilby Family . . . . .*, p. 37*n*, cited by Douglas, *op. cit.*, p. 29*n*.

[8] *D.B.*, ii, 168b, 169b.

Castle Acre priory mention gifts in these places made by Lambert de Rosei,[1] thus identifying the under-tenant. Lambert's son Walkelin[2] witnessed another of the Castle Acre charters, *c.* 1130 [3]; and Ralf and Walkelin de Roseio witnessed a charter of the same earl for the abbey of St-Victor-en-Caux which passed in Normandy, 1120–38.[4]

Rosay is 2 kil. SE of Bellencombre, the *caput* of the honour of Warenne in Normandy.[5]

ROUMARE, earl of Lincoln.

Roumare: Seine-Inf., arr. Rouen, cant. Maromme.

William de Roumare, earl of Lincoln, gave to the cathedral church of Rouen a yearly payment from his rent of Roumare.[6]

ROVILLE.

Rouville: Seine-Inf., arr. Le Havre, cant. Bolbec.

Gifts made by William de Roville to Eye priory were confirmed by his lord Robert Malet.[7] Rouville is 14 kil. E of Emalleville, the place of origin of another of the Malet tenants[8]; and there is no other place of the name in this part of Normandy. The spelling in the thirteenth-century *pouillé* is Rovilla.[9]

RUILI.

Rouellé: Orne, arr. and cant. Domfront.

In 1166 Geoffrey de Ruili held a third of a knight's fee of the new feoffment of Gervase Paynel.[10] Rouellé was the *caput* of Gervase Paynel's holding in the Passeis.[11]

It is probable that Ralph de Rolliaco, an under-tenant of Ralph Paynel, the Domesday tenant-in-chief,[12] took his name from the same place.

RUMILLY.

Remilly: Manche, arr. St-Lô, cant. Marigny.

Evidence for the identification of this place from which Robert son of Rainfray de Remilly, whose daughter Cecily de Rumilly brought Skipton and Harewood and other lands to her husband William Meschin, has been given in *Early Yorkshire Charters*, vol. vii, pp. 31–35.

[1] *Mon. Ang.*, v, 50.

[2] Farrer, *Honors and Knights' Fees*, iii, 371, where there are some notes on members of the family.

[3] *Early Yorks. Charters*, viii, no. 22.

[4] *Mélanges* (Soc. Hist. Norm.), 5me série, p. 380.

[5] This identification was noted by Round in *Genealogist*, xviii, 8.

[6] *Cal. Docs. France*, no. 10. For further references to Roumare see *Complete Peerage*, new ed., vii, 667*n*.

[7] *Mon. Ang.*, iii, 405.

[8] See ESMALEVILLA.

[9] *Rec. Hist. France*, xxiii, 285d.

[10] *Red Bk. Exch.*, p. 270.

[11] *Early Yorks. Charters*, vi, pp. 47–8, 134*n*.

[12] *Ibid.*, pp 68–9.

SACHEVILLA.

Secqueville-en-Bessin: Calvados, arr. Caen, cant. Creully.

In 1086 Richard de Sacheuilla was mentioned in the entry for Rivenhall, Essex, held by count Eustace of Boulogne.[1] Round has shown that the Richard who held Great Braxted, Essex, of Eudo dapifer was the same man[2]; and he seems also to have been the Richard who was the tenant of Eudo dapifer in Rockland, Norfolk.[3] As Richard de Sachanuilla (probably a false spelling) he held Aspenden, co. Hertford, of Eudo dapifer.[4] His lands ultimately passed through an heiress to the family of Anesti.[5] Secqueville-en-Bessin is 11 kil. SE of Ryes, Eudo's place of origin.

SACKVILLE, later dukes of Dorset.

Sauqueville: Seine-Inf., arr. Dieppe, cant. Offranville.

In 1166 William de Saukeville held one knight's fee of the old feoffment of the Giffard honour of Buckingham.[6] The details given by Round in *Peerage and Pedigree*, vol. i, pp. 285 *et seq.*, make the derivation certain.

ST. CLAIR, DE SANCTO CLARO.

Saint-Clair-sur-Elle: Manche, arr. St-Lô, cant. Saint-Clair.

William de St. Clair gave the church of Hamerton, co. Huntingdon, to St. John's abbey at Colchester, and also his 'tenura' in Greenstead, Essex, for the health of Hamo de St. Clair his brother, mentioning his lord Eudo dapifer.[7] An account of the family is given in Farrer, *Honors and Knights' Fees*, vol. iii, pp. 287–291.[8]

A letter of William de Sancto Claro to Richard bishop of Bayeux, 1114–29, states that he had given his land of Thaon (Calvados, arr. Caen, cant. Creully) and of 'Vilers' to the abbey of Savigny[9]; and a letter to Maud countess of Gloucester, described as his lady, makes a similar statement.[10] The Bayeux Inquest of 1133 shows that Thaon was held of the bishop of Bayeux[11]; and it can be deduced that 'Vilers' must have been held of the honour of Gloucester. A confirmation charter of Henry II for Savigny, 1156–58, included 'ex dono Guillelmi de Sancto Claro et Haimonis fratris ejus et concessione Stephani comitis Moretonii et Ricardi Baiocarum episcopi sextam partem de Taon cum omnibus pertinenciis . . . et terram de Villers cum ecclesia ejusdem

[1] *D.B.*, ii, 27.

[2] *Ibid.*, ii, 49. Round, in *V.C.H. Essex*, i, 379, adds that from this can be traced 'the origin in England of the noble house of Sackville'; but of this he subsequently supplied his own refutation when in *Peerage and Pedigree*, i, 287, he showed conclusively that the Sackville family, later dukes of Dorset, originated at Sauqueville, near Dieppe. The two families are quite distinct.

[3] *D.B.*, ii, 239b.

[4] *Ibid.*, i, 139.

[5] *V.C.H. Essex*, *u.s.*; Farrer, *Honors and Knights' Fees*, iii, 271.

[6] *Red Bk. Exch.*, p. 312.

[7] *Cartularium Monasterii . . . de Colecestria* (Roxburghe Club), i, 154–5.

[8] On pp. 287, 291, William's brother must be corrected from Hugh to Hamo. For a note on the two brothers see Round in *Genealogist*, xviii, pp. 10–11.

[9] *Cal. Docs. France*, no. 798.

[10] *Ibid.*, no. 799; dated by Round *c.* 1150.

[11] *Rec. Hist. France*, xxiii, 700h.

ville et decima et cum molendino et molta totius terre que fuit Ricardi de Villers.'[1] The mention of Hamo identifies the donors with Eudo dapifer's tenants in England; and 'Vilers' or Villers can be identified with Villiers (Manche, arr. St-Lô, cant. St-Clair), 7 kil. SSW of St-Clair-sur-Elle, for the abbot of Savigny was patron of the church.[2] A charter of Robert earl of Gloucester addressed to Philip bishop of Bayeux and therefore of date 1142–47 runs 'clamo etiam ei quietum hoc quod habebam apud Anaerias de dono Ricardi Samsonis filii Baiocensis episcopi, scilicet feodum Malleurer et totum feodum quod Eudo dapifer tenuit apud Sanctum Clarum præter meum proprium feodum et nominatim feriam et totum feodum quod idem Eudo dapifer tenuit apud Mattonum vel in ejus pertinentiis de Baiocensi ecclesia.'[3] A comparison of this charter with that of Henry II throws light on the feudal history of St-Clair. Having been held by Eudo dapifer, as was probably also Villiers, it escheated on his death in 1120, and was apparently granted by Henry I to his favoured nephew Stephen; on the conquest of Normandy by Geoffrey count of Anjou it would be lost to Stephen and presumably given by Geoffrey to his wife's half-brother and faithful supporter Robert earl of Gloucester.

Gerville failed to find any trace of a castle at St-Clair.[4]

SAINT-HILAIRE, DE SANCTO HILARIO.

Saint-Hilaire-du-Harcouët: Manche, arr. Mortain, cant. St-Hilaire-du-Harcouët.

Documentary proof that James de Sancto Hilario took his name from this place has been given in *Early Yorkshire Charters*, vol. v, pp. 86–7. James was the son of Harsculf de St-James, taking his name from St-James-de-Beuvron (arr. Avranches, cant. St-James-de-Beuvron) nearby. Gerville described the remains of the castle at St-Hilaire in 1827.[5]

ST. JOHN, DE SANCTO JOHANNE.

Saint-Jean-le-Thomas: Manche, arr. Avranches, cant. Sartilly.

On the conquest of Normandy William de St. John adhered to king John and his lands in Normandy were confiscated by Philip Augustus.[6] An entry in the Registers of Philip Augustus[7] makes the place of origin certain. William was the son of Adam de Port of Basing by Mabel,

[1] Delisle et Berger, *Rec. des Actes de Henri II*, i, 186; *Cal. Docs. France*, no. 824.

[2] A. Longnon, *Pouillés de la province de Rouen*, p. 123. In the index to *Cal. Docs. France* it is wrongly identified as Villiers-le-Sec (Calvados, arr. Bayeux, cant. Ryes) of which the patron was the abbot of Fécamp (Longnon, *op. cit.*, p. 109).

[3] *Antiq. cartul. Baioc.* (Soc. Hist. Norm.), i, 49. Asnières (Calvados, arr. Bayeux, cant. Isigny) is 21 kil. N of St-Clair-sur-Elle; 'Mattonum' is Mathieu (arr. Caen, cant. Douvres) which the Bayeux Inquest of 1133 shows to have been held of the bishop of Bayeux (*Rec. Hist. France*, xxiii, 702g).

[4] *Mém. Soc. Ant. Norm.*, vol. v (1830), p. 243.

[5] *Ibid.*, vol. iv (1828), p. 166.

[6] Delisle, *Cartulaire Normand*, no. 113.

[7] *Rec. Hist. France*, xxiii, 612g; and *cf.* Powicke, *Loss of Normandy*, p. 512.

heiress of Orval and through her mother of the St. John honour of Halnaker; and William adopted the name of St. John.[1] Gerville has given a description of the remains of the castle at St-Jean-le-Thomas.[2]

SAINT-LAURENT, DE SANCTO LAURENTIO.

Saint-Laurent-en-Caux: Seine-Inf., arr. Yvetot, cant. Doudeville. In 1166 Adam de Sancto Laurentio held half a knight's fee of the old feoffment of the honour of Giffard.[3] In Normandy Roger de Sancto Laurentio and Adam his son witnessed an agreement between Longueville priory and Jordan son of Herbrand de Sauqueville *ante* Sept. 1155[4]; and *ante* 1189 Ralf de Cressy gave to Longueville priory lands which he held of William de Sancto Laurentio in Omanville.[5] That place, in arr. Dieppe, cant. Bacqueville, is *c.* 4 kil. W of Longueville. It seems reasonably certain that the family took its name from St-Laurent-en-Caux, which was held of the count of Longueville in 1503,[6] and where there was formerly a 'vieux château' near the church[7]; it is 16 kil. SW of Longueville.

ST. LEGER, DE SANCTO LEODEGARIO.

Saint-Leger-aux-Bois: Seine-Inf., arr. Neufchâtel, cant. Blangy. In 1086 Robert de St. Leger held one hide and half a virgate in Bexhill, Sussex, of the count of Eu.[8] In 1166 Thomas de Sancto Leodegaro held four knights' fees of the old feoffment of the count of Eu[9]; and after 1176 Thomas de Sancto Leodegario issued a charter to Robertsbridge abbey.[10] In a general confirmation charter for the abbey of Foucarmont, 1156–61, Henry II confirmed 'ex dono Thome et Rainaldi de Sancto Leodegario sedem ville nemoris Ulberti cum dimidio ejusdem ville territorio et ecclesiam cum tota decima.'[11] 'Nemus Ulberti' cannot be identified, but Saint-Leger-aux-Bois and Foucarmont are close together and lie within the limits of the *comté* of Eu.

ST. MARTIN, DE SANCTO MARTINO.

Saint-Martin-le-Gaillard: Seine-Inf., arr. Dieppe, cant. Eu. In the *carta* of John count of Eu in 1166 Alvred de Sancto Martino was returned as a knight 'super dominium.'[12] Alvred was the founder

[1] *Complete Peerage*, new ed., xi, pp. 320–1.
[2] *Mém. Soc. Ant. Norm.*, vol. iv (1828), pp. 99 *et seq.*
[3] *Red Bk. Exch.*, p. 313.
[4] P. Le Cacheux, *Chartes du Prieuré de Longueville*, no. 7.
[5] *Ibid.*, no. 36.
[6] Beaucousin, *Reg. des fiefs . . . . de Caux* (Soc. Hist. Norm.), p. 110.
[7] Cochet, *Rép. arch. . . . . de la Seine-Inf.*, col. 513.
[8] *D.B.*, i, 18.
[9] *Red Bk. Exch.*, p. 202.
[10] Hist. MSS. Comm., *Lord De L'Isle and Dudley*, i, 35.
[11] Delisle et Berger, *Rec. des Actes de Henri II*, i, 309; *Cal. Docs. France*, no. 186.
[12] *Red Bk. Exch.*, p. 203.

of Robertsbridge abbey, Sussex, on land in the rape of Hastings which he held of Geoffrey de St. Martin.[1] He married Alice daughter of William earl of Arundel, widow of John count of Eu[2]; and they had a son Alvred.[3] The family of St. Martin can be traced in the cartulary of St. Michael of Le Tréport as under-tenants of the counts of Eu from the middle of the eleventh century onwards; in some entries their fee is expressly called St-Martin-le-Gaillard (*de Jaillardo*, etc.), thus clearly distinguishing it from St-Martin-en-Campagne in the same neighbourhood.[4] Alvred must have been a junior member of the family, for the succession to St-Martin is clear and he never held it.

SAINT-OUEN, DE SANCTO AUDOENO, of Hertfordshire.

Saint-Ouen-prend-en-bourse: Seine-Inf., arr. Dieppe, cant. Longueville.

In 1086 Germund, whom Round identifies as Germund de St-Ouen, held land in Hertfordshire of Geoffrey de Mandeville.[5] Apparently in or before 1135 Germund de Sancto Audoeno held four knights' fees of the honour of Mandeville.[6] The Registers of Philip Augustus show St-Ouen, named above, as a fief of Manneville, being then held by Injorrandus de Sancto Audoeno.[7] This St-Ouen is 3¾ kil. SE of Manneville.

SAINT-OUEN, DE SANCTO AUDOENO, of Kent and Suffolk.

Saint-Ouen-sous-Bailli: Seine-Inf., arr. Dieppe, cant. Envermeu. In 1086 Bernard de Sancto Audoeno held land in Folkestone, Kent, and Clopton, Suffolk, of William of Arques.[8] This points very strongly to his place of origin being the St-Ouen named above, which is 12 kil. E of Arques and is naturally attached to Arques and its district.

SAINT-OUEN, DE SANCTO AUDOENO, of Sussex.

Saint-Ouen-sur-Maire: Orne, arr. Argentan, cant. Ecouché.

In 1153 Ralf de Sancto Audoeno gave a salt-pan in Annington, Sussex, to Sele priory, the gift being confirmed by his lord William de Briouze.[9] In 1242–43 Ralf de Sancto Audoeno held two fees of the Briouze honour of Bramber.[10] This St-Ouen is 15 kil. E of Briouze and 10 kil. NW of Boucé (*see* DE BUCEIO).

1 *Mon. Ang.*, v, 667. Geoffrey's charter granting his land in England, held of the count of Eu, to Alvred to hold by the service of one knight is dated 1160 (Hist. MSS. Comm., *Lord De L'Isle and Dudley*, i, 33).

2 *Complete Peerage*, new ed., v, 158.

3 Farrer, *Honors and Knights' Fees*, iii, 12.

4 *Cartulaire . . . . du Tréport*, ed. L. de Kermaingant, pp. 6, 14, 114, 130.

5 *D.B.*, i, 139b; *V.C.H. Herts.*, i, 331.

6 *Red Bk. Exch.*, p. 345.

7 *Rec. Hist. France*, xxiii, 640k.

8 *D.B.*, i, 9b; ii, 431b.

9 H. E. Salter, *Facsimiles of Oxford Charters*, no. 9.

10 *Bk. of Fees*, p. 689.

St. Quintin.

Saint-Quentin-des-Iles: Eure, arr. Bernay, cant. Broglie.
Robert de Ferrers, first earl of Derby, enfeoffed William de St. Quentin of half a knight's fee between 1135 and 1139[1]; and William witnessed a charter of Robert the second earl dated 26 Sept. 1139.[2] Saint-Quentin-des-Iles, the next parish to Ferrières-St-Hilaire, was a fief of the Norman barony of Ferrières according to the 'aveu' of 1604.[3]

This derivation does not exclude that of other families deriving from other places of the name.

St. Valery, de Sancto Walarico.

Saint-Valery-en-Caux: Seine-Inf., arr. Yvetot, cant. Saint-Valery.
In 1086 Ranulf de Sancto Walarico was a tenant-in-chief in Lincolnshire, and a certain Ranulf was an under-tenant of the bishop of Lincoln.[4] In the Lindsey survey, 1115–18, the lands held of the bishop by Ranulf in 1086 were held of him by Gilbert de Novavilla.[5] The returns of 1212 and 1242–43 show that not only those lands, but also those held in chief by Ranulf de Sancto Walarico in 1086, were held by members of the Neville family of the bishop, and the service of the whole adds up to approximately five knights,[6] thus accounting for the five knights' fees held by Gilbert de Neville of the bishop of Lincoln in 1166.[7] It follows that at some time the King must have granted the superiority over the lands held in chief in 1086 by Ranulf de Sancto Walarico to the bishop of Lincoln. Moreover, the subsequent combination of the two sets of Domesday holdings in the hands of Gilbert de Neville suggests very strongly that Ranulf de Sancto Walarico and Ranulf the bishop's under-tenant were the same person. The latter must have been enfeoffed by bishop Remigius, who had been almoner of Fécamp.

By a charter of 990 Richard I, duke of Normandy, gave to the abbey of Fécamp 'sanctum Walaricum et quicquid ibi pertinet.'[8] The churches of St-Valery-en-Caux and St-Valery-près-Fécamp were both of the exemption of Fécamp, but the latter was merely a church in the suburbs of Fécamp and there is no evidence of its existence until later than the eleventh century, whereas the former was a place of comparative importance, and the charter also records the gift of Ingouville, only 5 kil. to the S of it. It seems safe, therefore, to identify it with the St-Valery of the charter, and as the original home of the Domesday tenant.

This Ranulf de Sancto Walarico must be distinguished from the well-known baronial family who derived from St-Valery-sur-Somme.

[1] *Red Bk. Exch.*, p. 338.

[2] Hist. MSS. Comm., *Earl of Essex* (*Various Collections*, vol. vii), p. 310.

[3] A. Le Prévost, *Mém. et Notes . . . . de l'Eure*, ii, 84.

[4] *Lincs. Domesday* (Linc. Rec. Soc.), pp. 164–5, 49–50.

[5] *Lindsey Survey* (Linc. Rec. Soc.), p. 250.

[6] *Bk. of Fees*, pp. 159, 169, 1013 *et seq.*

[7] *Red Bk. Exch.*, p. 374. See Neville, *supra.*

[8] Lemarignier, *Les Privilèges d'exemption . . . des Abbayes Normandes*, p. 292. On this charter see also Haskins, *Norman Institutions*, p. 252.

SAINTE-FOY, DE SANCTA FIDE.

Sainte-Foy-du-Bois: Seine-Inf., arr. Dieppe, cant. Longueville. Alueredus de Sancta Fide witnessed a gift of the manor of Blakenham, Suffolk, to the abbey of Le Bec made by Walter Giffard and confirmed by king William II.[1] In 1166 Roger de Sancta Fide held half a knight's fee of the old feoffment of the Giffard honour of Buckingham[2]; it can be identified as being in Chilton, co. Buckingham, where in 1242–43 Hamo de Sancta Fide held half a fee of the honour of Buckingham.[3]

In Normandy Gilbert de Sancta Fide witnessed twelfth-century charters for Longueville priory.[4] Sainte-Foy is the next parish to Longueville, the *caput* of the Norman honour of Giffard.

SAINTE-MERE-EGLISE, DE SANCTE MARIE ECCLESIA.

Sainte-Mère-Eglise: Manche, arr. Valognes, cant. Ste-Mère-Eglise. William de Sancte Marie Ecclesia, bishop of London from 1199 to 1221, is the subject of a lengthy biographical note in Delisle's *Actes de Henri II, Introduction*, pp. 496–500, where his connexion with this place is established by record evidence. Peter de Sancte Marie Ecclesia, who was treasurer of St. Paul's Cathedral, London, is there shown also to have come from this place.

There was another place of the name, in the twelfth century the seat of a small *vicomté*. It has now lost all importance and has disappeared from the map, being included in the commune of St-Pierre-du-Chatel (Eure, arr. Pont-Audemer, cant. Beuzeville).

SALCEIT.

Le Saussey: Calvados, arr. Caen, cant. Villers-Bocage, comm. Epinay-sur-Odon.

Raulfus de Salcet witnessed as a man of Roger son of Walter de Lacy a charter of Robert bishop of Hereford granting Holme Lacy, co. Hereford, to Roger in 1085[5]; and, as Ralf de Salceit, in 1086 he held Westuode (in Llanwarne), a manor of St. Peter's, Gloucester, in which Roger de Lacy held land.[6] Le Saussey lies 18 kil. N of Lassy; see further under ESCHETOT.

DE SANCTO CRISTOFORO.

Saint-Christophe-L'Anfernet: Calvados, arr. and cant. Falaise, comm. Ouilly-le-Basset.

In 1166 Ernaldus de Sancto Cristoforo held one knight's fee of the old feoffment of Henry de la Pommeraye.[7] St-Christophe, a commune now united with Ouilly, lies 4 kil. S of La Pommeraye.

[1] *Mon. Ang.*, vi, 1002; Davis, *Regesta*, no. 320.

[2] *Red Bk. Exch.*, p. 313. [3] *Bk. of Fees*, p. 881.

[4] P. Le Cacheux, *Chartes du Prieuré de Longueville*, nos. 66, 77.

[5] Printed, with facsimile, by Professor Galbraith in *Eng. Hist. Rev.*, xliv (1929), 372.

[6] *Ibid.*, p. 361.

[7] *Red Bk. Exch.*, p. 260.

de Sancto Germano.

Saint-Germain-la-Campagne: Eure, arr. Bernay.

In 1086 Roger de Sancto Germano was an under-tenant of Richard Fitz Gilbert in Suffolk.[1] Members of the family were benefactors of the priory of Stoke-by-Clare.[2] St-Germain is 5 kil. E of Bienfaite and 5 kil. N of Orbec, both important fees of Richard Fitz Gilbert. William Marshal, earl of Pembroke, who ultimately succeeded to a moiety of Richard Fitz Gilbert's lands, confirmed the church of St-Germain to Lisieux cathedral.[3] 'Aveus' of 1392 and 1407 show that St-Germain was held by the service of castle-guard at the castle of Orbec.[4]

de Sancto Manevo.

Saint-Manvieu: Calvados, arr. Caen, cant. Tilly-sur-Seulles.

In 1166 Adam de Sancto Manevevo (*sic*) held one knight's fee of the new feoffment of John de Port of Basing.[5] St-Manvieu is 26 kil. SE of Port-en-Bessin, but in the earlier part of the twelfth century the church belonged to Enguerrand de Port, who also had the church of La Folie, whence came a family who in 1166 were under-tenants of the old feoffment of Port of Mapledurwell.[6] See further remarks under Port of Basing.

de Sancto Planees.

Saint-Planchers: Manche, arr. Avranches, cant. Granville.

In 1166 William de Sancto Planées held half a knight's fee of the countess of Hertford, wife of earl Roger.[7] The countess was Maud daughter and heir of James de St-Hilaire (*q.v.*). St-Planchers is 35 kil. NNW of St-James, which supplied an alternative name for Maud's family. This is a considerable distance, but the patron of the church of St-Planchers was the abbot of Le Mont-St-Michel.[8] In 1165 a Hugh de Sancto Planchers witnessed on behalf of William de St. John an exchange of land between him and the abbot.[9] In view of the exceptional name it seems highly probable that William came from St-Planchers, though the evidence is scanty.

Sanderville, Salnerville.

Sannerville: Calvados, arr. Caen, cant. Troarn.

In 1166 William de Sanderville held four knights' fees of the old feoffment of the honour of Skipton; and a fifth fee was held by Gervase de Sanderville.[10] An account of these fees is given in *Early Yorkshire Charters*, vol. vii, pp. 95–101, one of William's fees being in Flitwick and Husborne

1 *D.B.*, ii, 392b, 448.

2 *Mon. Ang.*, vi, 1659–60.

3 A. Le Prévost, *Mém. et Notes . . . de l'Eure*, iii, 126.

4 *Ibid.*, p. 127.

5 *Red Bk. Exch.*, p. 209. In *Lib. Niger*, ed. Hearne, p. 73, it is Sancto Meneveno.

6 For particulars see Folie.

7 *Red Bk. Exch.*, p. 407.

8 Longnon, *Pouillés de la province de Rouen*, p. 286.

9 *Cal. Docs. France*, no. 777.

10 *Red Bk. Exch.*, p. 430.

Crawley, co. Bedford, and Gervase's fee in Enborne and South Moreton, Berkshire. In the earlier part of the twelfth century the honour of Skipton was held by William Meschin, a younger brother of Ranulf Meschin, earl of Chester and *vicomte* of the Bessin.[1] In the Registers of Philip Augustus is a list of fees of the then earl of Chester[2]; and in the arrondissement of Caen there are several within a radius of 7 to 25 kil. from Sannerville. These fees represent the hereditary lands of the earls of Chester of the second line, *vicomtes* of the Bessin, of which family William Meschin was a member. Sannerville occurs as 'Saunervilla' in 1169 and 'Salnervilla' in 1230[3]; and, although there is no express evidence as to its feudal position in the eleventh and twelfth centuries, its position on the edge of a considerable block of fees of the earl of Chester seems sufficient to connect these under-tenants of the honour of Skipton with it.

SARTILLY.

Sartilly: Manche, arr. Avranches, cant. Sartilly.

By a charter of twelfth-century date William de St. John of Halnaker confirmed to Boxgrove priory, Sussex, gifts of lands in England made by Humphrey, Gilbert and Geoffrey de Sartilla.[4] St-Jean-le-Thomas, the Norman home of the St. John family (*q.v.*), is in the canton of Sartilly.

SAUCY.

La Saussaye: Eure, arr. Louviers, cant. Amfreville-la-Campagne.

Anschetil, the ancestor of the family of Saucy of Newbold Saucy, co. Leicester, is shown to have been the man of Ives de Harcourt by a charter earlier than 1166.[5] La Saussaye was a fief of the Norman branch of the Harcourts.[6] In the Registers of Philip Augustus, 1212–20, in a list of the sub-infeudated fees of Breteuil is the entry 'apud Saucei unum quarterium quod tenet Ricardus de Harecort, sed ille negat.'[7]

SAVENIE, DE SAVIGNO.

Savenay: Calvados, arr. Vire, cant. Villers-Bocage, comm. Courvaudon.

In 1086 Ralf de Sauenie[8] held of Roger Bigot, who in every case held of the bishop of Bayeux, in the following places in Suffolk: Market Wickham, Charsfield, Cretingham and Kenton[9]; Hemingstone[10]; Ulverstone.[11] Roger Bigot held Savenay of the bishop of Bayeux,[12] and there can be no doubt that Ralf derived his name from this place.

1 *Early Yorks. Charters*, vii, 4–6.
2 *Rec. Hist. France*, xxiii, 620–1.
3 C. Hippeau, *Dict. topogr. du Calvados*, p. 267.
4 *Mon. Ang.*, iv, 646.
5 F. M. Stenton, *Danelaw Charters*, no. 461; *cf.* Nichols, *Leicestershire*, ii, part ii, pp. 766–7.
6 A. Le Prévost, *Mém. et Notes . . . . de l'Eure*, iii, 220.
7 *Rec. Hist. France*, xxiii, 617c.
8 Also Sauigno and Sauigni.
9 *D.B.*, ii, 373b.
10 *Ibid.*, 375b.
11 *Ibid.*, 376b.
12 See BIGOT.

SAY, SAI, of Shropshire.

Sai: Orne, arr. and cant. Argentan.

Picot, who was a substantial under-tenant of earl Roger of Montgomery at Clun and elsewhere in Shropshire,[1] is shown by the devolution of his lands to have been Picot de Say.[2] Robert abbot of St-Martin de Sées granted the privilege of burial to 'Roberto de Sayo qui cognominabatur Ficot et Adaloye uxori' and to Robert and Henry their sons; and in return Picot (as he is henceforth called) and his wife gave to the abbey 'edificium matris Picot cum virgulto quod habebat juxta ecclesiam sancte Marie de Vrou,' and confirmed a third of the church of Sai which Osmelinus de Sayo gave at the same time, giving also meadow land in the meadows 'de Juvigneio'; the charter is subscribed by earl Roger, Picot and his wife and two sons.[3] 'Vrou' is clearly Urou, the next parish to Sai, and Juvigni the parish immediately S of Sai. An agreement was made on 17 May 1086 in the court of Robert de Bellême between Picot de Saio and Droco de Coimis as to the dower which Droco's brother William had given to Adeloia his wife, who had been remarried to Picot.[4] This is further evidence of Picot's tenure under the house of Montgomery-Bellême, and suggests that the charter to St-Martin de Sées was considerably later than 1060, the date to which it has been assigned.

SCORCHEBOFE.

Ecorcheboeuf: Calvados, arr. Vire, cant. Condé-sur-Noireau, comm. Lassy.

In 1166 Roger de Scorchebofe held 100 'solidatae' of land of the new feoffment of Hugh de Lascy for which no service had been fixed[5]; and Simon de Scorchebof held a knight's fee of the old feoffment of Henry de Lascy.[6] The geographical situation of Ecorcheboeuf makes the identification certain. In 1610 it was a fief of Lassy.[7]

SCOTNEY, SCOTENI, SCOTEIGNY, ETC.

Etocquigny: Seine-Inf., arr. Dieppe, cant. Eu, comm. Saint-Martin-le-Gaillard.

The family were under-tenants of the counts of Eu at Crowhurst and elsewhere in the rape of Hastings. Walter de Scotiniis or Scoteni, *c.* 1180, issued two charters for Robertsbridge abbey, and his son Peter de Scotiniis one *c.* 1216.[8] In 1210–12 Peter de Scoteny held nine fees of the count of Eu and was his standard-bearer.[9] Walter de Scotenies

[1] *D.B.*, i, 258.

[2] Eyton, *Shropshire*, xi, 225, where there is an account of Picot and his descendants.

[3] *Gall. Christ.*, xi, Instr., col. 152–3; Eyton, *loc. cit.*

[4] *Cal. Docs. France*, no. 654.

[5] *Red Bk. Exch.*, p. 283.

[6] *Ibid.*, p. 422.

[7] C. Hippeau, *Dict. topogr. du Calvados*, p. 103.

[8] Hist. MSS. Comm., *Lord De L'Isle and Dudley*, i, pp. 38–9, 71.

[9] *Red Bk. Exch.*, p. 623.

witnessed a charter of William abbot of Le Tréport, 1181–83.[1] Between 1149 and 1153 Enguerand de Escoteignies witnessed Norman charters of John count of Eu.[2] Henry count of Eu, who died in 1183, confirmed to the collegiate church of St. Mary in the castle of Hastings the land of 'Betenessa' given by Engeler de Scoteniis[3]; this is clearly the Enguerand above-mentioned, who must have been Walter's predecessor in title. The statement in *V.C.H. Sussex*, vol. ix, p. 79, that the family descended from Lambert son of Walter, the Domesday under-tenant of Crowhurst, seems to lack anything in the nature of evidence to support it.

On general grounds it is probable that the Lincolnshire family of Scoteny is another branch deriving from Etocquigny, but no evidence has as yet come to hand to confirm it.

Scures.

Escures: Calvados, arr. Bayeux, cant. Ryes.

Roger de Scures witnessed a charter of Henry de Port of Basing, 1120–1130, for the abbey of Cerisy-la-Forêt.[4] In 1166 Matthew de Scures, Roger's son,[5] was holding four knights' fees of the old feoffment of John de Port.[6] Escures is 3 kil. S of Port-en-Bessin.

A family of Scures were under-tenants of the counts of Aumale in Holderness,[7] the earliest known member, Ansketil de Scures, holding land in Hackthorn, co. Lincoln, of Stephen count of Aumale in 1115–18.[8] There is, however, no evidence to connect them with Escures and the connexion is improbable. It is more likely that they derived their name from Ecuires by Montreuil sur-Mer in the Pas de Calais. Although it lies far N of Aumale, it belonged to the counts of Ponthieu,[9] and Enguerrand count of Ponthieu was the first husband of Adeliz, the mother of Stephen count of Aumale[10]; moreover in the first half of the eleventh century the counts of Ponthieu seem to have held Aumale.[11]

Sept Meules, de Septem Molendinis, Septem Molis.

Sept Meules: Seine-Inf., arr. Dieppe, cant. Eu.

In 1086 William de Sept Mueles held land in Bexhill, Sussex, of the count of Eu.[12] In 1166 a later William de Septem Molis held two and three-quarters knights' fees of the bishop of London.[13] In Normandy William de Septem Molis witnessed at Eu a charter of John count of Eu

[1] *Cartulaire . . . . du Tréport*, ed. L. de Kermaingant, pp. 73–4.

[2] Examples are in *ibid*. For an Inguerran de Esscotengiis (probably of an earlier generation) witnessing a charter of Henry count of Eu in 1106 see *Cal. Docs. France*, no. 399.

[3] *Mon. Ang.*, vi, 1470.

[4] H. E. Salter, *Facsimiles of Oxford Charters*, no. 14.

[5] *Ibid.*, no. 15.

[6] *Red Bk. Exch.*, p. 208.

[7] *Early Yorks. Charters*, iii, p. 64.

[8] *Lindsey Survey* (Linc. Rec. Soc.), p. 239.

[9] C. Brunel, *Rec. des Actes des Comtes de Pontieu* (Coll. Docs. inédits), p. 22.

[10] *Complete Peerage*, new ed., i, pp. 351–2.

[11] *Ibid.*, p. 351*n*.

[12] *D.B.*, i, 18.

[13] *Red Bk. Exch.*, p. 186.

in 1153.[1] A charter of Henry II, 1158–62, for the abbey of Foucarmont confirmed among other gifts that of Rainald and Roger de Septem Molendinis and Amabilis their mother[2]; and Mabilia de Septemmolis daughter of Gouduin made gifts to the abbey of Le Tréport for the souls of her husbands Hugh de Ulmeto and Robert de Gal.[3] In 1870 a motte at Sept Meules was still existing.[4]

SIFREWAST.

Chiffrevast: Manche, arr. and cant. Valognes, comm. Tamerville.

In a general confirmation charter for the abbey of St-Sauveur Henry II included the gift of Ralf de Siffrewast of the church of 'Salomonis Villa'[5]; and in a charter for the abbey of Montebourg he confirmed the gift of W. de Sifrewast and Halenas his son of tithe in his fee in Anslevilla.[6] As both abbeys are in arr. Valognes the identification seems practically certain.[7]

The association of Martinwast and Sifrewast both in England and Normandy, and the close proximity of the two places, have been noted above.[8]

SOLNEY, SOLENNEI, SULIGNEI, ETC.

Subligny: Manche, arr. Avranches, cant. La Haye-Pesnel.

Alvred de Suleinei held Newton Solney, co. Derby, of the earl of Chester *c.* 1170, and it continued in his descendants.[9] Subligny is 7 kil. N of Avranches, and the connexion of the earls of Chester with the Avranchin establishes the identification.

SPINEVILLA.

Epineville: Seine-Inf., arr. Yvetot, cant. Fontaine-le-Dun, comm. St-Aubin-sur-mer.

William de Spinevilla gave tithe in a place unnamed to Castle Acre priory, as recorded in a charter of the second earl de Warenne.[10] In 1242–43 a later William de Spineville held half a knight's fee in Barmer, and another half in Feltwell, both in Norfolk, of the honour of Warenne.[11] Epineville, which occurs in the thirteenth century as Espinevilla, is 3 kil. NNW of Bourg-Dun; and a charter of the second earl de Warenne for Longueville priory, *c.* 1130–1138, shows him to have been the overlord of Bourg-Dun.[12]

1 *Cal. Docs. France*, no. 235.

2 *Ibid.*, no. 186.

3 Coquelin, *Hist. du Tréport* (Soc. Hist. Norm.), i, 344.

4 Cochet, *Rép. arch. . . . de la Seine-Inf.*, col. 45.

5 Delisle et Berger, *Rec. des Actes de Henri II*, ii, 78; the church is indexed as probably Sénoville, dép. Manche, arr. Coutances, comm. Barneville.

6 *Ibid.*, p. 155; probably Hémevez, dép. Manche, arr. Valognes, cant. Montebourg.

7 It is so given in the index to *ibid.*

8 See MARTINWAST.

9 Farrer, *Honors and Knights' Fees*, ii, 41.

10 *Mon. Ang.*, v, 50.

11 *Bk. of Fees*, pp. 906–7.

12 *Early Yorks. Charters*, viii, no. 28.

STAFFORD.

Tosny: Eure, arr. Louviers, cant. Gaillon.

Robert de Stafford, otherwise de Tosny, was an important Domesday tenant-in-chief. In a charter for the abbey of Conches he is described as ' filius Rogerii de Totteneio '; it is witnessed by his son Nicholas and by St. Wulfstan bishop of Worcester.[1] Robert de Stafford confirmed to Conches the gifts in Wootton Wawen, co. Warwick, where there was a cell of Conches, made by his grandfather Robert de Tosny and his father Nicholas de Stafford.[2] The later house of Stafford descended from Hervey Bagot and Milisent daughter and eventual heir of this second Robert.[3]

STRABO.

Eu: Seine-Inf., arr. Dieppe, cant. Eu.

In the *carta* of John count of Eu in 1166 Robert Strabo was returned as a knight ' super dominium.'[4] A rent of 6*s*. was due from him to the college of St. Mary in Hastings castle.[5] Somewhat later a William Strabo gave to the abbey of Le Tréport a rent of money and salt in Le Tréport[6]; and in 1199 ' Robertus Strabo de Augo ' gave to that abbey five acres of land in Monthuon, a suburb of Le Tréport.[7] William Strabo witnessed a charter of Henry count of Eu, 1170–83.[8] The family clearly came from Eu or its neighbourhood.

STUR, WILLIAM son of.

Tourlaville: Manche, arr. and cant. Cherbourg.

In 1086 William son of Stur was a substantial tenant-in-chief in the Isle of Wight and Hampshire. By a charter, probably *temp*. William II, Hugh de Insula son of William son of Stur of the Isle of Wight gave to the abbey of Marmoutier the tithe of the mill of Torlavilla which he held by hereditary right.[9] The *Infeudationes militum* of 1172 show William son of Estur holding half a knight's fee in the district near Cherbourg.[10] Although it is not completely certain that Tourlaville was the original home of the family, the name not being territorial, it seems clear that William came from the Cotentin.

SURDEVAL.

Sourdeval: Manche, arr. Mortain, cant. Sourdeval.

Documentary proof that Richard de Surdeval, the Domesday tenant-in-chief, part of whose lands passed to the Paynels of Hooton Pagnell and part to the Brus fee, derived his name from Sourdeval has been given in *Early Yorkshire Charters*, vol. vi, p. 4 *n*.

[1] *Gall. Christ.*, xi, Instr., col. 131.
[2] *Mon. Ang.*, vi, 994.
[3] *Complete Peerage*, 1st ed., vii, 208*n*.
[4] *Red Bk. Exch.*, p. 203.
[5] *Mon. Ang.*, vi, 1470.
[6] *Cartulaire . . . . du Tréport*, ed. L. de Kermaingant, pp. 72–3.
[7] *Ibid.*, p. 94.
[8] *Cal. Docs. France*, no. 401, where the date 1190 must be subject to amendment.
[9] *Ibid.*, no. 1178.
[10] *Red Bk. Exch.*, p. 634; and see *V.C.H. Hants.*, i, 426.

TAHUM.

Thaon: Calvados, arr. Caen, cant. Creully.

In 1086 the son of William Tahum was an under-tenant of Odo bishop of Bayeux.[1] Among the fees of the bishop of Bayeux in 1133 the 'feodum Maminoth' consisted of five knights' fees in places including Thaon (*Taun*).[2] A charter of Richard bishop of Bayeux, previously dean of Bayeux, of *c.* 1164 shows that the dean had been the patron of the church of Thaon.[3]

TAILLEBOIS.

Cristot: Calvados, arr. Caen, cant. Tilly-sur-Seulles.

A note in the cartulary of La Trinité de Vendôme[4] mentions a copy of the grant of the church and patronage of Cristot by Ives Taillebois to the abbey. An account of Cristot is given in Béziers, *Diocèse de Bayeux*, vol. ii, p. 192.

TAISSEL.

Tessel: Calvados, arr. Caen, cant. Tilly-sur-Seulles.

Wimund de Taissel was a Domesday under-tenant of Beauchamp of Bedford. For the evidence see BROILG.

Between 1121 and 1128 a Rannulf de Taissel witnessed a charter absolving Robert son of Bernard who had burnt four houses belonging to the abbey of St. Stephen at Caen; two other witnesses took their names from places in the canton of Tilly.[5]

TALBOT.

Dept. Seine-Inférieure.

In 1086 Geoffrey Talebot was an under-tenant of Hugh de Gournay in Essex[6]; and Richard Talebot of Walter Giffard in Bedfordshire.[7] As this was not a territorial name it is impossible to derive the family from a particular place, though there is much evidence as to the different lands held by them in the Seine-Inf., where they were extensive under-tenants. Charter evidence shows them as under-tenants there of Giffard, the count of Eu, and Gournay; and as benefactors of Holy Trinity, Rouen, St-Lô, Rouen, Beaubec, Valmont, Bival, St-Victor-en-Caux, Le Tréport, and Longueville. The exact connexion of the family of the earls of Shrewsbury with these Talbots has not at present been established by satisfactory evidence, though such a connexion is in the highest degree probable.

[1] *D.B.*, i, 8b.
[2] *Rec. Hist. France*, xxiii, 700h.
[3] *Antiq. cartul. Baioc.* (Soc. Hist. Norm.), i, 161; *cf.* Béziers, *Diocèse de Bayeux*, iii, 392 *et seq.*
[4] Ed. Ch. Métais (1893–5), iii, 42.
[5] E. Deville, *Analyse d'un ancien cartulaire de . . . St-Etienne de Caen*, p. 36.
[6] *D.B.*, ii, 89b.
[7] *Ibid.*, i, 211.

TANCARVILLE.

Tancarville: Seine-Inf., arr. Le Havre, cant. Saint-Romain-de-Colbosc.

An account of the early generations of the Tancarville family, lords of Tancarville and its castle, who held the hereditary office of Chamberlain of Normandy, has recently been given in Appendix F of *The Complete Peerage*, new ed., vol. x, pp. 47–54; this is based on Norman and English sources.

TANI.

Saint-Aubin-du-Thenney : } Eure, arr. Bernay, cant. Broglie.
Saint-Jean-du-Thenney : }

Richard de Tani witnessed among the men of the honour of Gilbert FitzRichard a charter of Adeliz wife of Gilbert FitzRichard for Thorney abbey, 1136–1138.[1] These two communes lie respectively 6 kil. and 4 kil. E of Orbec, the *caput* of Richard FitzGilbert's Norman honour. The thirteenth-century form was Taneium or Tannei.[2] An 'aveu' of 1603 for the barony of Ferrières shows them to have been then members of that barony,[3] but they are more distant from Ferrières-St-Hilaire, its *caput*, than from Orbec, and there being no other place with a name at all similar it seems safe to derive Richard's family from one of these communes.

TERRA VASTA, TERRA GUASTA.

Terregatte: Manche, arr. Avranches, cant. Saint-James.

Roger de Clare, earl of Hertford, married Maud daughter and heir of James de St-Hilaire.[4] In 1166 Rualent de Terra Vasta held half a knight's fee of the fee of the countess.[5] St-Aubin-de-Terregatte is 5 kil. N of St-James-de-Beuvron and 16 kil. W of St-Hilaire-du-Harcouët; St-Laurent-de-Terregatte is 6 kil. NE of St-James and 14 kil. W of St-Hilaire. The family of the countess[6] was connected with both these places, being called sometimes 'of St-James' and sometimes 'of St-Hilaire.'[7]

TESSON, TAISSON.

La Roche-Tesson: Manche, arr. Saint-Lô, cant. Percy, comm. La Colombe.

In 1172 Jordan Tesson owed the service of ten knights for the honour of Thury [Harcourt] in the Bessin, having thirty and a half knights' fees there, and the service of five knights for the honour of St-Sauveur-le-Vicomte, where he had fifteen fees.[8] At the same time he held

[1] F. M. Stenton, *Early Charters from Northamptonshire Collections*, no. 18.
[2] Blosseville, *Dict. topogr. . . . de l'Eure*, pp. 190, 196.
[3] A. Le Prévost, *Mém. et Notes . . . . de l'Eure*, ii, 84.
[4] *Complete Peerage*, new ed., vi, 500.
[5] *Red Bk. Exch., p.* 407.
[6] *Early Yorks. Charters*, v, 86–7.
[7] See SAINT-HILAIRE.
[8] *Rec. Hist. France*, xxiii, 694k.

of the abbot of Le Mont-St-Michel the fee of La Columbe, in which parish La Roche-Tesson is situate.[1] He died in 1178, and was succeeded by his son Ralf, who held North Wheatley, co. Nottingham, and land in Kent.[2] These were lost in 1204 when Ralf adhered to Philip Augustus.[3] He died shortly afterwards, leaving daughters and coheirs; for further details and for the castle at La Roche-Tesson see Delisle, *Château et Sires de St-Sauveur-le-Vicomte* (especially Chapter II), and Gerville in *Mém. Soc. Ant. Norm.*, vol. v (1830), pp. 187 *et seq.*

TIBOUVILLA, TEDBOLDVILLA, ETC.

Thibouville: Eure, arr. Bernay, cant. Beaumont-le-Roger.

In a charter of the period 1181–89 Henry II confirmed to Le Bec, ' ex dono Rogeri de Thebovilla medietatem cujusdem manerii in Anglia quod dicitur Widone; et ex dono Willelmi filii ejus ecclesiam Sancti Lamberti et aliam medietatem predicti manerii de Widone cum ecclesia et decima ejusdem manerii cum omnibus rebus ad eundem (*sic*) manerium et eandem ecclesiam pertinentibus et decimam redditus sui de Ponte Autoni et redditibus extra positis et molendinum de Malassis cum terra molendinarii et quicquid habebat juxta predictam ecclesiam Sancti Lamberti . . . . '[4] The places in question are Weedon Beck, co. Northampton, the church of St. Lambert of Malassis in the commune of Fontaine-la-Soret, 5 kil. WSW of Thibouville, and Pont-Authou on the Risle, 12 kil. NW of Thibouville. The gift by William de Tibouville of the church, or rather the chapel, of St. Lambert at Malassis was made by a charter dated 1126 to which his mother Aldemeda and his wife Bertha assented.[5] A charter of Roger de Beaumont for the abbey of St-Wandrille in 1086 is witnessed ' S. Rogeri filii Roberti de Tedbolduilla,'[6] and another of the same for the Holy Trinity of Beaumont in 1088–89, ' Rogero de Thiboltvilla fratribusque suis Radulfo et Fortuno.'[7] In a charter of 1131 of Henry I for the Holy Trinity of Beaumont, among the ' Homines comitis Mellenti ' in the list of witnesses is ' Willelmi (*sic*) de Teobovilla,'[8] the genitive being an obvious scribal error for the nominative. In 1086 Weedon Beck was land of Hugh de Grentemaisnil, held in demesne,[9] and consequently the enfeoffment of Roger de Tibouville must have been after the acquisition of the Grentemaisnil lands in 1102 by Robert count of Meulan, the lord of Beaumont. On the other hand it was probably earlier than count Robert's death in 1118, when the honour of Beaumont

[1] *Ibid.*, p. 704h.

[2] *Bk. of Fees*, pp. 149, 230, 270, 286.

[3] *Pipe Roll* 6 *John*, pp. 87–8.

[4] Delisle et Berger, *Recueil des Actes de Henri II*, ii, 378.

[5] A. Le Prévost, *Mém. et Notes . . . de l'Eure*, ii, 117.

[6] F. Lot, *Etudes critiques sur . . . Saint-Wandrille*, p. 96.

[7] *Cartulaire de la Sainte-Trinité de Beaumont-le-Roger*, ed. E. Deville, no. (p. 6). This has been calendared by Round (*Cal. Docs. France*, no. 368) from a MS. in the Bibliothèque Nationale, where the list of witnesses is defective; Round's text reads ' Roberto filio Anschetilli de Tebotevilla, fratribus suis Radulfo et fortino,' ' et Rogero ' being omitted after ' Anschetilli.'

[8] *Ibid.*, no. 3 (p. 10).

[9] *D.B.*, i, 224b.

devolved on his eldest son Waleran count of Meulan and the honour of Leicester on his second son Robert earl of Leicester. On the loss of Normandy in 1204 the family adhered to the French king and the English lands were lost. In a list of lands of the Normans of the year 1205 Syston, co. Leicester, is shown as the land of Robert de Tilboville,[1] and in a list of the fees of the honour of Beaumont-le-Roger of 1204-1208 Robert de Tibouvilla is shown as owing the service of two and a half knights.[2] In Normandy the family continued in the male line until the closing years of the fourteenth century.[3]

TIGERIVILLA.

Thierceville: Eure, arr. Les Andelys, cant. Gisors, comm. Bazincourt.

A charter of Henry I to Belvoir priory confirmed the gifts of Ives de Tigerivilla and his sons Robert and Hugh in ' Dastuna ' and in Ropsley, co. Lincoln.[4] Ives can be identified with the Ives who in 1086 held land in Ropsley of Robert de Todeni.[5] Hugh son of Ives of ' Clacston ' confirmed to Belvoir the gifts of Ives his father in ' Clacston ' and of Robert his brother there and in Ropsley, and added gifts of his own.[6] A comparison of this with Henry I's charter shows the measurement of lands to be the same; and it is certain, therefore, that ' Dastuna ' is a corruption for ' Clacston,' which Round[6] identified as Long Clawson, co. Leicester—a Todeni fee. The family evidently adopted that name in place of Tigerivilla.

Thierceville occurs in the thirteenth-century *pouillé* of the diocese of Rouen as Tygiervilla,[7] and in the Registers of Philip Augustus as Tigervilla.[8] It is 14½ kil. NE of Guerny, a fief of Robert de Todeni,[9] and 16½ kil. ENE of Hacqueville, held by Roger de Clere of the lord of Tosny itself.[10] The only other place of the name in Normandy is Thiergeville (Seine-Inf., arr. Yvetot, cant. Valmont), which was held in the thirteenth century in part by Estouteville, and in part by the Chamberlains of Tancarville.[11]

TILLY.

[?] Tilly-sur-Seulles: Calvados, arr. Caen, cant. Tilly-sur-Seulles.

It was recorded in 1212 that Henry I gave the manor of Wonford, Devon, to Geoffrey de Mandeville, who gave it to William son of John in marriage with his daughter, and that Henry de Tilli had held it for life whose heirs were in Normandy[12]; and again in 1237 that Henry de Tilly, a Norman, had held an interest in Wonford and elsewhere in Devon.[13]

1 *Rot. Norm.*, p. 139.
2 *Rec. Hist. France*, xxiii, 710j.
3 A. Le Prévost, *op. cit.*, iii, 429.
4 *Cal. Chart. Rolls*, 1327–41, p. 295.
5 *D.B.*, i, 353.
6 Hist. MSS. Comm., *Duke of Rutland*, iv, 129.
7 *Rec. Hist. France*, xxiii, 311g.
8 *Ibid.*, 621k, 631j, 713j.
9 See NOYERS.
10 *Gall. Christ.*, xi, Instr., col. 132b.
11 *Rec. Hist. France*, xxiii, 642 l, m.
12 *Bk. of Fees*, p. 96.
13 *Ibid.*, p. 612.

William son of John gave land in Castrum Tillei to Bayeux cathedral before 1153[1]; he was the father of Henry de Tilli. In 1172, under the heading of the bailiwick of Falaise, Henry de Tilli held of the king the castle of Tilli and 10 acres of land in the vill.[2]

TODENI, TOSNY.

Tosny: Eure, arr. Louviers, cant. Gaillon.

The evidence that Todeni of Belvoir[3] was a branch of the Tosny family is strong, but the precise nature of the connexion is difficult to prove.

TOREIGNY.

Torigny-sur-Vire: Manche, arr. Saint-Lô, cant. Torigny.

In 1166 Peter de Toreigny was an under-tenant of the new feoffment of Walter de Mayenne.[4] A charter of Henry II, 1155–56, shows that Walter de Mayenne held interests in Montchamps (Calvados, arr. Vire, cant. Vassy), which is 20 kil. SE of Torigny, in Burcy (in the same canton), 23 kil. SE of Torigny, and in Truttemer-le-Grand (arr. and cant. Vire), 30 kil. SSE of Torigny.[5] The fact that there seems to be no other Torigny, combined with these holdings at no great distance, suggests that Walter had enfeoffed a man from Torigny.

TORNAI.

Tournay-sur-Dive: Orne, arr. Argentan, cant. Trun.

Gerard, who in 1086 held Kinnersley and other lands in Shropshire of earl Roger,[6] is shown by a charter of his son-in-law and successor Hamo Peverel[7] to have been Gerard de Tornai. In 1247 'Alexander dictus Abbas de Tornaio juxta Trun' stated that he and his 'antecessores' had held his land by the service of castle-guard at Exmes.[8] Roger de Montgomery was *vicomte* of Exmes or the Hiesmois.[9] Tournay is 6 kil. E of Bailleul-en-Gouffern.[10]

TRACY.

Dept. La Manche.

The earlier history of the honour of Barnstaple and the early Tracy pedigree have both to be taken into account. At the end of the eleventh century, or more probably early in the twelfth, the honour was granted to Juhel son of Alvred, who was living in 1123 when he witnessed a charter

[1] *Antiq. cartul. Baioc.* (Soc. Hist. Norm.), i, 195.

[2] *Rec. Hist. France*, xxiii, 698c, where in the index Tilli is identified as above. Mr. Loyd adds some pencil notes relating to a Tilly family who had an interest in Rotherham, co. York; he was doubtful whether or not the derivation of that family was from Tilly-la-Campagne (Calvados, arr. Caen, cant. Bourguébus), and his notes are unfinished.

[3] Ped. in Hist. MSS. Comm., *Duke of Rutland*, iv, 106. The name Berenger occurs in this family as well as in that of Tosny.

[4] *Red Bk. Exch.*, p. 196.

[5] Delisle et Berger, *Rec. des Actes de Henri II*, i, 127.

[6] *D.B.*, i, 258b; *V.C.H. Shropshire*, i, pp. 298, 338.

[7] Eyton, *Shropshire*, viii, 128.

[8] *Querimoniæ Normannorum* in *Rec. Hist. France*, xxiv, 72e.

[9] *Complete Peerage*, new ed., xi, 683. [10] See BAILLEUL.

of Henry I,[1] and was dead in 1130 when his son Alvred was paying relief for his father's lands.[2] Alvred the younger died without issue at some date earlier than 1139 when Henry de Tracy was in possession of a moiety.[3] In 1146 Henry issued a charter for Barnstaple priory in which he mentioned his son Oliver.[4] As the other moiety passed to the Briouze family by marriage with a daughter of Juhel,[5] it is probable that the Tracy moiety had descended in a similar way.[6]

By a charter dated 1110 William de Tracy, who had become a monk at Le Mont-St-Michel, made various grants to that abbey[7]; the charter was subscribed by his wife Rohese, his sons Turgis and Henry, and his sister Gieva; the places where the grants lay—all in dept. La Manche—were Montpinçon (arr. Coutances, cant. Cerisy-la-Salle), La Lucerne (arr. Avranches, cant. La Haye-Pesnel), Champrépus (arr. Avranches, cant. Villedieu), St-Vigor-des-Monts (arr. St-Lô, cant. Tessy), and Argouges (arr. Avranches, cant. St-James-de-Beuvron). It can be supposed that Henry named in that charter was the Henry de Tracy whose son Oliver, as will be noted below, held four knights' fees in that part of Normandy; and, if so, his elder brother Turgis must have died without issue. Since the Tracy interest in Barnstaple was not acquired before 1130, the Norman lands here mentioned must have been the original Tracy possessions.

In 1172, in the *Infeudationes militum* under the heading 'De vicecomitatu de Cerenciis,' is the entry 'Oliverus de Tracieio, j militem; et ad servitium suum iiij milites. Et isti iiij debent esse in servitio Comitis Moritanii uno die cum custamento suo, et deinceps cum custamento Comitis.'[8] 'Cerenciae' is Cerences (arr. Coutances, cant. Bréhal).[9] The places named in William de Tracy's charter of 1110 are somewhat widely scattered, but from an administrative point of view Cerences is a quite possible focal point for them, and the other tenants mentioned under this *vicomté* support such an impression. On the whole there seems good ground for attributing the places named in the charter of 1110 to this holding of four knights' fees.

The actual place from which the family took its name is a difficult question. At first sight there is much to be said for Tracy-sur-Mer (Calvados, arr. Bayeux, cant. Ryes), since among Oliver de Tracy's tenants of the old feoffment in the *carta* of 1166 is a William de Muncellis[10]; and there is a Monceaux 10 kil. S of Tracy. It is clear, however, that this Muncellis under-tenancy dates from a time anterior

[1] Round, *Feudal England*, p. 483 ; and see MONCEAUX, *supra*.

[2] *Pipe Roll* 31 *Hen. I*, p. 153.

[3] *Gesta Stephani* (Rolls Ser.), p. 52.

[4] *Mon. Ang.*, v, 198.

[5] See MONCEAUX.

[6] An agreement between Oliver son of Henry de Tracy and William de Briouze relating to a moiety of the manor of Barnstaple was made in 1196 (*Feet of Fines*, Pipe Roll Soc. vol. xvii, no. 100).

[7] *Cal. Docs. France*, no. 719.

[8] *Red Bk. Exch.*, p. 635.

[9] *Cf.* CHAMPERNOWNE.

[10] *Red Bk. Exch.*, p. 255.

to the Tracy acquisition of the honour of Barnstaple,[1] and when in addition it is shown by the Bayeux Inquest of 1133 that Tracy-sur-Mer was then held by William Picot,[2] such a theory becomes untenable. Two other places of the name remain—Tracy-Bocage (Calvados, arr. Caen, cant. Villers-Bocage) and Tracy a fief in Neuville (Calvados, arr. and cant. Vire). As regards the first it lies wide of any of the ascertained lands of the family, and beyond the name there is nothing to connect them with it. Tracy, the fief in Neuville, is somewhat more hopeful, for not only is it nearer the places in the charter of 1110, but according to C. Hippeau[3] there was 'une châtellanie d'ou relevaient les fiefs de Saint-Vigor-des-Monts.' This seems to connect it with the St-Vigor of the charter of 1110; but from another passage[4] it appears that this information comes from an 'aveu' of 1679 for the *vicomté* of Vire, whereas there is some ground for thinking that in 1172 St-Vigor belonged to the *vicomté* of Cerences. Moreover it is possible that the name of a fief of this description was derived from its former holders,[5] instead of it being a place from which they took their name. The matter, therefore, remains one of doubt, but it is of less importance since it seems clear that, whatever the origin of the name, for the purposes of feudal history the Tracies were under-tenants in the department of La Manche of the *comté* of Mortain. In view of this it is not without significance that Stephen was count of Mortain, and that Henry de Tracy of Barnstaple was the king's most prominent and persistent adherent in Devon.

TRAILEI, TRALGI.

Trelly: Manche, arr. Coutances, cant. Montmartin-sur-Mer.

In 1086 Geoffrey de Tralgi or Traillgi was an under-tenant of the bishop of Coutances at Yielden and elsewhere in Bedfordshire,[6] and as Geoffrey at Teign, Devon.[7] Trelly is 10 kil. S of Coutances.

TREGOZ, TRESGOZ.

Troisgots: Manche, arr. St-Lô, cant. Tessy-sur-Vire.

In 1172 William de Tresgot owed the service of one and a half knights in the Cotentin.[8] He was succeeded by Robert de Tresgoz, probably his son, who was bailiff of the Cotentin in 1195 and under John,[9] and who held lands in many English counties.[10] Robert adhered to John and lost his lands in Normandy; and in the Registers of Philip Augustus there is the entry 'Feodum de Tresgoz quod dominus rex tenet per

[1] See MONCEAUX.

[2] *Rec. Hist. France*, xxiii, 700j.

[3] *Dict. topogr. du Calvados*, p. 281.

[4] *Ibid.*, p. 206.

[5] See BIGOT for the 'fief Bigot' in Savenay.

[6] *D.B.*, i, 210.

[7] *Ibid.*, 103b; and see *V.C.H. Devon*, i, 428.

[8] *Rec. Hist. France*, xxiii, 696c.

[9] Stapleton, *Rot. Norm. Scacc.*, i, p. clxxiv.

[10] *Bk. of Fees*, see Index.

escaetam debet servicium unius militis et dimidium.'[1] By a charter dated at Paris in Nov. 1218 Philip Augustus gave to Miles de Lévis the usufruct of the land which Robert de Trégots had possessed at Trégots, Favarches and St-Romphaire.[2] Favarches is the next commune to Troisgots, and St-Romphaire is close by. There was a castle at Troisgots, described by Gerville.[3]

DE TRIBUS MINETIS.

Les Trois Minettes: Calvados, arr. and cant. Falaise, comm. Saint-Germain-Langot.

In 1130 Walter and William de Tribus Minetis occur in Devon and Cornwall.[4] In 1166 Joslen de Tribus Minetis held two knights' fees of the old feoffment of Henry de la Pommeraye; and William de Tribus Minetis held two knights' fees of the old feoffment of the abbot of Tavistock.[5] Les Trois Minettes, a hamlet of St-Germain-Langot,[6] is 7 kil. E of La Pommeraye. *Minata* or *mineta* is a measure of land.

TUIT.

Le Thuit: Eure, arr. and cant. Les Andelys.

A charter of Henry I confirming the gifts of Robert de Todeni to Belvoir priory reproduces much of Robert's charter, including the witnesses, among whom was Ralph del Tuit, described as the man of Berenger de Todeni, Robert's son.[7] A great part of Berenger's lands passed by the marriage of Aubreye his widow to Robert de L'Isle, and ultimately to Hugh Bigod, earl of Norfolk.[8] In his *carta* of 1166 earl Hugh returned certain fees held by him as 'de feodo Albrede de Insula,' and among them is one knight's fee held by Hugh de Tuit.[9] A notitia of gifts to Keldholme priory includes 'ex dono Hugonis del Tuit' the mill of Edston, co. York.[10] To this Farrer, in his section on the Bigod fee, has a long note giving several details; in this he says, however, that the family took its name from Thwaite by Aylsham, Norfolk, but he gives no evidence for a connexion with that place. The form of the preposition *del* indicates a place with the form 'Le'; and Le Thuit, which in the thirteenth century occurs as Tuit or Tuitum, is only 6 kil. N of Tosny. Moreover, it is reasonably certain that Todeni of Belvoir was an offshoot of the Tosny family.[11]

[1] *Rec. Hist. France*, xxiii, 612d.

[2] Delisle, *Cat. des Actes de Philippe-Auguste*, no. 1856, where in the index it is noted 'Trégots, mal à propos nommé Troisgots.'

[3] *Mém. Soc. Ant. Norm.*, vol. v (1830), p. 215; and see generally Stapleton, *loc. cit.*

[4] *Pipe Roll* 31 *Hen. I*, pp. 155–6, 160.

[5] *Red Bk. Exch.*, pp. 260, 251.

[6] C. Hippeau, *Dict. topogr. du Calvados*, p. 283.

[7] *Cal. Chart. Rolls*, 1327–41, p. 296.

[8] *Early Yorks. Charters*, i, 466.

[9] *Red Bk. Exch.*, p. 397.

[10] *Early Yorks. Charters*, i, 470.

[11] See TODENI, and *cf.* CLERE, NOYERS and TIGERIVILLA.

TURVILLE.

Tourville-la-Campagne: Eure, arr. Louviers, cant. Amfreville-la-Campagne; *or*

Tourville: Eure, arr. and cant. Pont-Audemer.

This family were under-tenants of the earls of Leicester.[1] Before 1131 Geoffrey de Turville gave a rent in England to the priory of Beaumont-le-Roger.[2] These details seem to point rather strongly to one of the two Tourvilles mentioned above as the family's place of origin. Tourville-la-Campagne is nearer to Beaumont than the other; and in addition it would be expected that a man living close to Pont-Audemer would benefit one of the two abbeys of Préaux in his immediate neighbourhood; but the evidence is insufficient to decide between the two places.

UMFRANVILLE.

[?] Offranville: Seine-Inf., arr. Dieppe, cant. Offranville.

Rodulf de Ulfranvilla witnessed the gift of Blakenham, Suffolk, to the abbey of Le Bec by Walter Giffard, *temp.* William I[3]; and a William de Hunfranvilla witnessed a charter of the last earl Walter Giffard *ante* 1164, giving land in Longueville.[4] Offranville is 10½ kil. N of Longueville.[5]

VALBADUN.

Vaubadon: Calvados, arr. Bayeux, cant. Balleroy.

In 1086 Ranulf de Valbadon was an under-tenant of Odo bishop of Bayeux.[6] In 1210–12 Richard de Vabadone was returned as doing castleguard at Dover for the Maminot ward.[7] At a later date the chapter of Bayeux had jurisdiction over the parish.[8] This with the individual nature of the place-name and its locality seems sufficient proof for the identification.

VALEINES.

Valognes: Manche, arr. and cant. Valognes.

In 1166 Roger de Valeines held half a knight's fee of the old feoffment in Kent of William d'Avranches.[9] As another under-tenant of William was Robert de Beseville, and there is a Beuzeville 15 kil. SE of Valognes, the case for the identification seems strong.[10]

1 *Beds. Hist. Rec. Soc.*, vii, pp. 204 *et seq.*

2 *Cartulaire de la Sainte-Trinité de Beaumont-le-Roger*, ed. E. Deville, no. 1 (p. 8).

3 *Mon. Ang.*, vi, 1002.

4 *Cal. Docs. France*, no. 221.

5 The whole of this entry is entered by Mr. Loyd in pencil, and suggests a late and uncompleted line of research.

6 *D.B.*, i, 11b.

7 *Red Bk. Exch.*, p. 617.

8 Béziers, *Diocèse de Bayeux*, i, 332.

9 *Red Bk. Exch.*, p. 192; in *Lib. Niger* he is given as Reginald.

10 The entry for Robert de Beseville was deleted by Mr. Loyd as he did not consider the evidence sufficiently good for a derivation from Beuzeville-au-Plain, arr. Valognes, cant. Ste-Mère-Eglise, as there is also a Beuzeville-la-Bastille in the same canton.

VEILLY.

Villy-Bocage: Calvados, arr. Caen, cant. Villers-Bocage.

Of this family, under-tenants of Lascy of Pontefract, Farrer has given some details in *Early Yorkshire Charters*, vol. iii, pp. 255–6. Villy is 3 kil. N of Epinay-sur-Odon, in which commune lie Ectot and Le Saussey, the places from which came Eschetot (*q.v.*) and Salceit (*q.v.*), under-tenants in England of Lacy of Hereford.[1]

VEIM, VEHIM, VEYN.

Vains: Manche, arr. and cant. Avranches.

Between 1129 and 1141 Ranulf earl of Chester addressed a mandate to Richard de Veim and his other 'vavassors' of Bisley, co. Gloucester.[2] Notes on the family are given by Farrer in *Honors and Knights' Fees*, vol. ii, p. 51. Vains itself had been granted to St. Stephen's, Caen, by William the Conqueror,[3] and was presumably of the ducal demesne; but it lies only 3 kil. W of Avranches, and the earls of Chester were hereditary *vicomtes* of the Avranchin.

VENUZ.

Venoix: Calvados, arr. and cant. Caen.

Miles, a marshal of duke William in Normandy, held land at Caen, Vaucelles and Venoix; in or before 1070 he was succeeded by his son Geoffrey the marshal, who held land in chief at East Worldham, Hants, in 1086. Geoffrey's successor, probably his son or grandson, was Robert de Venuz. Full details are given in *The Complete Peerage*, new ed., vol. xi, app., pp. 122–4, with references to English and Norman sources[4] and to the notes by Round in *The King's Serjeants*, pp. 89–90 and elsewhere.

VERDUN.

Verdun: A fief in par. Vessey, Manche, cant. Pontorson.

In 1166 Bertram de Verdon held two knights' fees in chief.[5] In a return of the knights of Le Mont St-Michel in 1172 there is the entry 'Radulfus de Fulgeriis debet facere unum militem de medietate de Buillun et de Chavei et de quadam parte Olivi. Istud autem servicium debet facere pro eo Bertramnus de Verdum, filius Normanni.'[6] The places are Bouillon (Manche, arr. Avranches, cant. Granville) and Chavoy (arr. and cant. Avranches). The entry makes it highly probable that Bertram derived his name from Verdun as above.[7]

1 *Cf.* LONGVILLERS.

2 F. M. Stenton, *English Feudalism*, app. no. i, p. 256.

3 Haskins, *Norman Institutions*, p. 98*n*.

4 They include the references given by Mr. Loyd in his MS.

5 *Red Bk. Exch.*, p. 271.

6 *Rec. Hist. France*, xxiii, 703h.

7 *Hist. de Guillaume le Maréchal*, ed. Paul Meyer (1901), iii, 98*n*.

DE VERLEIO.

Vesly: Manche, arr. Coutances, cant. Lessay.

William d'Aubigny, *pincerna*, enfeoffed Hugh de Verleio of two knights' fees and Roger de Verleio of one.[1] Vesly is 16 kil. NW of St-Martin d'Aubigny.[2]

VERE.

Ver: Manche, arr. Coutances, cant. Gavray.

In 1086 Aubrey de Ver, the ancestor of the earls of Oxford, in addition to his tenancies-in-chief in several counties, was an under-tenant of Geoffrey bishop of Coutances in Kensington, Middlesex, and two places in Northamptonshire.[3] This indicates that his place of origin was Ver as above, which is 18 kil. S of Coutances, and not Ver in the Bessin. In 1172 Ralf de Ver, whose connexion, however, with the family of Aubrey de Vere has not been determined,[4] held a knight's fee in the bailiwick of Gavray[5]; and in the Registers of Philip Augustus, 1212–20, William de Ver held a knight's fee at Ver 'ad servicium Gavraii,'[6] *i.e.* of castle-guard at Gavray.[7]

VERNON, of Haddon.

Vernon: Eure, arr. Evreux, cant. Vernon.

By an original charter now at Belvoir Henry de Neufbourg and Robert his son gave to Richard de Vernon land at Ashampstead and Basildon, Berks., in exchange for Richard's land at Radepont.[8] The limits of date are 1159, the death of Robert de Neufbourg, Henry's father, and 1181, the death of Humphrey de Bohun who witnessed a confirming charter of Henry II.[9] The possession of this charter by the Duke of Rutland, the representative of the Vernons of Haddon, identifies the grantee with Richard de Vernon of Haddon, information about whose family has been given by Farrer in *Honors and Knights' Fees*, vol. i, p. 163; and vol. ii, p. 276.

Radepont, dept. Eure, arr. Evreux, cant. Fleury-sur-Andelle, lies *c.* 32 kil. N of Vernon; but the fact that there is no other place of the name in dept. Eure, or indeed in Normandy, seems a sufficient indication of Richard's origin. Vernon was a considerable place, and it does not follow that Richard was related to its lords, a collateral branch of the earls of Devon and magnates in Normandy.

In 1086 Huard de Vernon was an under-tenant of William de Escoies (*q.v.*), and presumably came from Vernon likewise.

1 *Red Bk. Exch.*, pp. 398–9.

2 *Cf.* MILLIERES.

3 *D.B.*, i, 130b, 220b.

4 *Complete Peerage*, new ed., x, app. p. 110.

5 *Rec. Hist. France*, xxiii, 696d.

6 *Ibid.*, p. 611 l.

7 *Ibid.*, p. 608e.

8 Hist. MSS. Comm., *Duke of Rutland*, iv, 21.

9 *Ibid.*, p. 22.

VILERS, VILIERS.

Villiers-le-Sec: Calvados, arr. Bayeux, cant. Ryes.

In 1166 Roger de Vilers held a knight's fee of the old feoffment of the earl of Gloucester[1]; and in 1212 Roger de Vilers held two and a half hides in Stourpaine, Dorset, of the honour of Gloucester.[2] Villiers-le-Sec is 2½ kil. NW of Creully, an important stronghold of Robert FitzHamo, whose daughter and heir brought his lands by marriage to Robert earl of Gloucester.[3] In later times a fief in Villiers was held of the barony of Creully.[4]

At first sight Villiers (Manche, arr. St-Lô, cant. St-Clair) might seem to offer an alternative provenance, since the facts stated under St. Clair show it to have been a fief of the earl of Gloucester *c.* 1150; but for the reasons there given it could not have come to the earl of Gloucester before the reign of Stephen, and the Vilers tenure in England, being of the old feoffment, must have originated before the earl's acquisition of Villiers, dept. Manche.

WALTERVILLA, VATIERVILLE.

Vatierville: Seine-Inf., arr. and cant. Neufchâtel.

In 1166 Ralf de Waltervillla and Ralf de Grincurt (*q.v.*) held half a knight's fee of the new feoffment of Walter de Aincurt.[5] In the thirteenth-century *pouillé* of the diocese of Rouen Vatierville is Galteri Villa.[6] It lies at a considerable distance from Ancourt, but only 11 kil. S of Fallencourt, and Elias de Fanucurt (*q.v.*) was an under-tenant of Walter de Aincurt in 1166. These two places seem to support each other for the purposes of identification, suggesting that Aincurt held land in this district or at any rate was connected with it. It is significant that on the loss of Normandy Vatierville, equally with Ancourt, came into the hand of the king of France.[7]

WANCY, DE WANCEIO.

Wanchy: Seine-Inf., arr. Neufchâtel, cant. Londinières.

The family were under-tenants of the honour of Warenne in Norfolk and Suffolk from the time of Domesday.[8] Wanchy, where there is a motte,[9] is *c.* 12 kil. SW of Grandcourt and Pierrepont (*q.v.*).

WARENNE.

Varenne: Seine-Inf., near Bellencombre.

For this identification see Mr. Loyd's paper 'The Origin of the Family of Warenne' in *Yorkshire Arch. Journal*, vol. xxxi, pp. 97–113. The hamlet of Varenne lies on the river Varenne *c.* 2 miles S of Arques and

1 *Red Bk. Exch.*, p. 290.
2 *Bk. of Fees*, p. 88.
3 *Complete Peerage*, new ed., v, 685–6.
4 C. Hippeau, *Dict. topogr. du Calvados*, p. 302.
5 *Red Bk. Exch.*, p. 381.
6 *Rec. Hist. France*, xxiii, 268f.
7 *Ibid.*, p. 641c.
8 Farrer, *Honors and Knights' Fees*, iii, 380 *et seq.*
9 Cochet, *Rép. arch. . . . de la Seine-Inf.*, col. 233.

c. 13 miles N of Bellencombre. The latter place, arr. Dieppe, cant. Bellencombre, where there was a castle, became the *caput* of the Warenne honour in Normandy.[1]

WASPREY.

Guéprès: Orne, arr. Argentan, cant. Trun.

Henry de Wasprey, a household knight of Roger de Mowbray, was a benefactor of Byland abbey, where he became a lay brother.[2] Guéprès, the medieval Wasprée, was not part of the Norman lands of Mowbray, but was held in 1172 by William de Sancto Selerino.[3] It lies, however, 16 kil. NNE of Château-Gontier,[4] held by Roger de Mowbray, and 17 kil. E of Bazoches-au-Houlme, which Roger and his father Nigel d'Aubigny held of the count of Eu.[5]

WASPRIA.

La Vespière: Calvados, arr. Lisieux, cant. Orbec.

In 1136–38 Osmund de Waspria, described as a man of the honour of Gilbert FitzRichard, witnessed a charter of Adeliz wife of Gilbert FitzRichard for Thorney abbey.[6] La Vespière lies 2½ kil. SSE of Orbec, the *caput* of the Norman honour of Richard FitzGilbert, the Domesday tenant-in-chief and founder of the house of Clare. The twelfth-century form of the name would be Wasperia.[7]

WAST.

Le Vast: Manche, arr. Cherbourg, cant. Saint-Pierre-Eglise.

In 1086 Nigel de Wast was an under-tenant in Bedfordshire and Buckinghamshire of Nigel d'Aubigny of Cainhoe, and his descendants continued to hold of Aubigny.[8] A charter of William d'Aubigny *pincerna* was witnessed by Nigel del Wast, Ralf de Chieresburgh and Richard Caneleu.[9] The last name represents Canteloup, the next parish to Le Vast.[10] The identification of Le Vast has the authority of Round.[11]

1 *Early Yorks. Charters*, viii, 3.

2 *Mon. Ang.*, v, 350; F. M. Stenton, *English Feudalism*, p. 140.

3 *Rec. Hist. France*, xxiii, 695h.

4 Orne, arr. Argentan, cant. Ecouché, comm. La Courbe. It must not be confused with the better-known Château-Gontier in Mayenne, with which it is wrongly identified in the index to *ibid.*

5 *Cal. Docs. France*, no. 595.

6 F. M. Stenton, *Early Charters from Northamptonshire Collections*, no. 18.

7 *Cf.* Willelmus de Wasperia (Stapleton, *Rot. Scacc. Norm.*, i, 193).

8 *Beds. Hist. Rec. Soc.*, quarto ser., i, 96.

9 *Mon. Ang.*, i, 164.

10 *Beds. Hist. Rec. Soc.*, xix, 107.

11 *V.C.H. Bedford*, i, 199.

INDEX
OF FAMILIES, PERSONS AND PLACES

The names of families of which there is a separate section in the text are given in block type. Place-names in France are given with their departmental reference ; fuller details, with arrondissement and canton, will be found in most instances in the text.

INDEX OF TENANTS-IN-CHIEF AND THE FAMILIES HOLDING OF THEM IN ENGLAND

Tenant-in-chief	Families holding of them
AINCOURT	Fanecurt, Grincurt, Waltervilla
ANSEL	Martinwast, Sifrewast
ARQUES	Appeville, Auberville, St-Ouen
AUBIGNY (of Arundel)	Cherbourg, Costentin, Millières, de Verleio
AUBIGNY (of Belvoir)	Reines
AUBIGNY (of Cainhoe)	Caron, Wast
AUMALE, count of	Chamflur
AVRANCHES	Millières, Valeines
BALIOL	Dumard
BAYEUX, Odo bishop of	Bigot, Braiboue, Castellon, Corcelle, Crevequer, Giron, Maminot, Port (of Basing), Tahum, Valbadun
BEAUCHAMP (of Bedford)	Broilg, Locels, Ros, Taissel
BIGOT	Corbun, Cuelai, Savenie
BISET	Angens
BRIOUZE	de Buceio, Carteret, Covert, St-Ouen
BUSLI	Chevercourt
CHESTER, earls of	Dol, Marston, Massey, Praeres, Rhuddlan, Solney, Veim
EU, count of	Bailleul, Cruel, Daivile, Floc, Fraelvilla, Fressenville, Meiniers, Monceaux, Normanville, Ricarville, St. Leger, St. Martin, Scotney, Sept Meules, Strabo
EUDO DAPIFER	Amblie, Berners, Caron, Matuen, Sachevilla, St. Clair
FERRERS	Aukenvilla, Bachepuis, Boscherville, Cambreis, Curzon, Dun, Livet, Montgomery, St. Quintin
FITZGILBERT, Baldwin	Moels, Punchardon
FITZGILBERT, Richard (of Clare)	Abernon, Carleville, La Cressimera, Favarches, Friardel, Nazanda, Orbec, de Sancto Germano, Tani, Waspria
FITZOSBERN	Cormeilles
GIFFARD	Belnai, Bolebec, Cressy, Grenville, Langetot, Milleville Sackville, St-Laurent, Ste-Foy, Talbot, Umfranville
GLOUCESTER, earl of	Champernowne, Portmort, Vilers
GOURNAY	Talbot
LASCY (of Hereford)	Eschetot, Gamages, Salceit, Scorchebofe
LASCY (of Pontefract)	Campeaux, Longvillers, Raineville, Scorchebofe, Veilly
LEICESTER, earls of	Bois, de Bordineio, Bygore, Chiray, Harcourt, Malory, Poteria, Tibouvilla, Turville
MALET	Avilers, Clavilla, Coleville, Conteville, Esmalevilla, Roville
MAMINOT	Feugères, Nowers
MANDEVILLE (earls of Essex)	Criketot, Gweres, Martel, Oseville, St-Ouen
MARMION	Fontenay, Meisi, Quilli
MAYENNE	Toreigny
MEULAN, counts of	Mandeville, Neubourg
MOHUN	Chanfleur
MONTFICHET	Bacon
MONTFORT	Chandos, Mandeville
MONTGOMERY	Bailleul, Belmeis, Pantulf, Say, Tornai
MOWBRAY	Wasprey
PAYNEL	Ruili
PERCY	Morers
POMERAI	Estre, de Sancto Cristoforo, de Tribus Minutis
PORT (of Basing)	Anisy, Lingieure, de Sancto Manevo, Scures
PORT (of Mapledurwell)	Arguges, Folie, Fresne, Marinni

INDEX OF PLACES IN NORMANDY SPECIFIED AS FORMING THE CAPUT OF A BARONY OR HONOUR